# Two Week Window

## Living with Lyme and Thriving in Life

KRISTY WOOD-GILES

**BALBOA.**
PRESS
A DIVISION OF HAY HOUSE

This book is a work of non-fiction. Unless otherwise noted, the author and the publisher make no explicit guarantees as to the accuracy of the information contained in this book and in some cases, names of people and places have been altered to protect their privacy.

Balboa Press books may be ordered through booksellers or by contacting:

Balboa Press
A Division of Hay House
1663 Liberty Drive
Bloomington, IN 47403
www.balboapress.com
1 (877) 407-4847

Because of the dynamic nature of the Internet, any web addresses or links contained in this book may have changed since publication and may no longer be valid. The views expressed in this work are solely those of the author and do not necessarily reflect the views of the publisher, and the publisher hereby disclaims any responsibility for them.

The author of this book does not dispense medical advice or prescribe the use of any technique as a form of treatment for physical, emotional, or medical problems without the advice of a physician, either directly or indirectly. The intent of the author is only to offer information of a general nature to help you in your quest for emotional and spiritual well-being. In the event you use any of the information in this book for yourself, which is your constitutional right, the author and the publisher assume no responsibility for your actions.

Print information available on the last page.

ISBN: 978-1-9822-1134-9 (sc)
ISBN: 978-1-9822-1132-5 (hc)
ISBN: 978-1-9822-1133-2 (e)

Library of Congress Control Number: 2018910413

Balboa Press rev. date: 09/17/2018

Living with Lyme and Thriving in Life

An intimate memoir of misdiagnosed Lyme disease and the treatment that led to insight and healing, ultimately creating a life of knowing, self-love, and peace.

Kristy Wood-Giles

# NOTE TO READERS

This publication contains the opinions and ideas of its author. I am not a medical doctor, nor am I endorsing, dispensing, or recommending any particular treatments, products, or health services as a form of diagnosis or treatment for any physical, emotional, or medical condition. I simply wish to share what helped me and others in the search of answers.

The content of this book is anecdotal and written for general informational purposes only. This book is sold with the understanding that neither the author nor the publisher is engaged in rendering medical, health, or other professional advice or services. If the reader requires such advice or services, a competent and appropriate professional should be consulted. The content, ideas, theories, suggestions, and treatment protocols in this book may not be suitable for everyone. They are not guaranteed or warranted to produce any particular results. No warranty is made with respect to the accuracy or completeness of the information contained herein.

Both the author and the publisher specifically renounce any responsibility for any liability, loss, or risk—personal or otherwise—that is incurred as a consequence, directly or indirectly, of the use and application of any of the contents of this book. Neither the author nor the publisher shall be liable for any loss of profit or any commercial damages, including but not limited to special, incidental, consequential, or other damages.

Where I have provide names of doctors, I cite these doctors only as the authors of reference materials that may be consulted. I personally have not consulted these doctors for my own personal treatment or care. I encourage anyone who would like to investigate any ideas shared in this book to review the references provided and consult with the appropriate medical professional.

# REVIEW

*Two-Week Window: Living with Lyme and Thriving in Life* is author Kristy Wood-Giles' harrowing account of one of the most difficult passages of her life: being deathly ill and not knowing why.

As a lifelong athlete, one who completed many triathlons, and played every sport imaginable while growing up, Wood-Giles' mission in life has been to do far more than survive ... but to thrive. A mission she learned from her beloved father who battled cancer and died not long before she herself fell ill. His illness and his ability to get through each day was a critical life lesson that served her well during her own health ordeal.

Growing up with the message that you push yourself even if you don't know why, Wood-Giles found herself compelled to complete a 300 km hike along the Rideau trail soon after her father passed away. It was on this hike that her medical troubles began. But it was not until many years following her trek, after consulting her doctor numerous times as well as other medical specialists, after a litany of blood tests, EKG's, ultrasounds, after suffering day in and day out with a myriad of "weird symptoms" including colds that wouldn't go away, chest pain radiating into her back, nausea, vomiting, diminished appetite, exhaustion, shortness of breath, roaming pain from knee to shoulder to hip, night sweats, general malaise, crippling anxiety and panic, forgetfulness, feeling lost in space, diminished productivity, losing her train of thought, that she finally determined––only by chance––that she was suffering from chronic Lyme disease.

And it was then that she was presented with the greatest challenge of her life, one that made a 300 km trek seem like child's play––recovering from a debilitating, life destroying illness that is barely acknowledged by mainstream medicine, forcing her to experience a "do-it-yourself" medical odyssey that most chronic Lyme sufferers are all too familiar with.

Before long, she became "passionate, almost obsessive" about correcting the misinformation, falsehoods and confusion so that others would not have to endure what she has. Her activism quickly took on the same fiery determination as her athleticism once did and today Wood-Giles remains tasked with a personal calling to set the record straight.

We need more voices like Wood-Giles' to bring truth to this medical travesty. I, for one, am grateful that she chose to record her story in this raw, real, educational and engaging memoir.

—Lori Dennis, author of *Lyme Madness*

I dedicate this book to my husband, Brian, and my children, Haley and Warner. Without you, I would not be here. You gave me a reason to keep fighting and helped me feel like my life was as normal as possible. Seeing you, hugging you, and talking to you made every day worth fighting for. Thank you.

Brian: I know you felt you never knew how best to help, but you always managed to do it right. Your quiet patience, subtle support, and unwavering certainty that I would see the other side helped me get through this. I love you.

Haley and Warner: I will always hate the years that I was too sick to be the mom I wanted to be. I love you for all you did to step up and help me. You made being a mom really easy. I love you both so much.

# ACKNOWLEDGMENTS

To my friends and family: Many of you may not be blood, but you are most certainly my family. I can't imagine how I would have done this without you. I can't begin to thank you for all the support and help you provided. I will always be wealthy just having you in my life. Special thanks for the editing support from Suzanne, Tracey and Kaiti.

To my fellow Lyme warriors: I know some of you are suffering immensely, and I so wish I could lessen your pain and torture. I know it's no way to live and certainly not a humane existence for many reasons. Many of you talked me through dark times, and many of you inspired me to keep fighting. I'm so grateful to you all, and I promise to never stop fighting for you.

To my mentors: So many of you motivated me to push forward and achieve new things. Some of you have been in my life forever, and some are Lyme fighters for whom I have the utmost respect. The confidence you gave me to share my own gift has been a blessing.

To my dogs: First, to Keesha, who I now realize likely struggled with Lyme in the years before I was diagnosed—I miss our runs together and wish I could have done more to help you before I had to let you go. And to Aggie, whom I chose to get with my heart and not my head—I may have been too sick to have a puppy, but you healed me in more ways than you know.

To God: I thank you for the obstacles you've given me to make me strong in life, but this one almost went too far. I know you intend for me to do good in spite all of it—and I promise to do my best—but please help those who are now struggling. Knowing the pain and suffering of others is too much to bear.

# WHAT I WISH EVERYONE KNEW ABOUT LYME DISEASE AND TICKS

1. Infection transmission: You can be infected with Lyme disease in much less than twenty-four hours, and other infections can be passed on in minutes. Don't let that rule apply when considering treatment. You can easily be infected if the tick was stressed during removal or was not removed properly.

2. Rash: Many people end up with chronic Lyme because they were told their bite was from a spider. Many don't get a rash at all or the rash doesn't always look like a bull's-eye, nor does it have to be where you were bitten.

3. One-day dose: If you are prescribed a one-day dose after a bite, know that this treatment is based on one study that was only 80 percent successful in healing the rash, not in curing Lyme. Not a good idea.

4. Two-week window: Studies show that Lyme affects your immune system within two weeks of infection. Don't delay treatment. Lyme is easy to get and hard to treat if left for too long.

5. Coinfections: It's very rare to be infected only with Lyme from a tick bite. A person infected with Lyme is more likely than not to have other infections as well, which can sometimes be more harmful and deadly than Lyme.

6. Persistence: Studies show that after twenty-eight days of antibiotics, Lyme still survives. Treatment with a short course of antibiotics may cause symptoms to disappear for months— even years— but they can reappear at a later date, and doctors don't make the connection.

7. Transmission methods: There are many possible modes of transmission such as congenital Lyme that are often overlooked. Just know that you don't have to have a tick bite to consider Lyme as a diagnosis. Hopefully, with more research this will become better understood.

8. Testing: It's extremely unreliable in Canada, and diagnosis should be based on clinical assessment. Out-of-country testing is available but may require a Lyme-literate professional for interpretation.

9. Denial: When a doctor denies that you have Lyme or is reluctant to treat you, Lyme disease shouldn't be ruled out. To properly rule out Lyme, a patient should see a Lyme-literate professional to be sure.

10. Epidemic: Lyme disease is the fastest-growing vector-borne infectious disease in the United States and is prevalent in eighty countries worldwide.

# PREFACE

Writing has always been a healing outlet for me, even though I never excelled at it. Despite my lack of ability, one special teacher encouraged me to write and improve. I have been doing it for years and have realized it's better to share with the possibility of criticism than to keep inside and hide what may benefit others. I never claim to be a good writer, but I always share from the heart. This book is more honest, truthful, and *me* than anything I've ever done.

I've used writing to deal with loss in my life, and it proved especially helpful when Lyme took so much away. When living with Lyme, you never know if you're going to heal, how far you can go, or what all will be lost in the end. It's a very scary place to be. Writing helped me sort out my thoughts and manage my emotions as I traveled along the journey. It also made me understand so much more about living beyond Lyme.

I want to share some of that journey with all of you. I believe people need to better understand ticks and Lyme. I also believe the system has been misled—mainly due to greed and power—so there is great purpose in my sharing my story. This need to share also has helped me revisit and heal from the parts of my journey that seemed so painful at the time.

I hope that you find value in my story and that some of what I learned can benefit you. It has certainly taught me the value of life and, even more importantly, how to live a good life. I feel my purpose is to help as many people as possible, and the best way to do that is by sharing. We're all struggling in some way, and we all deserve a better life. I want to help you find that. If I can find happiness despite suffering with Lyme disease, then you can too.

# CONTENTS

# CHAPTER 1

# Hike

Why did I want to do it? I was asked that question several times, but I didn't have one specific answer. There were many reasons I couldn't answer the question quickly or easily. All I knew in my mind was that it was inevitable. I had to go on this seven-day solo hike.

I had torn the medial collateral ligament (MCL) and meniscus in my right knee during hockey provincials, so I knew running was out of the question for a year. Eighteen years prior to this injury, I had torn the anterior cruciate ligament (ACL) in the same knee. Although I hadn't had any issues in all my years of sports and adventures, I wondered how vulnerable my knee was. After the hockey accident, I had been told my knee would never be as strong as it once was.

Nonetheless, I still needed a challenge that would keep me focused and motivated. That's just how I operated. I set a goal, achieved it, and moved on to the next. Typically, these challenges were competitive sports, off-road triathlons, and adventure races, among other physical activities. I wanted a goal to work toward but always something different and fun. I also liked to include travel in the adventure, to add new experience to the mix.

Although I worked in park management, I also became a certified personal trainer so that I could work out properly. I loved being outdoors and developing fitness programs in the parks that I managed. As my interest in triathlons developed, I knew I had to increase my fitness level, but I couldn't fathom spending my spare time in a gym. As a professional who commuted two hours to work each day and who had two young

1

children involved in sports and activities, I knew that if I was going to have any time to myself, it would be outdoors. As a trainer, I could combine my two favorite worlds into one.

Although it was never my intention to train anyone else, I did start a fun run to raise money for a fundraising group I volunteered with. The run would support a different medical cause each year, helping families who were struggling within our community. I had organized runs as a fundraiser at a previous job, so I decided to revive the idea and encourage people to train and participate. I then invited a few friends to come train at the park twice a week for six weeks in advance of the fun run, so that I could share my newly acquired training knowledge. In just a day, that group turned into twenty-five women. I never intended to train anyone again, but when the fun run was over, many were eager for another program. During this experience, I learned a lot about what motivates women. And so began my seasonal outdoor programs and my introduction to personal training in the outdoors. I couldn't keep up with the demand, but I have to admit I loved the opportunity to expose new people to scenic areas and fitness like they'd never experienced before.

Now back to my injury. Since I had to take a break from running, I decided to train for a monumental hike. I wanted to make it a challenge, so I decided that it would be a rugged trail and I would try to do it in record-breaking time. When I was thinking about which trail to choose, I heard about a policeman who had hiked the Rideau Trail in fifteen days the year before. He said it had almost killed him. The running record for the same trail had been set by an ultramarathoner in just under four days, but he hadn't carried a backpack or set up camp every night.

There were two reasons I picked the Rideau Trail, a multi-day hike, close to home. First, it was free, so I wouldn't have any travel costs. Second, it travelled through some parks I managed for work, and it would be productive to get an intimate look at the trail from this organic perspective.

I also had decided I wanted to know my local trails better than those found elsewhere in the world. Although I was always looking for a reason to travel, I felt obligated to do this hike first. Once I finished it, I would be so well versed in long-distance hiking that I could travel anywhere in the world to hike challenging trails. I had once heard someone say that it was great to travel to so many different countries, but how well did you know the wilderness in your own region?

I had a good friend recovering from lung cancer who wanted a challenge that would help restore her precancer fitness level. Since she could no longer run or work out like she once could, I thought walking training would be great motivation for her. Training for this walk would be a good opportunity for her to get back into fitness by joining me.

However, if I am completely honest, inside, my deepest motivation had to do with failing to manage my grief after losing my dad. He had died three years earlier. I'd had a good childhood, but there had been some substantial stumbling blocks (I was kicked out a few times) that I had come to accept as my fault. My dad had run a trucking company, so he was away a lot during my childhood. Although he was often traveling, I had still managed to have a relatively close relationship with him. I think it was because he understood my flaws—likely because we shared them.

We were both impatient, short-tempered, and easily frustrated individuals. We were always hardest on ourselves. It was like he truly understood my greatest weaknesses. That doesn't mean he didn't get *extremely* frustrated with me at times. Growing up, I was hyper, not easily controlled, and always ready to speak my mind. And even though he was a hardened disciplinarian, we shared cherished moments on the rare occasions that he was home. Even when he was mad or disappointed, he would later tell me that he knew how I felt. To me, that is one of the greatest gifts someone can give: understanding.

After I went off to school, I still felt like we had a real chance to develop our relationship. When he was on the road, knowing I was alone at school, he would often call just to chat. He would sometimes visit too, if he was traveling the highway nearby. He had a way of challenging me to always do better, but I could sense his unconditional pride at the same time. I admired so much about him, including his personality, his work ethic, his accomplishments, his humility, his incredible sense of humor, and his extreme attention to detail. He was a true perfectionist, or at least he always worked toward perfection. I have often thought that the opposite of loneliness is having someone you admire, more than anyone else in the world, know and accept your greatest faults and love you just the same.

It's like knowing there's always a soft place to land, regardless of how hard life gets.

Sadly, you often don't realize these things as soon as you should. It's like the saying "If it wasn't for the rain, we wouldn't appreciate the sun." I always appreciated my dad, but I had no idea how lost and lonely I'd feel once I lost him. I was a married adult with an amazing husband. I never thought that I could feel so completely overwhelmed. I was unsure how to exist without my father.

Whom would I go to for advice that I could put faith in? He was the only one I completely trusted in everything he said. Who would tell me their honest opinion, even if it was hard for me to hear? He was the only one who knew what it was like to be me. Before his death, I'd been so focused on saving him from his cancer that I had never for a second thought of what would happen when he was gone. I had questions about our history that I wanted to ask, things I needed to know for my future. I had wanted to know he would always be there, but now he wasn't. I had never prepared for this.

By the time I began planning my hike, this grief had consumed me for three years. No matter what I did, nothing seemed to help. I went to therapy, read self-help books, and tried many healing exercises, only to return to the same place: feeling like life would never be okay without him. I knew I couldn't live like this any longer. I decided there was only one thing left to do: force myself to venture alone into nature— without distractions—so that I would have no choice but to feel whatever awful feelings I had inside. I had to explore every corner of my heart in order to move on. It was at least worth a try.

I decided that the best way to do this was to walk the three-hundred-kilometer Rideau Trail in as short a time as possible while carrying all the necessary gear and supplies. I had originally wondered if it could be done in six days, but as I began my training, I realized that even seven days would be a stretch. Regardless, I still wanted to try.

I started doing long walks once a week along sections of the trail. Soon the weather turned wintery, which brought crazy snowstorms, extreme winds, and freezing rain. It seemed ridiculous to spend hours walking in those conditions, but I swore I was going to properly prepare so that nothing would stop me when the time for the hike came. I kept thinking that if I could enjoy the hike in these conditions, then it would be a breeze in the nice summer weather. Eventually, I was hiking the forty-five to fifty kilometers a day that I would need to accomplish in order to finish the trail in seven days.

As the hike got closer, I started training with weight. I needed to carry a pack that would be over forty pounds. I started with ten pounds and kept building. It was this part of the trek that concerned me most. I knew I could walk, I knew I could hike rugged terrain, and I knew that I was happy doing this for hours at a time—even by myself. What I didn't know was how long and how far I could go with such heavy weight on my back.

Two friends decided they wanted to join me. Many had offered to join me for a day, but these two wanted to do the whole trek. I knew my husband also would be more comfortable knowing people were with me. I explained what I thought the conditions would be, but truthfully there was no way for me to know. They still seemed keen to do it, and for the first time it occurred to me that maybe I had worried too much. Maybe I had overtrained. I can't say I had ever overtrained for anything before, but there was a clear pass-or-fail line with this challenge. I wanted to be sure I made it to the end. That fear of failure made me train extensively and plan every angle I could possibly anticipate. This was more than I'd done for any triathlon or adventure race.

I bought my shoes months before and trained in them, not so much that I wore them out, but just enough to break them in. I bought trail runners and road-worthy ones too. I bought them a half size and a full size too big to leave room for my feet to swell. I even had extra pairs set aside for someone to deliver if needed. I walked trails, gravel roads, and pavement—every type of trail I would encounter along the way. People thought it was crazy that I was even training. To them, it was just walking, and everyone could do that. I agreed, but I needed to know I could do the distance day after day to finish the hike in a week. Some days I had to be prepared to set up camp: pitch a tent, light a fire, and eat before dark. It was much more than just walking. I was about to turn forty years old, and I thought it was about time to quit caring what other people thought. It was going to be up to me—and only me—to finish it or not. Only I could decide what made me feel prepared and capable. If I needed to overtrain to go in confidently, then that's what I would do.

At nearly forty years old, I had also developed the maturity to know how to properly plan and prepare for something like this—to give myself the best chance I had to make it. There had been many challenges that I hadn't properly prepared for but still had managed to finish. But I had finished those knowing I could have done better, I could have made it easier, or I hadn't given the experience the respect it deserved. This time I was determined to find peace and enjoyment while experiencing the challenges and obstacles.

On the first morning, after being dropped off, the three of us set out from the original head of the trail in Kingston. A scenic portion had recently been added to the trail to showcase the shores of Lake Ontario, but I had always used the original trail maps and decided to work from those. Here a bronze plaque had been placed alongside the trailhead sign. It seemed like an appropriate place to start. I'd decided to leave my dry bags at home because they made my pack well over forty pounds, and that scared me. My sleeping bag and clothes were wrapped in garbage bags because it had already started to rain. I had never minded walking in rain; sometimes I really enjoyed it. This time, however, the rain could be a problem for the next seven days, leading to wet clothes and gear and ruined food.

The Rideau Trail was quite unique in the section that led away from the city of Kingston, traveling through the cemetery where Sir John A. Macdonald was buried. Whether I'm traveling in a foreign country, in the backwoods, or on a trail such as this, there is something exciting about unexpectedly coming across something interesting. It seems much more sacred when you fall upon it as opposed to heading to a known attraction. I guess that's why I've always been intrigued by new trails; you never really know what will catch your attention. The cemetery was very beautiful, and the Rideau Trail Association had built a memorial bench on the grounds. This felt like an instant reminder that part of this hike was about my extreme grief—a grief that was still haunting me after the loss my dad. I just wasn't sure what part it was.

As we left the cemetery, the rain started to pour. Shortly after this point, we had to leave the railbed trail and head down a bush trail. I didn't think the rain itself was a problem until we had to travel through this overgrown path. It was during this 1.5 kilometers that everything got soaked. My feet were drenched, my pants were soaked, and my pack was wet from the bottom up. When we stopped to eat, we realized just how drenched everything was. I had known rain was likely to be a problem at some point, but I hadn't anticipated heading off into the overgrown bush. The growth was so thick that when I looked back, I couldn't even see the others. This small section of trail proved very challenging. As we exited the bush, we had to follow the railbed in the ditch for a short distance. When we stepped up onto the railbed, I didn't reorient myself as I should have, and we continued to walk in the same direction.

I realized major mistake number one when we hit an unexpected crossroad. I double-checked the map and realized we had gone 1.5 kilometers in the wrong direction. I didn't know how to tell the others. We had about 47 kilometers to travel that day. Secretly, I had hoped we could go 51 kilometers, but now I knew that wasn't going to happen. We tried to make the best of it as we turned to retrace our steps, but I felt bad for misleading them. The last thing we needed was an extra three kilometers to walk. Things only got worse from there, as the blisters started to develop. We had to sit and care for our wounds, bandage our feet, and then start walking again. This was repeated many times. I started to get anxious. At this rate, we wouldn't make it to a suitable camp location for the night. Then what would we do? I had a backup plan, but it was another twenty kilometers away, and it was now well past three o'clock. Within the hour, we were encountering more problems; one friend was having hip trouble and could barely walk. I felt trapped. Although I didn't want to leave my friends, I would never reach the daily distance I needed to if I sat with them. This would put me behind for the next seven days.

Just as I thought the hike was going to be over before it began, I got a text message.

A friend I'd had since birth sent me a message asking where we could meet. She'd decided to meet us and was bringing a camper that we could spend the night in. It was like someone had heard my prayers. It had always been in her character to do things like this (she had saved me many times before). She didn't want to do the hike and probably thought it was a ridiculous idea, but she always found her own way to support me. At this point, I decided to walk ahead while the other girls decided what to do.

As I was walking and texting my friend to figure out where to meet, I realized my phone battery was quickly dying. I pulled out my solar charger and couldn't believe my luck—or lack thereof—as I noticed the clouds rolling in. Solar-charging my phone would not be an option. As quickly as things had seemed to be looking up, they now seemed to be falling apart all over again. I managed to send a message with the name of the conservation area I was heading to before my battery died. I had no way to get back to the others without retracing many kilometers, and I had no idea whether my friend would know where to meet me. But then again, we had traveled many places together over the years, and we each understood how the other thought. I knew she would find me eventually.

I didn't know if luck was with or against me, so I decided to enjoy the solitude. It was shortly after this thought that I got lost in a hayfield. I couldn't find the next orange marker. The trees were overgrown along the edge of the field, not only covering the markers but also making it impossible to see any signs of an exit.

The field was extremely wet, but I had been drenched the whole day, so this seemed normal now. I was thankful for the drawstring on my pants because the pants were so heavy that they would've fallen off without a tie. As I walked on, an orange marker caught my eye a distance across the field. If I went directly toward it, I would have to cross a barbed wire fence. There's certainly a trick to making sure you miss all the barbs, but I had crossed many of these fences in my life. I had forgotten about the forty pounds on my back, though. As I was almost over the top, the weight of my pack forcefully pushed me over. I stopped just short of landing on my head. I remember thinking the fall was going to hurt, but somehow it didn't, and it took me a minute to figure out why. My pants had caught the wire on the fence, and there I was, hanging completely upside down. I remember wishing my pants didn't stay on so well after all.

The wire was not only hooked through my pants but also nicely hooked on the zipper that was designed to change them into shorts. I really had no idea what to do, so I hung there and just laughed; I really did. It was not like me to laugh in this type of situation, but I did. When you're completely upside down, suspended by your own clothing with a large pack on your back, you had better be able to laugh about it. I couldn't have done this again even if I tried. I had no cell phone, I wasn't anywhere near where someone would find me, *and* I was hung up on barbed wire. It felt good to laugh. Nothing had gone right that day, and I think I just needed to laugh off the situation. I was impressed that I could do that. My well-laid plans going completely off the rails was not something I usually would find funny. Laughing was what my best friend would do. She had helped me laugh many times in my life even though it wasn't in my nature. She wasn't doing this trek with me because she was, she said, "too smart to do something so stupid." Had she been there with me, I knew she would've been laughing really hard at this point, so that's what I did. Then I ripped my pants, pulled them off the wire, and fell to the ground.

As I stood up to carry on, it was a like a new me heading out on the trail. For whatever reason, I was happy to be where I was. I knew my friend would find me if I just kept walking to the conservation area I had told her I would get to. I marched on, confident that I'd see her soon.

Later, I found out that only part of my text had reached her. She had stopped at the provincial park (my original destination) and worked with the ranger to figure out where I was actually heading. It still wasn't clear, but she knew she had to go with her gut instinct as to where I'd be. And that was exactly where she found me. It's amazing to have someone in your life who knows you that well, supports you despite your differences, and always finds a way to be there for you. We tracked back on the road and found the girls where I had left them. She fed us the lasagna she had brought for us, gave us a warm, dry bed, and planned to take the other two girls home in the morning.

I felt very grateful as I went to bed that night; I knew I had amazing people in my life. Even though part of me had wanted to prove that I could do this on my own, it wasn't necessary at that moment. Instead, I was able to simply live in the moment with my friends, feeling safe and content. I recognized the flaw in my plan: the trail was not meant to be done in one trip. I realized too that my other goals were much more important than proving my independence. There was no denying that things would've completely fallen apart had I not gotten help. As I sat with my gratitude, I decided I would move on with my plan for the next day.

Tomorrow would be a fresh start, and things could only get better from there, I was sure.

# CHAPTER 2

# **Bite**

I set off the next morning with the motivation of a fresh start. I was by myself and responsible only for myself. I was off to accomplish whatever this hike was meant to accomplish. It felt right and like this was how the trip was meant to go; I must be meant to do this solo.

I thought that yesterday must have happened so that I could appreciate the solitude of this adventure. I had many friends who wanted to join me for the last day of the hike. I saw this time by myself as a chance to sort out whatever I needed to while looking forward to that last day with them. At least that's how I pictured it.

There was a jump in my step as I traveled the early sections of the trail that morning. I had renewed energy and excitement for this excursion and was sure it couldn't get any worse than it had been the day before. The trails were rocky, forested, and meandering with beautiful outcrops that posed a constant workout; it was an enjoyable hike. I climbed a steep cliff to find the most amazing view at the top—just like in the movies. It seemed unbelievable that I was in Ontario. So very few had seen this view because of the difficulty of the trail.

The greenery was so overgrown that I was again having trouble finding the markers. The trails were completely flooded by water, and the swamps were overflowing. In some situations, I couldn't even find a route around the flooding, no matter which way I tried. I attempted bushwalking off-trail, but I had to bend over to crouch below the heavy brush and my pack kept getting caught on branches. I walked far into the bushes just to get around some sections and then decided it would be more efficient to walk through the water. In some cases, I had no choice. This issue would later be the most significant factor in deciding whether to end my trip.

At this point in the hike, it was obvious that no one had traveled this trail at all recently. Though it was well marked, I had to find the markers through the underbrush of the trees. It had been such a wet spring that the plant life was flourishing. It was also early in the season, so no trail maintenance been done. It was slow going finding my way.

Despite the wet spring, I had planned the hike for the end of June because it fell after black fly season and before the deer flies would appear. I knew I could handle mosquitoes. With a little bit of bug spray, mosquitoes were never much of a concern. I also thought it would be warm enough but not so warm that sunstroke or heat exhaustion would be an issue. But the man who had hiked the trail the previous fall (during a record-breaking dry year) had done so in fifteen days and hadn't had to deal with the wet of the spring season. I started to panic. Maybe planning would be my downfall.

I had planned to travel my shortest distance this day. I had thirty-seven to thirty-nine kilometers to hike versus the forty-two to fifty kilometers per day I planned for the remainder of the trip. I knew it was going to be the toughest terrain, so I was prepared.

I started at 7:00 a.m. as planned, an hour earlier than I was planning to start any other day. I was prepared to continue walking until between 7:00 p.m. and 8:00 p.m. that night. I started to watch my time and distance and soon found I was averaging only 2.5 kilometers per hour. That was not going to be enough to make the distance. Typically, I averaged four to five kilometers on trail and five to six kilometers on gravel. Conservative hiking would have been around three kilometers per hour, and I wasn't even meeting that.

I've never feared much in life except for failure. I rarely get anxious even when I probably should; yet when I sit with my thoughts and consider how I might fail, I do get anxious. I knew this wasn't why I was doing this trek—it wasn't about success or failure.

I wanted to be immersed in nature, and I was. I wanted to feel peace, be by myself, and be so out of touch that I had no choice but to appreciate my surroundings. I wanted to be physically challenged and tired, so that

I had no choice but to feel the moment. I really had all that I wanted, and yet I was disappointed that it wasn't happening exactly as I had imagined.

A few moments later, I reached the top of a hill and looked over to find a beautiful running river. There were massive granite rock outcrops and trees all around. True wilderness, and I was only hours from home—this was exactly what I had wanted to experience. I set my pack down, took a picture with my phone, and posted it on Facebook with the caption "This is why I am doing this." It might have seemed like a message to everyone else—to let them know I was okay—but it was more of a message to myself. It also might seem like I was too focused on modern technology (because my first thought was to post it), but I stood there for a long time and just stared. I tried to really take it all in—the view and the peace I felt just being there. Despite my efforts to stay in the moment, a nagging concern about my time constraints crept in. I knew I needed to keep going if I was going to reach camp before dark.

Throughout the day, I walked through rugged terrain, pools of water, and more poison ivy than I'd seen in my life; it was like a forest carpet in some areas. I had always thought I was somewhat immune to its effects, but this hike would be the true test. Surprisingly, I decided that I preferred walking through poison ivy; it was drier and more solid than the wet, swampy areas. I also thought my wet clothes would possibly repel the poison ivy oils.

I walked under the branches to try to avoid the wet spots, but my pack kept getting caught on the trees. I had to walk sideways more than ahead, and I realized I would never make camp at this rate. I knew I had no choice but to get back on the trail. Having been a park manager for almost twenty years at that point, I knew that "stay on the trail" was an important rule for safe hiking. I'd always thought, however, that when a site instates that rule, there should be some onus on the trail manager to ensure the trail is passable. This trail would not have been classified as passable. Regardless, I had known that I would encounter these types of situations, although I had hoped not to this extreme. It was still no excuse to stop. If I wanted to find an excuse to stop, there had already been many to choose from. To me, the true test of perseverance is what you do when you have all the excuses to stop. Going on was my only choice.

It was an incredibly long day, and I knew I was getting close just as the sun was starting to set. I came to an intersection where the sign was twisted, so it was difficult to figure out whether I needed to go straight or right. I looked at the map. I read and reread the text description but could not make sense of which way I had to go. After much internal debate, I decided to go right. Later I would realize that this turn took me more than a kilometer out of my way, though the decision still got me where I needed to be. I laughed out loud when I was almost to the road. I came to a small water crossing where I could see the wooden planks that were usually used by ATVs and walkers to cross the stream. It was more like a small river now, and the boards had washed just far enough away to be out of reach. It seemed like one last reminder of the kind of day I'd had. Just when I had thought the water levels along the trail couldn't get any higher, they had. I now had to cross a stream that was waist-high. I jumped in and was feeling positive as I got to the other side. If I could survive today, I could survive any day!

After thirteen solid hours of hiking with no breaks, I finally reached a campground just before dark. My feet were really sore, and they'd been wet all day. I was afraid to take off my shoes for fear of what they might look like. My feet felt so swollen that I half-expected them to expand like balloons. I knew I'd be moving to larger shoes the next day and probably wrapping some sores. I hadn't anticipated this much wetness and couldn't help but wonder if waterproof footwear would've been a better choice. I imagined what a marathoner's feet would look like after forty-two kilometers in rubber boots and figured they would probably be worse than mine. It was a tough call, but it was too late to revisit the shoe decision now.

I tried to find someone at the main office of the campground, but there was no one there. As time went on, it became more obvious just how much my feet hurt. All I could think about was taking my shoes off. My husband had arrived to drop off food and bandages, and we talked for a bit. He was horrified to see how sore my feet looked already, but he knew better than to suggest that I stop. He was quite used to my challenges and stupid ideas, and he had never tried to hold me back. He rarely even commented; he just supported. I was lucky to have someone who seemed to understand me so well. Truth be told, I didn't understand myself most of the time—doing this kind of stuff just fueled me and kept me happy. It was the only way I knew how to be. I knew if there ever came a day that I couldn't do these things, it would be crippling to me—probably mentally more than physically. I was always motivated to stay active and do adventurous things. I hoped that the day when I couldn't do these things would never come.

After my husband left, I was laying out my sleeping bag when I noticed a tick. I brushed it off, unsurprised because I'd noticed one on my leg earlier that day. I knew I was going to have to find the showers and do a tick check before bed. I wasn't worried because I'd sprayed 30 percent DEET on myself that morning. I had even added tea tree oil around my feet and legs since I'd been told that it too was a tick deterrent. I had worn long, tight running leggings that day, and because it was cold and wet, I had on a T-shirt, long-sleeved shirt, and rain jacket. And of course, I had been wearing my forty-pound backpack all day. You can imagine my surprise when, as I was getting ready for my shower, I found five ticks on my back. The lighting was horrible in the bathroom, and since it was dusk, very little natural light filtered in through the windows. I was, however, able to swipe most of them off. Your back is a horrible spot to find ticks, especially when you're alone. There was one that seemed really attached under my right shoulder blade—the one spot that was hardest for me to reach, of course. I went back to camp and got a flashlight and tweezers, neither of which seemed to help the situation at all. I couldn't get at the tick easily and had to keep trying until I felt it was all gone. I did not remove it well—there is no doubt about that. I removed it in tiny pieces, none of which I could collect to have tested.

I wasn't really concerned, though. I had always been told that a person was safe if the tick was removed within twenty-four hours. That tick couldn't have transmitted Lyme already. I did, however, decide that I would be smart and see a doctor when I was done with the hike. As park staff, I had received annual training on Lyme and on tick identification and removal. I was well aware that this was not something to overlook. My younger self would've brushed it off, but the smarter, more mature me was learning not to take anything for granted. I didn't worry about the ticks again and felt that seeing a doctor would be an adequate safety precaution.

After my shower, I headed back to my campsite, where I had to scare off raccoons. I had promised my husband that if I was alone, I would go to a proper campsite. I originally had planned to camp at a clearing along the trail, but he was concerned for my safety due to the black bears in the area. I had worked on a black bear project many years earlier that involved filming them in the wild. I had come prepared with precautions such as bear spray, and I was ready to employ all the bear-prevention measures related to my food. Regardless, I had kept my promise and gone to a campsite.

I hadn't really thought about raccoons; I had always really liked them. As a young child, I rescued four babies whose mother was killed on the road. That lasted about two nights because I couldn't keep up with the hourly feedings they needed. Eventually, I had to give up and take them to a wildlife rescue center. The owners of the stables where we kept our horses also had a pet raccoon, BJ, whom I had fallen in love with. After that, I had always really wanted a pet raccoon. That night at the campsite, however, they became my nemeses.

I ate a little more food and then decided to pack the rest away for the next day. That sounds easier than it is when you have only a backpack and a one-man tent. The tent was the smallest and lightest on the market, meaning my backpack had to stay outside; I had bought it specifically to add as little weight as possible to my pack. The raccoons eventually won, getting food out of my pack through a little hole in the bottom made for the hydration hose. I then brought my pack into the tent with me. The only way to fit it in was for me to lie on my back with the forty pounds on top of me. I couldn't move at all that night, but at least the raccoons were no longer driving me nuts. Once again, I started to laugh. If anyone could see me now, crammed into this tiny tent with a large backpack lying on top of me, that person would most certainly think I had lost my mind. I also thought that I had better leave early the next morning because my silhouette must look very strange from outside the tent. I was still laughing, though, and that was important.

My feet were sore and raw the next morning. A wave of concern came over me: even if my strength and endurance lasted, what would happen to these sore and raw feet? I still had five more days to go at this distance and pace. I didn't know what to expect from the condition of my feet and what it would mean for the remainder of the hike. My fear grew when I put on my larger shoes that were now too tight.

I had friends joining me in the afternoon that day, and the timing was going to be great. I called and asked them to bring me even larger shoes. By the time they found me early that afternoon, I was frustrated, drenched (again), worn down, and simply depressed. I felt overwhelmed by the fear and dread that this trip wasn't going to go as planned; I would not accomplish my goal. But as my friends have been known to—and have done many times in my life—they picked me up when I was down. They distracted me from the pain in my feet and made me laugh again. I was almost out of food, so we ventured off trail to have lunch. It was a perfect distraction to get my mind and body to rest. The remainder of that day went more like how I had hoped the hike would be.

That night as I was settling in, I felt tremendous gratitude for the amazing friends who were supporting me on this journey. I knew I was blessed beyond words to have people like this in my life, but I didn't know how to tell them that I was no longer sure I could do this. It wasn't my physical fitness or mental desire that I was worried about; something just felt off. I had my shoes off, but the pain was still so intense that I had to walk on the outsides of my feet. I didn't even know what was wrong with them. I'd had many reasons for doing this hike, but I had been sure that one of them would reveal itself as the main motive. At this point, however, all seemed lost. I wasn't enjoying the scenery, and it had become a test of endurance just to get to my destination each night. I wasn't finding the solitude I needed to deal with my emotions because I was wrestling with my thoughts too much. I felt like I was simply playing a game of faith because if left to my own devices, I knew I wouldn't complete this hike. That night, I tried to resolve it all in my head. I didn't understand the purpose of the hike anymore, and I no longer knew how to finish. I felt like it was completely out of my hands at that point. I feared that ultimately the lesson was going to be about failure—learning what it was like to fail at a challenge no matter how determined you were. The next morning, I wrote the following post:

> I woke up this morning at 5:00 a.m. and realized my feet were just as swollen as the night before, and the blisters had all filled up again. I elevated my feet some more and realized this challenge was going to require something greater than myself. So I prayed: I was willing, but if I was really meant to do this, I would need some help.

I slept for one more hour and woke up without the miracle I was hoping ... nothing had changed. I decided to take each minute at a time and start to prepare myself for the day. I wrapped my feet, and things started to seem better. I headed out, planning to take one step at a time and see what I was able to do. I ended up having the best day yet and did the 42 km (maybe even 44 km) that I needed to.

I realized today that this is not the challenge of endurance, strength, or willpower that I thought it was; it's purely a challenge of faith. I found faith that there is something more powerful than me that is willing to help if I just let Him.

My feet are still sore, but I was able to keep them dry; that seems to make a world of difference. Funny, though ... I am wearing size 8.5 shoes, and my feet are size 7, but they fit perfectly ... lol.

This challenge has been easier in areas that I thought would be hard but very hard in areas I never thought would be a problem.

The next few days were the same but less wet, which was nice. I spent some days by myself, and other days I was joined by friends. I was amazed by the number of people who put me up for a night, fed me, joined me in walking, sent me notes, and just generally supported me in any way possible. I'm really not sure why they did it. From the outside, this must have just seemed like a stupid challenge that I had created for myself. It wasn't a challenge that I had encountered due to conditions or life situations, so it was confusing that everyone was supporting me. It was as if all of these people understood me more than I understood myself. I didn't know why I had to do this, but my friends also knew I had to. It seemed to make even more sense to them.

As the hike went on, I started to see concern on some of their faces. I had already lost a lot of weight. My mood had deteriorated; this wasn't fun anymore, and the laughing had stopped. My feet felt like they were constantly on fire. I knew I needed to eat, but I couldn't seem to find my appetite. My friends' biggest concern was that I wouldn't quit even if the conditions suggested I should. And they were right: I wouldn't quit. I had to finish. It was strange to feel so compelled to finish something without really knowing why. At this point, my sole purpose was to finish.

As I was struggling one day, I thought about my dad's fight with cancer and how he had been willing to do almost anything if there was a chance it would save his life. He had struggled each day to do something to make his life feel meaningful. Some days, the task was simply getting some wood to start a fire in the fireplace. I remember the day I came in and he couldn't keep the fire going; he was upset and frustrated. It seemed like such a strange thing to be so upset about. He then explained that he felt like he had no purpose and wondered why he was still alive. If he couldn't even have a productive day, then what was the point? He just wanted to be able to say he had accomplished something that day, and he couldn't even do that. It was clear that he was being hard on himself, but that didn't matter. He wanted to matter; he wanted to know what he was fighting for and have something to show for his day. I felt like this wasn't too much to ask. Unfortunately, as time went on, it did become too much to ask. I could see that this tore him apart.

If someone had told him this hike would cure him, he would have done it. He would've taken as long as he needed, but he never would have quit. He would've wanted to give up many times, but he never would have stopped for good. I felt like I was replicating that feeling—his feelings. I asked myself: would I stop if this hike was the only way I could survive? I knew I wouldn't. Then I thought of my dad, who no longer had the choice of whether to hike or not. I did have a choice, and many would love to be so fortunate. I continued to walk, feeling thankful that I had the ability. Next, I shared this post:

> I so appreciate that everyone thinks I am so tough. It does give me strength. But as too many of us know, loved ones who struggle with disease are the tough ones.
>
> I kept thinking today … if someone had told my dad he could be rid of cancer if he hiked 300 km of the Rideau Trail, he would have done so without complaining about the challenges or discomforts. And he was not a

hiker. So today I walked without complaint for any of my discomforts in honour of him and anyone who has ever battled disease.

I would eventually finish the trail in the seven days allotted. It took much more work than I'd ever imagined, but the sense of satisfaction was intense. I was scratched and bruised, I had lost close to twenty pounds, and my feet looked like they'd been through a war. I got dizzy and nauseous every time I ate, so I wasn't gaining strength back in the days following the hike. I definitely had to see a doctor as soon as possible.

Once the trek was over, I did a lot of reflection on the hike and my adventures. I had been so sure I had to do this to bring clarity to my life, yet things now seemed blurrier and more confusing than ever. I hadn't dealt with my dad's death, I hadn't found peace within myself, and I'd discovered I needed people and their help more than ever. Proving my ability to be self-sufficient was certainly not the outcome of the hike. I just didn't get it—why had I needed to do it so badly? What did I have to prove? Maybe I'd found a determination and resilience that I had always thought was there but had never really tested. If that was the case, then I was satisfied, but I worried I had missed a huge lesson along the way.

I finished my trip with one last post to try to explain or make sense of the excursion. I don't think it really clarified anything, but it was the best explanation I could come up with at the time.

> I worked very hard to get ready for this challenge: training, research, and months of preparation. My dad always said, "Plan for all the situations that you can anticipate so that you can deal with crisis when it happens." And so I was able to deal with many of the conditions: the rain, the 40 lbs. on my back, the long distance, the navigation of the trails, camping, food and water supplies, and physical wear and tear. I was not prepared for the chronic wet, swampy conditions on days 2 and 3, which resulted in trench foot–like symptoms that made walking very painful. Regardless, I believe my dad's advice allowed me to deal with that crisis, and I did so by doing the following:

- Taking each day, hour, and step at a time
- Accepting overwhelming support and generosity from incredible friends and family
- Practicing a whole lot of faith

I originally thought this hike was about putting myself to the challenge, testing my mental and physical strength, and honoring a friend and loved one. I have since learned it was about learning to enjoy the experience despite its challenges and that you're often your strongest when you believe in yourself. I also learned the importance of accepting support from friends and loved ones. I believe it took many of us (living and passed) to get me over 300 km along the Rideau Trail. And I am happy to say, "We did it!"

I decided to live with the satisfaction that I had accomplished this. Many would never understand how hard it was because even I had never imagined it could be that hard. I was okay with that; maybe it was just for me to know and understand. Maybe I'd had to prove this to myself and know only for myself. What I didn't know was that this challenge that I thought I had conquered was only the beginning. It had barely even begun.

# CHAPTER 3

# Race

I sat in the doctor's office feeling a little irresponsible, knowing that I had more or less brought this illness upon myself. Once I was with the doctor, I felt awkward explaining my reasons for doing the hike and admitting that I had inflicted this sickness on myself. I felt guilty—as though I was abusing the medical system—because I had done this to myself, and now I was using up the doctor's time and resources.

She asked a lot of questions to which I didn't have great answers. She noted that my feet were badly infected; there was even a rash on my right foot, a weird amoeba-shaped rash that seemed darker around the edges. She explained that parasites and malaria were potential concerns. I'd been very careful about the water I drank, but I obviously couldn't avoid walking in it. But malaria in Ontario? What? She explained that there was a very small chance that malaria could be spread by mosquitoes even in this province. It seemed strange that I'd never heard of local malaria threats. West Nile virus was freaking everyone out, yet the risk of being exposed to malaria seemed the same. How could one have constant media coverage and the other nothing at all?

While that question reverberated in my mind, the doctor decided to do several tests: blood, fecal, and so on. She then decided to put me on a short course of general antibiotics. She thought that I might have cellulitis in my foot and that I was likely just fatigued and stressed. My body needed time to recover. She also mentioned something about my never doing something like this again. I agreed and felt a little horrified; I still wondered how it wasn't okay that I had hiked in my own province. I managed parks all over the area and promoted hiking as much as possible. Was it really wrong that I had done this? I knew that I probably wouldn't push myself as hard next time; however, doing something like this in the future was inevitable. I decided that she meant that I shouldn't go so hard—that I should be smarter next time. I didn't ask for clarification, deciding that it was best to stick with my own conclusion.

After several days of rest, at which point I should have felt better, I was even sicker. I had no appetite, and if I did eat, nothing stayed in my system very long. My seven days' worth of antibiotics was finished, so I visited my doctor again. She decided that it would be best to follow up with an infectious disease specialist. She had already tested me once for Lyme disease as well as malaria, the results of which were negative. I felt reassured that a trip to an infectious disease specialist would cover all the illnesses I would need to consider. Even if I was sick for a little while longer, I would eventually get the proper help I needed. As it turned out—not that I was surprised, based on typical wait times to see specialists—my appointment couldn't be booked for another two months.

As summer continued, I was supposed to start training for an Ironman race that I planned to do the following year. As much as I enjoyed hiking and weight training, I was excited to get back to what I truly loved: triathlons. But this time training wasn't the same. I couldn't put a finger on it; it just seemed harder than normal. I'd never had an issue motivating myself to train. I loved running—it was my happy place. It was the only time my mind felt clear. When I was out for a run, I could solve problems, figure out my feelings, and find happiness. I couldn't pinpoint whether I feared the training ahead or whether I maybe just wasn't fully recovered from the hike. I decided to give myself more time to get well—a little more time to miss running—so that I could jump back into it completely healthy.

It was later in the fall that I started to pick up my training again. Strangely, it wasn't going any better. I was constantly catching colds and viruses. I used to exercise even when I wasn't well; a light workout usually made me feel better. Now it didn't at all, and I didn't ever feel like training. I wondered if I'd lost my love for these sports. I was never in the mood anymore. I didn't even have the energy or passion to train others. These were activities that previously had fueled me to do better, to go harder—they had given me a high. Now everything took effort.

Just before Christmas, I fell quite ill again. I tried to treat myself, but it became too much over the holidays. My sinus infection had become so bad that it had moved into my jaw and teeth. It hurt to talk and swallow, and my eyesight was also affected. I had a headache that was constant and profound; there was nothing I could take to ease the pain. The ache had even moved into my neck and shoulders, so much so that I could barely move them. I was sure this was just from trying to compensate for the pain in my sinuses and jaw. I put off seeking medical attention until after the holidays and by then was quite sorry I'd left it so long. By the time doctors were back in their offices in the new year, I was in a lot of pain and experiencing constant discomfort. The sinus infection that had gone into my teeth and jaw was causing continuous severe pain. The headache never went away; I had it all day long, every day. Nothing would relieve it or any of the pain I was in.

In the earlier stages, I hadn't wanted to burden the system with a stuffy nose. Well, this had turned into much more than a stuffy nose. I'd never been so sick from what I'd originally thought was a cold. I couldn't figure out how it had gotten so bad with all I was doing to take care of myself. I felt like it appeared to the doctor as though I was not taking care of myself at all if I could end up so bad, with so many issues. She treated the sinus infection and did a few other test, but the underlying suggestion was I should not have let myself get so run down.

In the new year I went back to training. I decided that resting wasn't helping me recover, so maybe I just needed to get back to my old lifestyle. I decided to push myself even when I didn't feel like it. Maybe I just needed to fake it until I could make it, and then I would find the old me. Apparently not. All that followed was weird illnesses, and I never seemed to fully recover from the sinus infection. Whenever I went to my doctor for new health reasons, she would tell me that I still had the sinus infection. I seemed to be catching everything going around, which wasn't like me at all. I wasn't fixing the old issues and new ones were adding up.

Once I'd finally accepted that my health wasn't what it used to be, I developed a symptom that concerned me more than any other. I was having trouble breathing whenever I worked out or ran. That was incredibly out of character for me. In fact, in many of my classes, I taught proper breathing techniques to runners, including regularly at one of the Running Room run classes. People had often told me that they increased their distances, improved their time, or were able to take up running after learning how to breathe using my technique. I knew that in many cases anxiety or a knee-jerk reaction to breathing difficulties caused people to disrupt their breathing. I spent time teaching runners how to relax their breathing and explained the mechanics of how their bodies used the oxygen—how improved breathing helped their bodies do more in more efficient ways. Now I couldn't even do it myself.

I knew my breathing was labored. I especially noticed it while I was teaching fitness classes. I had never had an issue catching my breath to speak, but I was now having problems a few minutes into each program. I thought I'd somehow managed to get out of shape even though I was still working out. I asked my doctor if she could hear the raspiness in my breathing. She said everything sounded clear. I was caught off guard and a little embarrassed; I had been sure she would be able to hear or sense what I was experiencing.

My doctor took me seriously enough to send me for multiple respiratory tests, assuming it was exercise-induced asthma or something similar. The tests revealed nothing.

I decided I was overreacting and returned to full-time training. I vowed to be hypervigilant in monitoring by breathing. Maybe I just needed to relax to get my breathing back to normal. I pushed forward and headed to California to run a half marathon with friends. The circumstances weren't ideal because we arrived late the night before the race. Regardless, I was excited to have this experience with my friends. It turned out to be one of my worst races; I lost steam at seventeen kilometers and never got it back. I finished, but I didn't feel like myself. It felt like I had given up mentally more than physically—I didn't use up all my energy; I just lost motivation. That had never happened to me before. I decided that I just hadn't trained well enough and that the heat and elevation had gotten to me. I let it be.

But after returning home, I knew something was definitely wrong. I wanted to avoid going to the doctor because I was sick of feeling like a hypochondriac. My doctor had once said she thought I played down my symptoms—which I did—but I got the feeling she didn't think that anymore. She was away from the office, so I saw a registered practical nurse. I had heart palpitations, trouble breathing, abnormal muscle fatigue, and low energy. She couldn't find anything and decided the issues must be due to overtraining. I tried to convince her that I knew what overtraining was and that I wasn't physically able to do it—not even close. But eventually, her insistence would even convince me I was wrong.

The next day I was working out of town when I got a call from the nurse. She was a little concerned because I'd flown recently and run a marathon, making me susceptible to issues such as blood clots. I mentioned that I had a bump on the back of my knee, and she insisted that I head to an emergency department as soon as I could. A part of me was relieved because this could finally be it; we could solve the problem, and I could get back to training. End of story.

They were prepared for me when I got to the emergency department. I was to have an electrocardiogram (EKG), ultrasound, and x-ray—again. A young, fit doctor was assigned to take care of me, and I could tell he was competent. He would know that I was taking care of my health and that it must be something serious if this many health issues had developed out of the blue. Once again, the tests revealed very little. He stated that endurance athletes could sometimes be hypervigilant about health concerns and suggested that maybe I was just reading too much into my symptoms. I was mortified. I had everyone jumping to my aid and doing double-time because I was too obsessed with my health. How could I be like that? That wasn't me. As I left the hospital that day, I swore that I would ignore symptoms from now on. If they didn't stop me from doing what I wanted, then I shouldn't bother anyone with my concerns. Even if my symptoms did make everything harder, I was still able.

I got very sick about six weeks before I was scheduled to run the half Ironman in Muskoka, Ontario. I was in and out of bed for two weeks; I just couldn't bring myself around. I thought the doctors and nurses must have been right that I was overtraining because how else would I get this sick? Not only could I not train, but I couldn't even get out of bed anymore. I wondered if I was even going to be able to run the race. I'd done many triathlons before, but I really wanted to do an Ironman and had hoped to train for a full Ironman the following year. If I wasn't able to do this one, it would push my plans back at least a year. I was going to be forty, and it felt like I didn't have time for this race to fall through.

I felt lost as to what I should do. I started to get better and talked to a fellow triathlete at work about how to proceed in the last few weeks of training. He told me to train at a level that was comfortable and stay well and rested until the race. I wasn't going to gain anything by trying to do more in such little time, so his suggestion was exactly what I did. Rest became my most important priority. The rest of my training would just have to stand as is.

Perhaps it was knowing that I wasn't properly trained; maybe it was the magnitude of the race itself. Whatever the reason, as the race got closer, anxiety started to overtake me. I wouldn't say I was the best at managing my anxiety. It ran in my family, but I'd always thought I managed to disguise it. I sometimes believed it was why I did these extreme activities. The buildup and release of completing each challenge was a nice break from constant anxiety. The anxiety I was experiencing now was different— much more intense than it had ever been before. It was crippling me at times, even while I was swimming.

I grew up in a very small town where we swam at the beach in the summer and skied at a small ski hill in the winter. That was all there was to do. In the summer, you would wake up, grab your towel and bathing suit, and bike down to the beach for lessons. Afterward, we stayed at the beach all day, playing tag and swimming. The town was built around a small river. We were so familiar with it that we would swim through weeds, attract bloodsuckers on our legs, and collide with fish with no qualms at all. Nothing in a river or lake had ever concerned me. Now I would head out to swim and panic, but I had no idea what I was panicking about.

I started swimming with a huge paddleboard in tow; this way I would always have a place to rest. It didn't seem to help (and I looked ridiculous towing this massive board), but I was willing to try anything to ward off panic. A friend finally came with me to time my swim since we thought making the cutoff time was the cause of my concern. I was really slow— slower than I'd ever been in my life. Even so, I still thought I could likely make the cutoff, so head to the race I would.

I took some time off work so that I could get to the race a few days early. I decided that I needed time to myself, and an early arrival would give me time to contemplate all aspects of the race. I wanted to feel as comfortable as possible before the horn. I followed my dad's philosophy by preparing for all I knew so that I could manage all that I didn't know. I had a feeling that this strategy would be more important now than ever. I went for a bike ride as soon as I arrived, and I thoroughly enjoyed it. The terrain was hilly, which I excelled at. I didn't like the monotony of flat races. I always seemed to thrive with the push and relaxed style of hilly rides. The scenery was amazing, so I stopped for a bit to take in the view. I decided right then and there that I would just enjoy the experience of this race; I wouldn't worry about my time or pushing myself too hard. This time it would be only about enjoying the race. Again, not like me, but maybe I was maturing with age.

The next morning, I went for a practice swim. I was swimming by myself, but there were many people around. I decided to do a short, relaxing swim out to one corner of the course and back. Well, that didn't happen. Minutes into my swim, I started to panic. I tried hard to relax, but I couldn't overcome it. Every time I started to swim again, panic immediately set in. I had no idea why or what was going on, but I knew I had to get out of the water. This wasn't going to get any better; in all likelihood, it was going to get worse. I couldn't tell if people on shore knew I was panicking, and I was trying really hard to hide it. I'm sure they figured it out once they noticed I was staying in the same spot for a long time. I eventually turned around and came back in. I was mortified, to say the least, when I walked up on shore. I thought, *And you think you can do an Ironman tomorrow? What a fool.*

The next morning, *fool* was one of the nicer things I was calling myself. My anxiety was through the roof; I'd been pacing the grounds since 4:30 a.m. I had set up my transition zone and double-checked it over and over. I walked to the swim start and back many times. I just couldn't relax and felt like I'd really over-planned this time. Some friends had arrived the night before, and they knew my nerves were overtaking me. But I don't think they knew how much. It was starting to feel crippling—like I couldn't sit still, but like my body was freezing up at the same time. I promised myself then and there that I wouldn't commit to any more events like this. It was clearly too much for my body to handle.

I'd prayed all night that a power would overtake me to help me through this race. Much like the hike, I felt like it was beyond my control. I would need something more powerful than myself to make this happen. This wasn't just my pessimistic side coming out; I hadn't completed a swim in weeks. How was it that all of a sudden I was going to do it in my race? I looked my husband in the eyes that morning and started to cry. He was used to my taking on these challenges and getting a little emotional over them too. He said the same thing he always said; he told me that it would all be okay and that I would do fine. He was always right, but this time I wasn't reassured.

What came next had to have been a divine intervention brought on by my prayers. Moments before the race, I ended up chatting with another participant. She must have noticed my nervousness because she asked if this was my first Ironman, to which I responded, "Yes." I explained to her that I was having anxiety during the swim and wasn't sure I was going to make it through. She asked if I realized that everyone in the race went through the same thing. My surprised look must have answered her question. She went on to explain that heightened anxiety was normal at the start—my adrenaline was flowing, and I had to regulate my breathing while being exposed to the pressure of water. It was almost like a physiological reaction to everything at once, a reaction that felt like a panic attack. She said that some people worked through it better than others but that most participants would experience this reaction until their bodies and minds regained balance. Wow, I thought, she was talking to me like I talked to runners about breathing. At this point, I knew I'd be okay.

It's funny how coping is easier when you know other people are going through something similar. Maybe for me it was knowing that my experience was a normal physiological response and not a weakness on my part. Regardless of the why, I was determined to swim (or tread) through the panic and race on. That's exactly what I did when the time came. I had a moment of panic, and I just flipped on my back and did the backstroke for a few minutes until I was able to resume a front stroke again. It worked brilliantly. I did, however, have to apply this strategy once more when a wave of men behind me began closing in at a rapid pace. They were all wearing baby-blue swim caps. When I looked behind me, all I could see was blue hats bobbing up and down with arms flailing. They were getting closer and closer. I knew I wasn't going to be able to stay ahead of them, so

I prepared myself: I rolled on my back and tried to stay afloat. They swam around and what felt like over me. In a second they were past me. As I caught my breath, I watched them create distance between us.

I was smiling inside as I neared the end of the swim course; I knew I'd done it. I was going to complete the swim well before the cutoff. I realized that I'd been talking to myself and actually cheering myself on, addressing myself by my nickname, Woody. I had to laugh about that. I'd spent many years playing sports with friends cheering me on: hockey, rugby, broomball, adventure races, and triathlons. Now I was echoing their cheers in my head. I just kept repeating, *You got this, Woody*, over and over in my head. I was smiling. I was proud of myself, and I knew I would keep my promise and just enjoy the experience for what it was.

As I came to the transition zone, I was shocked to see that no one was there to cheer me on. When I took off for the bike portion, I noticed a few of my friends wandering aimlessly. When I caught the attention of one, I realized I'd come in much faster in the swim than I had expected; they didn't even think I'd be back yet. Things were turning out way better than I'd imagined! And of course, my husband had been right again.

I headed out on the bike, which was always my favorite part of the triathlon. I had my fueling down to a science. I had honey-based gels and bars because being sugar-free was very important to me. I knew when to eat and when to drink so I'd have enough energy. I knew better than to consume so much that it would slow me down. The biking was going well until the halfway mark. At first I thought I was just bored with a short, flat portion of the race, but I soon realized I'd lost steam. I didn't worry too much because I was still biking—I was just going at a more moderate pace and wasn't able to push up the hills like I had before. A woman in my age category with whom I'd been taking turns passing each other eventually passed me one last time, and I never saw her again. I felt deflated, but I stayed focused on saving energy for the run.

When I got back to the transition zone, I knew I was going to finish the race. I decided to yell at my friends to say I was going to be a little longer in the run. I knew my energy level was lower than it should've been, and I accepted that. I would soon be glad I had shared my thoughts with them because things were about to fall apart during the run. The joys of being female were about to present themselves in a very physical way. I'd managed not to notice during the other portions of the race, but it quickly became obvious that I'd gotten my period. I typically wouldn't share this story beyond my friend group, but the ridiculousness has value. I could only laugh. I had to visit the water stations to splash my legs, and I stopped at most outhouses. If I'd had money (which I didn't), I probably would've gone to the drugstore as I passed one during the run. Needless to say, my run was even longer than I had anticipated. I'm not sure if I could even call it a run, but I finished just like I'd promised I would. And despite everything, I absolutely loved every second of it. I couldn't wait to do the next one.

# CHAPTER 4

# Decline

This time I was set on allowing the appropriate time for my body and mind to recover after the race. I knew I needed mental and emotional rest along with the physical recovery. I committed to being kind and gentle with myself for as long as it took.

Something along the way scared me a little. It actually scared me so much that I believed I'd pushed myself too hard. Mentally, I just felt out of sorts—not myself. My daughter had left for university weeks before the race. I hadn't expected this to impact me so deeply because I had always encouraged her to do anything she wanted: to travel, to try new things, and to dream big dreams. But after she headed off to university, I was devastated. I thought maybe these strong, new emotions combined with training and a prolonged illness were finally taking a toll. I really wasn't sure. I just knew that for the first time in my life, it was time to back off and truly recover.

Of course, I felt a sense of satisfaction after finishing the race. I'd checked a lot of things off my bucket list in my life, the Rideau Trail hike and the half Ironman being two events that were major triumphs for me. I had always lived with the fear of not being able to accomplish things that made me happy. What if someday it would be too late? Now I felt like I had enough under my belt that I could sit back for a while. That didn't mean I was done challenging myself; I just wasn't hell-bent on tackling the next obstacle just yet. I had time to recover. I thought my next feat would be a full Ironman, so that might be why I was so committed to recovering properly. Regardless, I knew it was time to give myself a break, and that was what I was going to do.

As weeks passed, I felt that letting myself heal was the right thing to do. I wasn't noticing any major improvements, but I also wasn't rushing the process. I was content with my progress even though I had initially thought the recovery would be around three weeks. As week 3 came and went, I started to do more research on what a typical recovery should be. The information was mixed—as it always is on the internet—but I found the average recovery time to be around three to six weeks. That's when I noticed a few disturbing articles. Some athletes were saying it had taken them three months to recover, and there was one who had never recovered at all. That seemed ridiculous to me. It did, however, re-up my resolve to recover properly.

During my recovery, to keep in shape, I would occasionally go for a light jog or try one of my favorite high-intensity interval training workouts. They sure didn't feel good; I didn't get the normal rush of energy or natural high that I usually felt. I knew I had to give my recovery more time. I tried to keep up with stretching, yoga, and a few muscle-toning exercises, but they also didn't feel very good. I even found them hard to do, which was really discouraging.

As the three-month post-race mark approached, I started to push myself out of sheer determination. Three months was without a doubt enough time to heal, so I started a light training regime. Running—my absolute favorite exercise—felt awful. I tried to work up to ten kilometers again, and I just couldn't do it. After several weeks, I finally worked my way up to six kilometers, and it was the most pathetic six kilometers I'd ever done. I walked a lot, and I lost my breath and was never able to recover it. I felt completely drained before it was even over. I was so depleted that I had to call one of my kids to come pick me up. I took this setback to mean that I actually had taken *too* much time to recover, and now I was out of shape. I was disgusted with myself.

Over the next few weeks, I started my workouts at a lower level, so that I could build up my endurance again. This seemed like a very reasonable plan, but I got sicker and sicker as I went. Every time I worked out, I would feel so sick the next day that I'd barely make it to work. It seemed

ridiculous to miss work because of a workout, so I tapered off even more—
so much so that I was barely exercising at all.

I went back to my doctor and tried very hard to explain how I was
feeling. It proved much more difficult than I had imagined. After I
explained that, after many months, all I could do was a labored six-
kilometer run, she said, "Do you know how many people would be happy
to run six kilometers?"

I knew she hadn't understood my complaint. I was an experienced
athlete, not a beginner. And yes, I did understand how many people would
be happy they could run six kilometers because I used to train people to
do it. But I really couldn't explain it any more clearly. I still had all the
symptoms I'd been describing to her for the last two years, but I'd lost sight
of how long I'd actually been sick. I thought describing new symptoms
might help with a diagnosis, but in the end this only seemed to make my
issues look petty—the worries of a high achiever. I was embarrassed and
felt selfish to be burdening the health care system with such insignificant
and maybe even vain symptoms. Boo-hoo, I couldn't run ten, twenty, or
thirty anymore. Suck it up.

As I looked for help beyond my family doctor, I found an alternative
health clinic that addressed health issues from an all-inclusive perspective.
After my initial consultation, I thought the clinic had the potential to
help me. The plan was that I'd go in one to two days per week for four
to six weeks. Each day would be a full day of treatments: homeopathy,
naturopathy, osteopathy, acupuncture, psychology, and massage. It would,
of course, be paid out of pocket, which I was willing to do because I was so
desperate to be healthy. After a few weeks, I saw some improvement with
many symptoms but noticed my chest pain was getting worse. I hadn't
even mentioned the chest pain to my doctor because I thought the constant
chest tightness—which felt almost like bruising—was brought on by my
stress and anxiety. After some improvement, it seemed that the days after
visiting the clinic, I would get really sick, so much so that I couldn't go to
work. I eventually had to quit the program; it was making me feel worse. I
would miss two days of work a week to go to the clinic and then miss the
next two days because I was sick. At this rate, I would lose my job.

I felt a little defeated, but I was happy that some symptoms had
lessened. Since my chest pain was radiating into my back, I decided to

try a chiropractor. I hadn't realized how bad my posture had gotten, and I was told that I had a few ribs out of place—a potential cause of the breathing issues and chest pain. I was relieved that there could be such a simple solution. Was it possible that a small issue like this could cause so many symptoms? I was hopeful and committed to finding out. After a few treatments, I thought my breathing was better, but I wasn't sure. After a few weeks, however, it was clear that my chest pain was still out of control. I started to feel ill the day after each treatment. I tried to explain this to the chiropractor, but he didn't seem to think it was related to the back adjustments. How was it possible that they were making me nauseous, weak, and fatigued? I had to take a break.

I thought my energy was picking up, and I considered that simply going to all these appointments might be wearing me down. I was waking up feeling sick and nauseous every morning—it was like that feeling you get when you're coming down with something, so you go back to bed. It was as if I hadn't slept all night; I was exhausted far beyond anything normal. I would tell myself to just go and shower in hopes that it would wake me up and make me feel better. But after the shower, I would feel worse. How was it possible that a shower, which usually left me feeling rejuvenated and awake, made me feel worse? I could barely keep my eyes open or hold my head up, and I'd just woken up.

I called in to work—again—to let them know that I was working from home. I knew I couldn't get myself to the office, but I had work that had to get done. I was starting to spend many days working from my bed because I was simply too tired to sit up. When I did go to work, by midafternoon I'd often think, "I have to head home; I'm coming down with something." I would hang on, only to end up feeling the same way the next day. I knew I had to be sick with something. I assumed it was just a lingering virus that wasn't presenting itself, and it was simply wearing me down as I tried to fight it. At least that was the story I started to tell myself.

When the "virus" did finally get me down, I'd be down for a week. When my coworkers talked about getting the latest cold or virus going around, I'd say, "Wasn't that the worst one ever?" They'd often give me a strange look. I'd tell them that normally when I got sick, I'd have one bad day when I couldn't get off the couch, didn't want to eat, and couldn't do anything. But then it would pass. Now when I caught a cold, it leveled me for three or four days. The first day when I felt something coming on would be followed by many days where I couldn't function at all. A full recovery took a week or more when it used to take days. People seemed to have no idea what I was talking about. I couldn't figure out why I seemed so unhealthy compared to everyone around me. No one I knew ate healthier or focused more on their health and fitness than I did. Yet I was always so sick.

My chest pain was so bad one night that I actually considered going to the emergency room; however, it was very late at night, and all I could think was that if I went, I'd be too tired to go to work the next day. I could *not* miss another day; I'd missed too many days already.

I stayed home and looked at websites about heart conditions in women. I checked all the symptoms and warning signs in females who were unaware they were having a heart attack. My thoughts were so conflicted. I was convinced I had heart attack symptoms. But no—it was ridiculous. There's was no way I was having a heart attack. I was a very healthy and fit woman. I had run marathons and endurance races; I was taking good care of myself. There was just no way I was having a heart attack. All I could imagine was how embarrassing it would be to go into the ER and tell someone that I thought I was having a heart attack. I'd humiliated myself in front of doctors too many times already; I wasn't going to do it again. Had I become a hypochondriac? I couldn't believe I was like this.

It was a horrible night. I went back and forth between thinking that something really bad was happening and telling myself I'd lost my mind. In the morning, I called my doctor's office as a precaution. When they asked if I wanted an appointment, I said no—I couldn't waste the doctor's time again. I instead asked if I could I leave a message, so that she could decide if I needed to come in or not. I got no phone call that day. I thought that I must have really been overreacting despite my symptoms that seemed to be worsening. It seemed like a clear message that I needed to change my perspective. If the doctor wasn't concerned, then I sure wasn't going to be.

The next day, my symptoms seemed better, so I went to work. Our secretary called me out of a meeting because she'd received a call from my doctor, who didn't want to leave a message. When I called back, the doctor scolded me over the phone, saying that I should've gone to the hospital immediately if I'd had those symptoms. "You should never fool around with those kinds of symptoms," she said.

I explained to her that I thought they'd passed, and maybe I was making them seem worse than they actually were. The doctor responded that those types of symptoms all together were serious regardless of how strong they were. She then told me to leave it be if I was comfortable but to head to the emergency department if the symptoms returned at any point. That afternoon, her office set me up for an appointment with a cardiologist.

Wow, I thought. Apparently, I wasn't overreacting. What a relief. Maybe this had been the solution all along. Perhaps, finally, the cardiologist would find out what was wrong with me. I just had this feeling that I would finally find some answers to my varied symptoms: the blood clots, the trouble breathing, the chest pain, and the lack of stamina. Yes, a heart issue just might explain it all. Thank goodness help was on its way. I couldn't have been happier.

My first appointment was underwhelming and didn't reveal much. The cardiologist explained that the growth on the back of my leg was a Baker's cyst and not a blood clot as the ultrasound had indicated. Looking back, I don't know why I didn't dig deeper to find out why I had a Baker's cyst. The doctor felt it wasn't a big deal, and that was good enough for me. He then did some stress tests and said that if nothing was found, there were still more tests that he could do. We could book those assessments if we needed them.

The cardiology testing was a lengthy process. The doctor reviewed the results of each test over a period of weeks. After his review, I'd get a call to book another test that I'd have to wait another couple of months for. It took all summer and into the fall just to find out that I had absolutely no heart issues. The cardiologist summed up the process and the "good" news by saying, "You're one of the healthiest patients in my clinic."

I don't know if the news felt crushing because I didn't have answers or because I felt completely embarrassed. I'd thought I was having a heart attack, and he didn't know anyone healthier. It *had* to be all in my head. Who could possibly think they were that ill when they were so well, except for someone who always believed the absolute worst? I was mortified that I could create so much drama in my head when there was absolutely nothing wrong with me.

My doctor scheduled more appointments with different specialists; it was months before I could get in to see them. By that time, I'd decided nothing was wrong, but I wanted to go anyway just to see if something had been missed. I didn't have much faith that anything would turn up. Clearly, I'd developed some sort of mental condition where I was identifying symptoms that didn't exist. I was disgusted with myself. I had always thought I was so tough that I could overcome anything, yet I'd become this drama queen. I truly believed I was the problem.

I was also so sick of telling my story. I was sick of answering the same questions and receiving test results that showed nothing. I was most sick of being told how healthy I was. Either I was sick in the head and creating all these health issues, or I was really and truly unwell. At this point, I could no longer handle my mental state being put into question. In an effort to move forward, I'd assume it was all in my head and work on turning my perspective around. Clearly, I'd become neurotic, though I had no idea how. I had some major work to do on my attitude and my outlook on life. It was up to me to change and get better.

Stress was a recurring theme during my doctors' visits and tests. I was told that I needed to get my stress under control before I would see change. I'd already started to slowly back out of physical commitments that I hadn't been able to keep up with for months or maybe even years. I pulled out of a fundraising committee I'd sat on for twelve years, and it was heartbreaking. Close friends and I had formed this committee in memory of a very special person in my life. I felt like I was abandoning them, but I had no choice. I quit training along with all my fitness programs, health seminars, and personal training. I backed out of committees at work and set very clear priorities and small goals for myself. I tried not to focus on health issues, and instead I listened to fitness and motivational podcasts. I thought I saw small improvements in my health; I was hopeful.

Then came the day when I had to give up exercise altogether. I'd been struggling to walk even ten minutes on a treadmill. Many months before, I'd had to quit running and even walking outside because I would crash and have to be picked up every time. It was embarrassing. I kept decreasing my distance and still failed to maintain enough energy to walk. What had happened to the woman who walked over three hundred kilometers through pain and illness and never fatigued? Now I couldn't walk two kilometers down the road without worrying that I wouldn't make it back home. No medical professional seemed to think this was abnormal. I needed to take responsibility for this.

I committed to waking up early some days to walk for ten minutes on the treadmill. I felt nauseous and dizzy every time I did it. I'd be okay for about two minutes before extreme fatigue would set in. I chalked it up to a lack of motivation and a hatred of treadmills. I wanted to be outside on a back road or trail in the fresh air. I was sure it was my attitude that was causing this breakdown.

Then I had an idea. I used to always drink Coke or Pepsi when I needed a last-minute push while playing in hockey tournaments, working overtime, or even running in triathlons. I drank a bit now to see how long it would carry me on a treadmill. After two minutes, I felt like my legs could no longer carry me, and I couldn't catch my breath. Clearly, the caffeine wasn't helping at all.

I remember the details of that day very clearly. I lay on the cool floor beside the treadmill for about ten to fifteen minutes. I was just going to rest for a minute, and then I would see how much longer the caffeine would give me a boost. It was early in the day; I shouldn't have been that tired. I climbed back on the treadmill, and after just thirty-seven seconds, I felt like I was going to pass out, throw up, or fall over. I was done. That was the day I knew I could no longer exercise. I'd tried every trick I knew—and every exercise option I could find—and I was still barely able to walk two and a half minutes at a slow pace on a treadmill. I never reflected on how unrealistic it was for someone to go from running an Ironman to not being able to walk for more than two minutes over a period of only two years. The expert opinions and the "good" test results had convinced me that it was all in my head and that my situation was normal; my health issues were my own doing, and it was my responsibility to figure out what I was doing wrong. I hoped that stopping everything would give me some answers.

I was wrong. My commitment to giving up exercise was the beginning of my demise.

I had been listening to motivational, spiritual, and religious podcasts on my way to work every day. I thought this was helping me have a more positive outlook as I made my way to work. Regardless of how ill I felt when I woke up, I would force myself to get in my truck and drive to work, insisting that a different perspective would change everything. I even tried to ignore that I was so sore and stiff when I arrived at work that I had to loosen up my legs before I could get out of my truck. I would have to stand beside it for a few seconds to make sure my legs would support me. It would take the whole walk into the office before they no longer felt like I was recovering from an ultramarathon. My leg muscles felt more sore now than they had after the hardest workout.

In an effort to change my perspective, I decided to ignore some of my more concerning symptoms, hoping they weren't as bad as they seemed. After months of pain in my left shoulder, I lost all feeling in it. I lost feeling in my right foot and left hip. Every time I got up from my desk, I would quickly lose my balance and fall. At some point during every day, I felt so sick and tired that I thought I could roll up and sleep just about anywhere. Sometimes I couldn't think clearly and would have to tell my staff that we needed to talk about a particular issue on another day. I couldn't even figure out simple things.

I got caught daydreaming a lot, and it was embarrassing. That had never happened to me in my life. People would come into my office and find me staring into space. I'd make up an excuse as to what I had been thinking about, but the truth was that I hadn't been thinking about anything. I'd had no idea that I was even daydreaming. Sometimes it even took a minute to get my attention. I was forgetting everything—and I mean *everything*. I used to have a great memory, and I had excelled at multitasking (or at least I thought I had). Now I had to ask people what we'd decided in a previous conversation or if we'd even talked about a certain topic. The weirdest feeling was when I felt like I was losing time in a day. We all have those days when we don't feel very productive; we question how we could have only sent one letter in eight hours. This was how I was feeling every day.

I never had quiet, productive days at work anymore—days when I got a lot done or caught up on work. Even sending an email felt like it took effort: thinking, writing, editing, and then hitting the send button. Sometimes it would take me all day to produce an email. Again, I thought it was my attitude, so I wanted to hide these setbacks until I got my act together. I shared my health concerns with my boss because I feared reprimand for my numerous sick days and lack of production. It was, however, often humiliating to say that nothing had been found through the tests or specialist visits. I just wanted her to know that I wasn't myself and that I really didn't know what to do about it.

My own doctor said she had no idea what else to do, so I was left to my own devices. At this point, things were getting scary. I was struggling to even make notes at work. By the time I picked up a pen to write something down, I had already forgotten what it was. I would drive to meeting locations—locations I'd driven to countless times before—only to end up sitting on the side of the road, confused, with no idea how I had gotten there or how I was going to get home. I'd be quietly driving home when I'd be overcome with such intense anxiety that I'd have to pull over and wait for it to pass. I'd often call my husband to talk—not to share what was happening, but to distract myself so I would recover faster. I didn't know what was causing such anxiety.

My tolerance level at work was very low. Everything upset me so much that I started to decline meetings so that I could hide in my office as much as possible. I felt like I was rapidly deteriorating—my mind, body, and soul—and I couldn't even help myself. The list of daily activities that were major hurdles started to grow. If I had to walk up one flight of stairs, afterward I had to wait to catch my breath before I could speak to anyone. I wasn't much of an athlete anymore, but my body felt like I was participating in the most grueling challenge every single day.

I knew I'd physically deteriorated too far when I started having trouble walking in the mornings. This wasn't trouble walking on the treadmill—I literally could not step out of bed and know that my legs would hold me up. I had to practice getting my legs and feet working. It was like they were temporarily paralyzed every morning. I had a routine: I would sit on the edge of the bed, wiggle my feet and toes, tap them on the floor, and then slowly add pressure. Once I could stand comfortably, I would try to take a step. I'd then have to lean against a wall or use a railing because my ability to support myself would take a few minutes to kick in. I knew now that something major was happening; I knew this couldn't be right. This was when my brain started to dramatically fail me too. This was much more than attitude—I was seriously failing, and I couldn't fight this on my own anymore.

For months, I'd been telling my husband that something was seriously wrong. He had done his typical thing in response, trying to comfort me by saying, "No, it's not that bad. It will pass. You're okay." Now he wasn't saying that anymore. He had to help me catch my breath while we were walking across our yard. He had secretly started to watch me do things such as get up from a chair. He couldn't believe how much I struggled. Even a few minutes of sitting left me so stiff and sore that it took me a minute to stand without experiencing pain. He then saw my confusion. I started messing up words, losing my train of thought, and just plain not understanding simple conversations. Now even he was getting scared.

# CHAPTER 5

# Help

You feel powerless while watching your life and the world you know slowly slip away. This is the case especially when no one—not even the people who love you most—can do anything thing to stop it. I'd seen all the doctors and specialists I could, and even my favorite doctor had thrown up her hands in defeat. I'd given up almost everything that had previously defined me. Most of my passions were out of reach, my moods were dark, and my level of frustration was very high. It took all my energy just to hang on to the basic pieces of my life that I had left. My only job now was to maintain some sense of normalcy as things slowly fell apart.

The religious podcasts I listened to on my way to work encouraged me to pray to God for help. I had a somewhat selfish relationship with God; I thought of Him only when I needed something. It felt like He usually came through for me in my moments of need, but I'd been sporadically praying for months at this point. I wasn't sure whether to give up or give it more effort. Regardless, my morning drive turned into an hour of tears in which I would beg for help and promise the world if only someone could stop this downward spiral.

I felt like praying and pleading with a higher power was all I could do at that point. I was doing everything in my power to keep my body healthy, but my health was declining every day. And now it was happening faster. My face was incredibly swollen, and I had a mild case of Bell's palsy that caused the right side of my face to droop a bit. I ignored this problem and tried to tell myself that one side of my face was just more swollen than the other. When I looked in the mirror, I didn't recognize the person looking back at me. It might sound cliché, but I would literally look in the mirror and say, "I have no idea who that is." I wasn't sure if it was because my face had changed so much or because a glaze had covered my eyes. It felt like those eyes didn't belong to me. Of all my symptoms, that one was the weirdest and the hardest to explain, so I told no one. I knew that someday—when this seemingly inexplicable situation was all sorted out—I'd be able to explain this daily experience to someone who would understand. For now, I just saw that person in the mirror as someone I did not know.

I started to wonder if I was disassociating from myself as a survival mechanism. Was this my way of dealing with the struggle, pain, and confusion? I had an incredibly weird thought that perhaps something had taken over my body, and that was why I wasn't me. You can imagine why I kept these crazy thoughts to myself. If professionals had originally thought this illness was in my head, then they would have had me committed at this point for sure. The thoughts remained private while I worked hard to convince myself that I wasn't crazy. I no longer had an objective perspective on my mental health. My physical health was clearly diminishing, and I was starting to believe that my mental health was sliding right behind it on this slippery slope.

I was doing my best to practice every coping mechanism available in order to survive the challenges I faced daily. I was doing everything from using a GPS to make sure I didn't get disoriented or lost (even if I was going to a familiar place) to writing everything—absolutely everything—down, to strategizing every moment of every day to maintain as much energy as possible. I knew I couldn't maintain this forever, but I had a strong feeling that I was trying to buy time until … something. I just didn't know what was coming.

I had been missing work and working from home on and off. Eventually, I was expected to attend a meeting in Toronto every few months as part of my job. The old me would have driven up the morning of the meeting, attended, and then driven home. It made for a long day, and my travel time was twice as long as the meeting, but I was used to it. This time, there was much debate about whether I could even get myself there, but I felt an overwhelming need to go. I booked a hotel for the night before and the night after the meeting. I knew it would be impossible for me to drive even one way without rest. What I didn't know was that I wouldn't even be able to make it the whole way there. I had to pull over halfway and sleep in my vehicle. I woke up feeling worse, but I knew I needed to either drive home or continue on, so I kept going. I crashed hard in the hotel room that night and struggled to get up the next day for the late-morning meeting. It was becoming glaringly obvious how weak my body was. A good night's sleep did nothing to rejuvenate me—ever.

I had a deep desire to make the meeting, and I couldn't understand why. It didn't seem like the appropriate thing to do given how horrible I was feeling. My worst fear was realized when I struggled to follow the conversations despite battling with my mind to stay focused. I lost track of any conversation or presentation within minutes. I was getting nothing from this meeting other than the desire to run. To make matters even worse, when I was asked a routine question, I could tell by the looks on others' faces that I was making no sense. It was a horrifying experience. It was like I was speaking gibberish—I just wasn't following a thought process, and no one knew what I was trying to say. The more I tried, the worse it got, so I just stopped. I criticized myself for having come and wondered why I had even considered it.

It was then that another participant said a few words about a colleague who had battled chronic Lyme disease. She was describing my symptoms. It hit me like a ton of bricks: maybe I was meant to hear this. I had considered Lyme throughout my illness, but the blood tests had all been negative, and every doctor had insisted that it wasn't the right diagnosis. One friend had kept suggesting that it was Lyme, but the information I looked up was so conflicting. The doctors in turn kept confirming that it wasn't Lyme, so why would I think otherwise? In this work meeting I discovered that a doctor had sent this colleague to the United States for diagnosis. She further explained that the Canadian medical society didn't understand, test, or treat Lyme properly. *What?* I thought. I'd never heard that before. With all the Lyme awareness and prevention training I'd received, this fact had never been disclosed. It was like the missing piece of the puzzle. How could I not have known this?

I left the meeting shortly after, feeling like my head was going to explode. It was all so confusing to me. Could it be possible? How could all the specialists have missed this? I started to pass it off as crazy talk. There was no way I could've had dozens of tests and visited so many specialists only to have a missed diagnosis. The doctors knew about my tick bites and my at-risk job. If Lyme was a possibility, then it would (should) have been the first thing they'd considered. I figured my mind was so desperate for help and for an explanation that I was grasping at straws. I decided to let it go.

I felt okay for a few days before I ended up losing my vision at work. My eyes were so blurry that I felt like I was walking around drunk. I was dizzy, nauseous, and unable to keep my balance. I struggled to even type and spelled every single word wrong—the letters were mixed up in every word, as though I'd developed dyslexia. I wasn't sure whether to go home, call someone, go to the hospital, or just sit tight to see if it would pass. At that moment, I felt compelled to email the colleague who had been mentioned at the Toronto meeting to ask her a few questions. She replied that she didn't mind helping me. When I sent her a short paragraph explaining what was happening, she came back with the answer that would change my life forever: "Kristy, you're describing my situation exactly."

I wasn't sure whether to be happy or sad, but at least it was a lead. It was a new start, and she was pointing me in the direction of possible help. It was at least something after months and months of hopelessness. It was something.

I quickly learned that seeking the assistance of a Lyme-literate professional was going to be the first and most difficult step. Who would've known that the Canadian medical profession was so uneducated when it came to Lyme and especially chronic Lyme? I couldn't have imagined all the misinformation and misunderstanding that was out there. It was no wonder I hadn't been able to figure this one out for myself. I contacted a Lyme-literate doctor in the United States who set me up with a good introductory package. I'd never received anything like this from a doctor in Canada before. The package explained what happens when a patient visits a Lyme-literate doctor but also provided guidance for the patient's family doctor, to allow that doctor to be involved in the process. I couldn't believe how full and complete this package was. I instantly called my doctor's office to set up an appointment to share it with her.

When I called, I was reminded that my doctor was on leave for a one-year specialized training program, so I'd have to meet with the replacement doctor who was covering for her. This was a little disappointing. I thought that I'd have to explain the last three years of illness, but then I realized that most of that should be in my files. I would, however, have to explain the last few months of decline because much of that was new since I'd given up seeking medical help. I was sure these new symptoms would now make sense because I'd received more information about Lyme. I also had a symptom checklist from the American doctor's office. I'd experienced forty-nine of the fifty symptoms of Lyme—with many of my symptoms very high on the scale for frequency and severity. It was all making sense to me, so I was sure it would make sense to the doctor as well.

I never imagined I would be treated as unfairly as I was during that appointment. I had heard stories about Lyme-related appointments going sour but had always thought it was likely due to the patient's attitude or a miscommunication. I know without a doubt that neither of those factors was the cause of my experience. I went in armed with a lot of information about Lyme in Canada; I knew the tests that could be performed to get the ball rolling and how a partnership with a US doctor could be helpful, plus all the symptoms that could support a clinical diagnosis. The doctor refused to even look at the papers. It was like I'd suggested that she give me all her money. Her back was up from the start, and the conversation only deteriorated from there. It went something like this:

I explained that I wanted to investigate some options because my symptoms had continued to get worse, and some were very concerning.

The doctor asked, "What kind of symptoms?"

I explained the memory loss, confusion, and complete lack of comprehension I was experiencing on top of the symptoms from the last few years.

The doctor smirked at me as though I was being ridiculous. It was hard for me to explain all the symptoms I was having, so I said, "It could be possible that I have Lyme from a tick bite. I got really sick three years ago, and the symptoms really started then."

While looking at the computer files, she said, "All I can see is that you had diarrhea back then."

I knew that didn't cover it because I'd had a rash on my foot that they had thought was cellulitis. I'd had to return for other medications because the symptoms had not improved after ten days. That was when I had been sent to see an infectious disease specialist. I'd had more than just diarrhea.

Next, the doctor asked, "Why would you want it to be Lyme?"

I tried not to look horrified at this insulting question. I sure as hell didn't want it to be Lyme, but I sure wanted to stop whatever was happening to me. I tried to explain that the symptoms were escalating, my health was declining quickly, and I was getting scared that it was something more serious. I said, "Do you not think it could be something serious?"

"Yes, it could be something serious like MS or ALS," the doctor replied. "But you would have to wait until more symptoms develop."

"Wait for symptoms to develop?" I exclaimed. "I have a checklist of fifty serious symptoms right here."

"I bet you got that checklist from the US doctor?" she said, refusing to look at the paper.

I was so confused as to why she was acting like I was a criminal trying to scam the system. I tried to talk to her about the research from CanLyme (the Canadian Lyme Disease Foundation) and share the information from the US doctors, but the doctor refused to look at the papers; she wouldn't even touch the files.

I set the files on her desk and asked if she would at least consider doing the blood tests that the other doctor had recommended. She very reluctantly asked what the tests were. After learning that one test was for celiac disease, she said, "I refuse to do that for you."

With a frustrated tone, I said, "Well, that's okay because I've already been diagnosed celiac." I thought to myself but stopped myself from saying, *Good thing that wasn't my health problem, though!* Instead, I said, "So if you think that this could be serious and that I'm dealing with it all wrong, what do you suggest?"

The doctor replied, "I think we should start over and repeat the tests you've done so far."

I then said, "Those tests took three years and gave me no answers. I feel like I'm running out of time. I think it's best for me to at least visit the doctor in the States, just in case."

She stood up and headed out of the office without any more discussion. She didn't take the papers or even make any notes on her computer. She stopped, turned, and said, "I hope you find what you're looking for."

I sat there and just cried. I felt like I'd done something wrong, but I couldn't figure out what. Why should I be treated like this when I was so willing to do all this to help myself? I tried to regain my composure because I had to walk out through the main reception area. I held it in as best I could, but I broke down once I got outside.

I was so confused as to why a doctor would refuse to help me when I was clearly suffering so badly. I felt like a solution was so close, but I didn't even know if the US doctor could help me without my doctor's support. It was the last reaction I ever would have expected from a doctor. I thought it would've been appropriate to at least check my vital signs since they'd proven to be of concern in the past. If I was this sick, should that not have been a mandatory step? Clearly, she didn't think there was an issue, or she simply didn't care.

I traveled to the United States and spent three and a half hours in my first appointment. Both the doctor and nurse reviewed every specialist exam and test I'd had, as well as every detail of my history. This was followed by physical exams and numerous blood tests. This appointment was the only time I'd had physical exams over the past three years.

I was amazed at their ability to explain so many of my symptoms—symptoms I'd ignored or found other explanations for. As they questioned me further about my health, I quickly realized there were issues that I'd never considered as part of my illness; I'd attributed them to getting older or simply to an increase in the severity of existing symptoms. I then realized that keeping a list of all of my symptoms—whether I thought they were related or not—would've been valuable and not necessarily negative thinking. As time went on, I started to recommend that everyone concerned about Lyme, or any chronic illness, record their symptoms. If someone was too focused on the negative, I'd recommend adding a gratitude section to their symptom list. You shouldn't ever neglect what's happening to your body.

Here's a complete list of my symptoms as my illness progressed.

## Head

- Headaches (tightness, hot head, and migraines)
- Blurry vision (circular haze, floating spots, and light sensitivity)

- Chronic sinus infection
- Drooped face (due to Bell's palsy and swelling)
- Memory loss
- Confusion and disorientation
- Recurring cough and throat infections (sore throat with a consistent need to clear it)
- Vertigo and light-headedness (extreme dizziness when attempting to stand)
- Intolerance to smells
- Hair loss and color change (unhealthy appearance)
- Mood changes (sadness, irritability, and low tolerance)
- Hearing problems (tinnitus)
- Verbal impairment (difficulty with speech, pronunciation, and finding words)
- Brain fog (lack of mental clarity, inability to concentrate, feeling lost and indecisive)
- Interchanging numbers and letters
- Difficulty swallowing
- Bad breath
- Dark circles under eyes
- Anxiety
- Frequent sighing

## Joints and Extremities

- Swelling all over body
- Numbness and paralysis in varying body parts
- Overactive nervous system (something rubbing or too tight on my skin felt like burning)
- Joint pain (constant pain moving from one joint to another)
- Muscle pain, aches, and fatigue
- Muscle twitches (regularly in my feet but could be other places)
- Tingling (mostly in extremities but could be throughout body)
- Aching hands and feet (ankles/wrists or any joint)
- Poor balance and impaired coordination
- Cysts/boils (Baker's cyst)

- Tremors (mostly in my hands and arms)
- Poor muscle endurance
- Extreme stiffness in the morning (not sure if joints would support me)
- Neck stiffness

## Organs and Internal Systems

- Recurring flu or virus (fever or feverish feeling)
- Diarrhea
- Weight loss
- Stabbing pain between shoulder blades
- Overwhelming fatigue (constant and more intense than the worst day before the illness)
- Upset stomach
- Breast pain, swelling, and tenderness
- Trouble breathing (feeling of not getting enough air or wheezing)
- Heart irregularities (fast, slow, or irregular beats)
- Chest pain (extreme tightness radiating all around my core)
- Hot sensations throughout body
- Cold sensations
- Bruises and cuts slow to heal
- Frequent urination
- Frequent thirst
- Difficulty losing weight
- Acne
- Hormonal imbalances
- Pungent body odor and increased perspiration
- Heartburn
- Loss of appetite
- Food cravings (salt and sugar)
- Night sweats
- Irregularities in menstrual cycle
- Low back pain

- Low tolerance for cardio exercise
- Swollen glands
- Rib soreness

**Fatigue**

- Constantly tired (yet jittery or anxious)
- Exhausted when waking up
- Afternoon fatigue
- Fatigue after eating
- No longer experiencing energy bursts
- Constant low energy level
- Crashes (naps where you feel like you're out cold and wake up feeling sick)
- Restless sleep
- Insomnia
- Lack of motivation
- Emotional numbness ("too tired to care")
- Mental sluggishness
- Constant need to sit or lie down

I was eventually diagnosed with chronic Lyme (borreliosis). However, of just as much concern were the coinfections babesiosis (from the bacteria Babesia) and bartonellosis (from the bacteria Bartonella), with which I'd been clinically diagnosed based on my symptoms. It seems ticks are infected with more than Lyme these days, and some of these infections can cause death within minutes. Studies also show that these bacteria can be transferred from a tick within minutes rather than days. The previous rules of attachment (i.e., you're safe from infection if the tick wasn't attached for more than twenty-four hours) are no longer valid. These infections added symptoms to my illness, making diagnosis harder. This proves that if a doctor simply states that your symptoms don't match those of Lyme disease, that doctor doesn't know what he or she is talking about. It could be Lyme along with many other infections. Babesia is one of the worst in my opinion; it travels to the brain, causes air hunger, and can damage your heart. It's often hard to conquer too. Lyme wasn't the only concern and shouldn't have been the only thing my doctors looked for.

As the nurse was finishing some of the blood tests to be sent for analysis, she asked me what I was thinking. I tried to answer a few times and then finally said, "I'm not sure. My mind is so full. I feel so confused."

She told me that my reaction was common and that patients often couldn't believe that someone finally believed them—that someone had really listened for a change, and there was hope for a recovery. She said, "After years of being treated one way—not believed and not helped—it's weird to all of a sudden have support."

I was told that the road to recovery with chronic Lyme was no walk in the park—it would get worse before it got better. The doctor said that I would want to give up many times and would wonder if treatment was making me worse. She said to look past the recovery—I could live a better life, a life I'd thought was gone forever. I would just have to go to hell and back first. She wasn't kidding.

I was going to have to take many antibiotics along with a multitude of supplements to support my body as the antibiotics started the healing process. The scary thing about this illness is that the bacteria morphs, hides, and is difficult to kill. Not only that, but it also creates immunosuppression, which opens the floodgates to all kinds of other infections, parasites, molds, other fungi, and retroviruses such as Epstein-Barr.

I was told that we couldn't get help in Canada because the length of the antibiotic treatment wasn't permitted there. In fact, some doctors had been investigated and even charged for trying to treat illnesses using long-term antibiotics. Understanding and treating Lyme wasn't something any doctor would want to do when they knew that the College of Physicians and Surgeons would come after them. The result was that some doctors understandably tried to fly under the radar so their treatment protocols wouldn't be attacked.

It felt like I was in another universe. I couldn't believe this was true—especially in Canada. My last doctor's visit, however, had definitely suggested that something was wrong with the system. What kind of doctor would discourage me from looking for the truth when she herself had no answers?

Admittedly, part of me was relieved that I was truly sick (and diagnosed no less). I was happy to move on from the lack of support in my own country. I'd found an answer and a treatment, and soon I'd be back to myself (or so I thought). I hadn't really processed what the doctor had meant when she said that the recovery process would be hell. How bad could it be when you knew you were going to get better? I wasn't focusing on the fact that she had said it would be a two-and-a-half-year recovery for a *potential* return of 75 to 85 percent of my abilities. As is my nature, I was going to hit the recovery process hard regardless of how sick it made me. Then I could finally move on with my life. I was flying high on the solution; it was either all I could focus on or all I could manage to deal with at the time.

A month later, it felt like everything was falling apart again. Everyone in my family had trouble with antibiotics—we'd always had weak and sensitive stomachs—and I was having difficulty keeping many of the antibiotics down. I panicked. How could I stop this disease from ruining me if I couldn't take the meds? As it turned out, my stomach wasn't the cause; I was having Jarisch-Herxheimer reactions. It was a horrible part of the Lyme recovery process, and the reactions were hitting me hard. Dr. Richard Horowitz, international Lyme-literate doctor and author, describes the Jarisch-Herxheimer reaction in his book *How Can I Get Better* as a "temporary worsening of the symptoms of Lyme disease that occurs when the Lyme spirochete is being killed off by antibiotics, creating inflammation … These JH reactions produce cytokines (TNF-alpha, IL-6, and IL-8), which then create inflammatory symptoms, including increased fever, muscle and joint pain, headaches, cognitive impairment, and a general worsening of the underlying symptomology" (Horowitz 2016, 37).

I was struggling with dizziness and nausea, and I was also choking when I lay down. More areas of my body had gone numb, and I really struggled to speak or form a thought. My labored breathing would barely allow me to walk around the house. It was a scary place to exist; I just wasn't getting better. When I couldn't keep the antibiotics down, I was even more scared that I'd never get better. I felt like I'd lost so much time already. These new issues were defining the seriousness of this illness, and now I was losing even more time. I was freaking out.

I researched clinics in Switzerland and Germany. My dad had traveled to a clinic in Switzerland when he learned he had terminal cancer. It's hard to say if or how much it extended his life, but I can tell you without a doubt that it improved his quality of life right up until the end. I didn't have the money to travel to these clinics, so I had to decide what to do. There was no cure for chronic Lyme; a million treatments existed, but there were no clear solutions. The best I—and others with the disease—could hope for was to find a treatment, get as healthy as possible, and then manage quality of life from that point on.

I found a clinic in Utah with help from a friend who is a nurse and paramedic. It was closer to home and a little less expensive than the other clinics. The treatments seemed similar to others, but the hyperthermia treatments were less severe because they were based on more recent research. This clinic also taught patients how to replicate some of the treatments at home. This way, you could manage the illness on your own in the years to come. There was even an exercise with an oxygen therapy component (a fitness solution) that really spoke to me. I talked to my doctor in the States, and she agreed that I should suspend the antibiotic regimen and try the new treatment. After my return, we would review the progress and decide what other courses of action would be necessary. I felt good about this approach because I was keeping an open mind and not eliminating any treatment options.

I wrote a daily blog to keep family and friends updated on what was going on. My treatments were alternative therapies, so I too was learning as I went. People often questioned how I knew to take that route of treatment. My simple answer was that I had no other option at the time; it was the only treatment I could afford that showed promise. No decision there—I needed help and fast.

My initial meeting with the doctor at the Utah clinic was very encouraging. He reiterated what my other US doctor had said about the number of false negatives in North America and how our testing system was failing us. Canadians needed to start diagnosing clinically. Doctors needed to start learning about the symptoms. There were so many symptoms that this in itself became a clue to the diagnosis. Lyme affects so many parts of your body that when a patient starts to display numerous, seemingly unrelated symptoms, Lyme should be a consideration. Lyme mimics the symptoms of other illnesses such as ALS, multiple sclerosis, and Alzheimer's disease. It should be the first illness considered because it is more treatable than the others. Lyme-literate doctors are finding clinical strategies to diagnose it, but no one is listening. One clinical clue to Lyme is roaming pain that, for example, may start as a knee issue, move to your shoulder, and then move to your hip. You don't link the pains because they seem like separate issues, but once you are diagnosed, you realize that this is typical of Lyme. Babesia, on the other hand, is known to cause excessive night sweats, and I mean *drenching* night sweats: clothes, sheets, the whole shebang. You'll know if you have them.

The doctor in Utah was well aware of how far behind Canada was regarding recognition and treatment of Lyme. Canada's statistics say that there were 522 cases of chronic Lyme in 2014 and 917 cases in 2015 (Gov. of Canada, 2018). That makes the experts laugh. Canada is stating that there are fewer than a thousand cases there when there are over 350,000 cases a year in the States? Hmm.

I am often asked whether the clinic cured me. Sadly, there's no cure for chronic Lyme unless it's caught early. Early detection was not the case for me, but I did get much help from this clinic. It gave me my strength back—both mental and physical. It relieved me of the intense joint and muscle pain. It fixed a lot of the extreme sensitivities I had within my nervous system. The clarity of my vision was better after most treatments, though it would still cycle from bad to good each day. I even started to regain my short-term memory. Things were better, and some symptoms were gone, but my brain—my cognitive skill set—was still challenged.

When I returned home to consult with my other American doctor, she was thrilled to see such evident improvement in such a short time. Since I was able to handle the medicines and my symptoms had diminished, she felt we could now target specific issues. That was all good news to me! I thought recovery would now be right around the corner.

But it was around a corner on a very long, windy road with boulders, potholes, cliffs, and quicksand.

# CHAPTER 6

# Insight

I started to see improvements from the treatments at the clinic. Old thoughts and behaviors started to resurface—signs of the old me. My face seemed familiar when I looked in the mirror. I couldn't go so far as to say it was all better; the battle wasn't over yet. But seeing signs of the person I used to be peeking through was motivating. And the old me? She was a person who liked to fight for what was right, and the treatment I had previously received at my primary doctor's office was far from right. I needed to know how many people who sought support for Lyme were neglected and abused by the system. How many of them didn't try to rectify or at least bring awareness to this spirit-crushing system?

I sent a letter to my original primary clinic. I tried to be tactful because I truly needed help finding another doctor who would support and follow my US treatments. Having a local doctor's support would make everything easier because there was a requirement for monthly blood testing. I was constantly dealing with specialists in the States, but I didn't have a local physician whom I trusted to handle my day-to-day medical concerns. When it came to my general health, I was still floundering for support in my own country.

After I gave the executive director of the clinic some background information on my condition, I got to the heart of the matter: my demeaning appointment with the replacement doctor. My letter read as follows:

For my appointment, I brought in all the paperwork from the US doctor. I understand this is a tough position to put a new doctor in that doesn't know me. But I encountered resistance that I did not understand at the time:

She could find very little in my medical history to represent how bad I have been. I felt sure the 35 pages of tests and specialist visits I sent to the US should have been enough. But I also knew there had to be more in a paper file somewhere. She wondered why I had decided I had Lyme. I had not; I was investigating every option to try and help myself. She agreed that I could potentially have something serious but [said] that we would have to wait for more symptoms to develop. Or we could repeat all the tests that had been done to date.

I showed her my list of symptoms, of which there were 50, which she would not look at. I tried to describe a few but felt I was not making a compelling argument. I explained that the US doctor had asked for the following baseline blood work to be done. She said she would request some, but not all.

She also did not order what is the best Lyme test in the States. Although I had tested negative for a few Lyme tests in Canada, I now know that doesn't mean much. I also wish I had known I could have ordered the US test myself. So it wouldn't have been so devastating when I couldn't get a doctor to order it for me.

I also explained that the US doctor would like her to follow my treatment, monitor with blood work, and help with my prescription, to which she responded, "Don't think I am going to do anything without the proper documentation to support it." This sounded reasonable (not sure it had to be said that way), but I was devastated to later realize that likely meant a positive Lyme test.

I left that appointment, sat in my truck, and cried. I was shocked at how the doctor's words and attitude made me feel. The visit with the US doctor that followed would explain some of the challenges that Ontario doctors have when helping patients with chronic Lyme disease or "hypothetical Lyme."

I was diagnosed in New York with two strains of Lyme, as well as Babesia and Bartonella. They also brought to my attention symptoms that I wasn't aware of and hadn't even added to my list, including tremors, paralysis on my left side, and additional cognitive impairment. So the doctor should not have said that I was looking for symptoms because I was actually denying several.

I'm writing with two questions:

1. Is chronic Lyme disease something that your clinic will recognize?

2. Is there a doctor in your facility that is open to the concept of chronic Lyme, willing to support me, and willing to work with the doctors at the FAR Clinic in Utah to monitor me?

I've been battling this illness for three years, have undergone one month of antibiotics, and will be returning home from three weeks of treatment. I need to find a doctor immediately. More than anything, I beg you to let me know if I should go elsewhere so that I don't waste time waiting for a reply.

Thank you for your consideration.

I expected a fairly diplomatic response, so I knew I'd have to read between the lines. I didn't expect direct answers to my questions, but I was hoping that I'd made my case for being assigned to a new doctor. I feared that I wasn't going to get what I was asking for—that I would end up getting a shuffle of different doctors over the next few months. Clearly, they didn't consider my medical issues to be serious. I couldn't imagine anyone with a chronic illness being moved to four or more doctors over the same number of months. It was ridiculous.

The response I received from the executive director read as follows:

I'm sorry to hear what you've gone through over the past few years; it must have been a very frustrating experience.

To answer your questions, the _____ as a medical clinic is not in a position to recognize the state of a specific disease; the physicians will do so or not based on their individual experiences. I discussed your request for support to work with the FAR Clinic with Dr. _____, who is covering for Dr. _____ currently. I recommend that you make an appointment with her to discuss your needs going forward. Dr. _____ will return at the end of October this year. Dr. _____ is covering Dr. _____ until the end of August, and Dr. _____ is covering her for September and October.

Please let me know if I can do anything to assist you.

I tried to contact the executive director by phone because he insisted that we no longer discuss the issue by email. We even set up a day to talk, but he never answered the phone. I decided this wasn't worth my effort; it wasn't going to get me anywhere. I had to do what was best for my health. Trying to work with doctors who didn't support my effort to find solutions was not going to get me anywhere.

This situation did force me, however, to look into why this disease was so badly understood in Canada and elsewhere. Once I was diagnosed and I better understood the illness, it seemed like I was a pretty textbook case. Consequently, I thought I must have somehow fallen through the cracks. In typical fashion, I managed to blame myself for the predicament I was in. I needed to understand what I'd done to now be straddled with a lifelong illness when all I ever had tried to do was maintain my health. I quickly realized that wading into Lyme land was like spiraling into a bottomless hole of corruption, misunderstanding, and medical negligence. The medical profession's purpose was to help people, and yet they failed to treat thousands—if not millions—of Lyme patients for their symptoms. I couldn't fathom how this was even possible.

I had no choice but to dig deeper. Sadly, the more I tried to make sense of everything, the more I was horrified by the truth.

My first objective was to understand why I hadn't been treated for

Lyme after my tick bite, especially when I had all the typical symptoms of the disease. The following is what I was able to uncover:

My blood was tested many times; however, each test came back negative. What I didn't know at the time was that the testing is unreliable. My doctor clearly didn't know this either. Three months after my diagnosis, the Ontario Minister of Health sent a letter to Ontario doctors stating the following: "In the early stages of this infection, results of laboratory diagnostic tests provide only supportive evidence and not the sole evidence for a diagnosis. The Ministry of Health and Long-Term Care emphasizes that physicians should exercise their own clinical judgment to diagnose Lyme disease and treat it without positive laboratory test results when clinically warranted" (Hoskins 2016).

The same letter referenced the Ontario College of Family Physicians website, which reads: "The diagnosis of Lyme disease, especially in the early stage, is a clinical diagnosis. Testing is to be seen as supportive only. This is because false negative test results are common in the disease's early stages as Borrelia burgdorferi specific antibodies may not be demonstrated in a patient's serum" (Hoskins 2016).

Still, it wasn't until 2017 that the Centers for Disease Control announced that the testing for Lyme disease was less than reliable. The agency continued on to say that it could take multiple tests before an infected patient would receive a positive result (ABC, 2017). Well, what kind of testing is that?

That's when I realized my mistake: I had assumed the professionals knew everything about Lyme and could provide the most up-to-date information on the illness. When they said my test results were negative for Lyme, I had walked away confident that this was the truth. As I came to terms with the fact that this lack of information had probably resulted in my new, lifelong illness, I realized that this was only the beginning of the misinformation.

I'd been told that I couldn't have Lyme because the tick wasn't attached for more than twenty-four to thirty-six hours. I had given many of my staff this same information in the past. This rule provided clear guidelines as to whether you should be treated after a bite. Now I wish I'd never shared this rule. Besides, how could I have been sure that the tick wasn't attached on the first day of my hike? I had been walking through terrain and conditions that were ideal for ticks. How well had I really done a check on the first day? The answer was not well at all.

I soon learned that infection was possible even if a tick was attached for only one day. The reasoning behind the 24- to 36-hour rule is that a tick usually feeds for this length of time before it becomes overfilled and regurgitates back into its human host. As gross as this sounds, I was far more disturbed knowing that infection could happen well within the first twenty-four hours after a bite.

A doctor explained to me that reliance on the 24- to 36-hour rule left many people infected and without treatment because they didn't know they were at risk. The public health agencies always says that the proper removal of ticks is crucial. Why? Because if the tick is stressed or put under pressure, it will prematurely regurgitate the infection into your body. If the Canadian medical profession preaches and preaches proper removal, then it must know that infection can happen during the extraction. In turn, they must know that infection can happen at any point while the tick is attached.

I was further horrified when I found a peer-reviewed study that showed Lyme bacterial infection in animals within sixteen hours of attachment. At a *minimum*, medical practitioners shouldn't be permitted to state that infection isn't possible within the first thirty-six hours. Infection is clearly possible at this stage—and twenty hours earlier no less. Should we not have a multitude of studies showing at what point infection occurs if we are going to provide the public with treatment guidelines and rules?

Assuming that this rule was correct could have been what put me in this dire situation. The US doctor explained that the pressure from my backpack alone could have caused the tick to transfer the infection. Regardless, like so many others, I had walked away confident that I wasn't infected because the tick had been attached for only a day.

To make matters worse, some studies showed that other infections carried by ticks could be even more detrimental, causing paralysis and possible death within ten to fifteen minutes. There were many studies contesting the 24- to 36-hour rule, so why were patients denied care based on such horrible, outdated science?

It was also becoming better-known that only a small number of people with Lyme are likely to get a bull's-eye rash. What seems less well-known is that only 9 percent of these individuals will have the typical bull's-eye rash. People are being told that they don't have Lyme because their rash doesn't resemble a bull's-eye—but it doesn't always have to. There are at least seven types of rashes that indicate a person has been infected with Lyme disease. A rash, in general, always suggests that there's an infection.

I became passionate—almost obsessive—about informing friends and family about the misinformation surrounding Lyme disease. This way, I knew that they could protect themselves from infection. I felt panicked that more people like me would be neglected due to an outdated rule or the absence of a rash.

Eventually, I would be part of an interview on *CTV News at Noon* that would spark a series of advocacy opportunities. At first, this made me feel like I was making a difference; however, this feeling was quickly followed by the stark realization that this issue was far greater than and too complex for any one single advocate to fix.

As a result of that interview, I was asked by a Minister of Parliament (MP) to come speak to ministers and senators at a roundtable discussion on Lyme disease. The Government of Canada was trying to develop a new framework to help assist with the diagnosis, treatment, and recognition of Lyme. Deep in my heart, I felt like this was the opportunity that could actually make a difference in fighting this disease.

I'd have five minutes to speak to approximately forty federal ministers and senators. I'd get to explain my story and represent chronic Lyme patients across the nation. The MP who had invited me was a runner, so my story really struck a chord with her. She felt I was a good example of someone who had worked very hard to stay healthy and yet still had succumbed to a horrible illness. My story also carried meaning because I'd had to pay out of pocket to travel and find treatment outside of the country.

As I prepared my speech, it became obvious that I was being tasked with a very important job. I had five minutes to represent *every* Lyme patient in Canada and to make a plea strong enough to effect change. It was up to me to express how horrible this illness was and explain the inadequate care available. All of a sudden, the task overwhelmed me.

I prepared a rough draft of the speech and called some friends over to help me polish it. I felt like I'd lost perspective as to whether or not this presentation was representative of my experience. What had happened to me and how I was managing it had become a blur. I could no longer identify the important points or remember the perfect examples; there was just too much in my head. I also didn't know how to handle the responsibility of the task. So many people were depending on me to influence a positive response.

I put my final speech together with much assistance and input from friends. The following is what I presented at the roundtable discussion on the Federal Framework on Lyme Disease in the House of Commons, to members of Parliament. It's my story and a plea for Lyme victims everywhere.

> With my professional background, I had a good handle on tick and Lyme prevention. Yearly training at work always told me, "If you're showing symptoms of Lyme, let the doctor know your profession. You're high risk." Yet while by myself on a 300-kilometer hike along the Rideau Trail, it all failed.
>
> One night, I had five ticks on my back—one of which was embedded in a place that was impossible to reach. I eventually removed it and promised myself I would go to a doctor as soon as I got back from my trek. I tested negative for Lyme and was sent to the Centre for Infectious Diseases, where I also tested negative.
>
> Later that year, I struggled with many illnesses. My doctor said that I seemed to be catching everything that was going around. Some described me as the unhealthiest healthy person they knew. My symptoms continued to build, and in turn, my doctor became more concerned. More specialist visits—and more tests—revealed nothing.
>
> I slowly but consistently declined. I lost feeling in many parts of my body. I also lost my balance on a regular basis. My short-term memory and reading comprehension were almost nonexistent. I could barely follow a story line on a television show. I was reverting to old habits and frequently getting lost and confused. When I spoke, the wrong words came out. I couldn't walk in the morning

without needing support and experiencing fatigue. In a few short years, I went from running an Ironman to barely being able to walk.

In one last effort to seek help in Canada, I visited a locum at my doctor's office to investigate Lyme as a diagnosis. She wondered why I "wanted" my illness to be Lyme. After refusing to review my list of symptoms, she could only suggest that we revisit the tests I'd done over the last three years. She wanted to wait for more symptoms to develop in case it was MS or ALS. This left me with no choice but to travel to the US, spending what has now amounted to $70,000 of my own money on treatment.

In the US, I was diagnosed with Lyme and two coinfections called Bartonella [bartonellosis] and Babesia [babesiosis]. I was put on a strong antibiotic protocol, which I would have to maintain for an estimated three years. I sought out complementary treatment, which led me to attend another clinic in Utah. I've resolved many of my physical symptoms and am now on a new protocol to help my cognitive and cardiovascular issues.

After some improvement, I decided to return to my doctor's office to see if they would support or follow my treatment in the States. The new locum insisted that I go off my meds because doxycycline was the only treatment for Lyme in Ontario. I explained that I was dealing with chronic Lyme, which I'd had for over three years. There was no response, no suggestions, and no assessment of my basic health indicators.

A few months ago, my original doctor returned to the office. Her positive response gave me hope. I spoke of my last year since diagnosis, to which she replied, "I read through the history—no need to go through it again." I brought up Lyme, to which she responded, "That's between you and your specialist." No questions asked.

After [I had seen] three doctors in Ontario, no one had taken my basic vitals or had any interest in my condition.

Like so many, I've been denied long-term disability support. While I go further into debt fighting this decision in court, I'm one of the lucky ones who might be able to go back to work. The only problem is that I work with and manage people who work outdoors and in parks. How do I do that knowing I'm responsible for their health and safety? If they're bitten, the chance of them getting diagnosed, treated, or even acknowledged is immensely low.

I've endorsed the benefits of nature for decades. How do I do that now, knowing that I'm sending people into a danger zone which could cause them to suffer physical, mental, and financial trauma?

How do I send them out there when my horror story started in one of our famed provincial parks? When the provincial health care system neglected me at every turn? This year, we're really encouraging people to visit our parks and natural areas. I hope we'll also be there for them if Lyme prevention fails.

I agree that the science needs to improve, but the compassion surrounding this illness must improve first. This is not an illness without a cure. It simply needs to be recognized and treated immediately. Clinical diagnosis will only be effective if doctors are willing to learn about Lyme and its early to chronic symptoms. If there continue to be consequences for doctors who treat Lyme, the situation has little chance of improving.

Please take note: I, along with hundreds of others I know, are not part of the Lyme statistics in Canada. Many have tested negative in this country and have been diagnosed or treated elsewhere. If we had access to all of the numbers, we would be faced with an epidemic.

I feel like hundreds of thousands of suffering people are dependent on the words I choose to share with you today. You see, the unfortunate part of this illness is that for many decades, many patients have been too sick to fight for what is right. We're at a critical point where those who are able are trying to influence change using what little resources are available. I plead with you now to recognize this desperate need for change. For many, this is their last hope—both for themselves and for those at risk. Ultimately, our whole country is at risk.

After speaking, I felt so encouraged by one of the members of Parliament, who said, "There must be something to be learned here. That one lady, Kristy, stated that she was having trouble speaking and walking, and I just saw her get up here, speak, and walk off. There must be something to be learned from what they're doing."

Another MP stated, "If there is one goal we should have today, it should be to make sure, from this point on, that not one more Canadian needs to travel to the US or pay out of pocket for treatment."

How could I not be encouraged by these statements?

As we left the meeting room, one of the participants asked an expert witness, "Do you think this will make a difference?"

I was deflated when I heard the following response: "Unfortunately, no. The government will have to provide an overarching document that will be valid for many years, so it will have to be general."

At the meeting, it also had been explained that treatment guidelines are developed at the provincial level. A change in policy would therefore have to begin with a clear directive from the Government of Canada, which would then be considered and weighed in each province. The chance of all that coming together felt almost impossible. If it was possible, it would be years—maybe decades—in the making.

I had gone from feeling such purpose in making my presentation to feeling so useless afterward. What was the point? Was it enough that we were trying to influence change? The expert's comment was soon validated when the Federal Framework on Lyme Disease came out repeating the same prevention information that had been shared for decades. There was no reference to new treatments or plans to help those who were already suffering. At this point, it was obvious: there was no point.

The real issue is that there are a few schools of thought out there, including the following:

1.  The Infectious Disease Society of America (IDSA) guidelines, which are very restrictive, suggest that someone can be cured of Lyme after two weeks of antibiotics or after one dose of antibiotics immediately after a bite. These guidelines don't address or recognize untreated Lyme or chronic Lyme that was not treated adequately.

2.  The International Lyme and Associated Diseases Society (ILADS) guidelines very clearly explain the issues related to treatment, one-day "prophylaxis" or preventive treatments, and two-week antibiotic protocols. Many studies have shown that Lyme and other coinfections morph to hide from your body; they persist and last longer than a short course of antibiotics; and they develop biofilms that make it hard for the antibiotics to break through to kill the bacteria.

3.  One view—which isn't necessarily linked to an association—states that chronic Lyme is *not* an infectious disease but rather an immunosuppressive disease. Advocates of this view believe that Lyme is an illness in which the spirochetes or bacteria shed blebs known as OspA. This creates a fungal post-sepsis condition that shuts down the immune system, inhibits natural B-cell death (apoptosis), and creates a bio-terrain that's vulnerable to other infections and retroviruses such as Epstein-Barr. This school of thought clearly explains why long-term antibiotic use doesn't reduce symptoms for the majority of chronic Lyme sufferers.

I worked really hard to understand all of this. It seemed to explain why I might not have been treated when I was first showing symptoms. The IDSA guidelines (which Canada follows) suggest that Lyme isn't dangerous and that the illness can be easily treated with two weeks' worth of antibiotics. What was even more disturbing in my situation was that I had been treated with only one week of antibiotics. Furthermore, the medication I had been prescribed wasn't suggested—by any guideline—for the treatment of Lyme disease.

Looking back, I realized that the two-week window after my bite had been the critical turning point in my life. If I had been better-informed, I wouldn't have become chronically ill or spent all my savings on treatment. I wouldn't have wasted three years struggling to live a normal life. The realization crushed me; it literally took my breath away. It hurt my heart to realize this had happened because I had trusted the experts and not second-guessed their diagnoses and prognoses. I would do anything to go back to that two-week period.

A fire started to burn inside me. I might not have been able to influence the government, and I might not have been able to influence public educators, but I *could* educate colleagues and friends. I had friends and family who lived, worked, and played in the most remote areas—hunting, ATVing, hiking, logging, and farming in areas now plagued by ticks. I would do my best to share the right information with them so that their two-week window would save them instead of send them spiraling down a road of torment, neglect, pain, and suffering.

# CHAPTER 7

# Truth

In the weeks following my presentation, I was contacted by CBC Radio to do an interview with another very knowledgeable and passionate Lyme advocate. She was familiar with numerous studies that made for an interesting and revealing discussion. The conversation reiterated the sentiments that scientists and Lyme-literate doctors had expressed to the federal MPs during the roundtable discussion. I was really happy with how it went.

The next day, I got a call from my aunt asking if I'd heard the CBC interview that had been broadcast in response to my segment. I hadn't heard the interview, and to be honest, I'd had no idea they were even following up on our discussion. I then found out that CBC had aired a phone interview with the president of the Association of Medical Microbiology and Infectious Disease (AMMI)—the organization that was basically Canada's IDSA. At first, it was very upsetting to hear the president deny almost everything we had said. After more consideration, however, it seemed that she didn't have any counter-explanations. She seemed unaware of the science that had been developed in the last decade.

I'll never pretend to know more than a microbiologist, but this lady was just plain wrong in her statements. I was upset because even though she was wrong, her words took the validity away from my interview. The segment had the Lyme community up in arms. Several scientists and doctors also came forward, citing a number of studies proving the association president's claims to be inaccurate. In short, these experts told

CBC that, during the interview [the doctor] made eight statements relating to science, of which six were factually incorrect.

I was also very grateful to the Canadian Lyme Science Alliance (CLSA) for publishing much of the transcript and rebuttals to the comments, in our defense (CLSA 2017).

In my profession, if I made statements that were mostly false, I would be fired. How was it, then, that a medical professional, whose information could make the difference between someone being properly treated or becoming chronically ill, could make such flawed statements with no repercussions whatsoever?

CBC considered following up on the story and eventually came back stating that it had shown both sides of the story and felt it necessary to leave it there. When you show one side of a story and only give the second side a chance to rebut, you're not truly showing both points of view. During the AMMI interview, CBC actually played statements that I'd made and then let the AMMI doctor respond. Where was my chance to respond? Why hadn't I been told that this interview was happening?

It's taken some time, but I've gathered some information and proof to show that the AMMI president did not present all the facts. I share the information here and will continue to share with anyone who cares to listen. Someday, the truth will come to light, and the Lyme warriors won't look so crazy. Those in power, who have much to gain from concealing the truth, will eventually be exposed. Eventually, the simple facts—which could have saved us all—will be revealed. Until then, I share the truth here.

> CBC: We heard from Kristy Giles yesterday. She says that she and many others are paying out of pocket for treatment in the US. Some people are getting no treatment at all because their diagnosis isn't even recognized in this country. How would a new framework help people in a situation like Kristy's?
>
> AMMI: Well, I think the goal of the framework was to try to better understand what's happening with Lyme disease in terms of prevention, education, and research. This was the reason why it'd been put together by the Public Health Agency of Canada. So what we've seen on

the internet recently was the first iteration of the summary
of that conference.

In her response the AMMI president said nothing about diagnosis
or treatment. The Framework was lobbied to improve these elements but
ended up including absolutely no reference to improving early treatment
or helping those already infected.

> AMMI: In fact, there's no scientific evidence in medical
> literature that states that Lyme disease can become
> chronic—whether it's from the Infectious Diseases
> Society of America or Canadian associations, including
> AMMI Canada.

In reality, there are more than seven hundred peer-reviewed scientific
studies suggesting that Lyme can become chronic. Clearly, the AMMI
didn't do a literature search prior to this interview, or else its president
would have known this.

A formal medical definition for chronic Lyme disease was being written
and was published in a medical journal two months after the AMMI made
this statement. "For years, Lyme disease patients with chronic symptoms
have been denied care because there was no formal recognition of their
disease. Now for the first time researchers from the International Lyme and
Associated Diseases Society (ILADS) have published a groundbreaking
case definition of chronic Lyme disease in the prestigious medical journal
*Chronic Diseases International*" (Stricker and Fesler 2017).

> AMMI: What we know is that Lyme disease is transmitted
> by tick bite. It can show up as an acute illness or a later
> disseminated stage. Once treated with antimicrobials
> for a maximum of four to six weeks—sometimes with a
> repeated treatment—there's no evidence that it actually
> becomes chronic.

To the contrary, there are many studies on the persistence of Lyme,
with the most recent suggesting that Lyme can still persist after twenty-
eight days of antibiotics (Embers et al. 2017).

Researchers have conducted many studies on this topic. They have used a variety of methods (i.e., in vitro and in vivo testing in mice, monkeys, and humans) to demonstrate the persistence of Lyme following infection and treatment. The AMMI may disagree with some studies, but to say there is no evidence is false.

> AMMI: Now, what's very complicated is that some patients who have been diagnosed with Lyme disease will report symptoms that will become chronic. The fatigue, joint pain, and muscle pain have been diagnosed as chronic Lyme in the US by an alternative lab and by clinicians without any lab tests. That form of chronic Lyme or post-treatment Lyme syndrome is not, however, recognized currently by the medical community.

Clearly, the AMMI is unaware that the vast majority of Canadians don't receive any treatment whatsoever. It's the misdiagnosis and mistreatment of Lyme that is causing problems (as in my case). ILADS refers to this as late undiagnosed Lyme.

The president of ILADS, Samuel Shor, recently presented to the Tick-Borne Disease Working Group in Washington, DC, on a study by Stricker, Hodzic, and Embers. In this study, short-term antibiotics failed up to 71 percent of patients with chronic and late-stage Lyme manifestations. (Horowitz, 2017b)

> CBC: How are those labs making a diagnosis without testing?
>
> AMMI: So, right, so—there's a lab in the US that has an alternative test that's not recognized by the medical community, and we have no evidence in literature that it actually detects Lyme.

"Alternative lab," a phrase the AMMI president used just before this, is definitely not a scientific term, so which lab and test she is referring to are unclear. She's most likely referring to private Lyme disease testing, which includes serological diagnostics based on enzyme-linked immunosorbent assay and immunoblot (Western blot) testing. These methodologies are well-established and routinely used in Borrelia testing and the testing for many other diseases. These are the exact same procedures as those used in Canada.

For decades, the Centers for Disease Control has said that the blood testing for Lyme is accurate. In 2018, the agency finally came out and stated that a patient may need several blood tests to detect Lyme. However, no formal press release was issued to the medical community, and I can't find any reference to this statement on the agency's website. In my opinion, this is highly valuable information that should be made available. What about the hundreds of thousands of doctors and patients who relied on this one test? What about those who are now infected like me?

> AMMI: And so, that laboratory, when you pay for your test to be sent there, will diagnose you with Lyme. On the contrary, the disease wouldn't be picked up or diagnosed here because in all our laboratories in Canada and the US, it's not considered to be Lyme.

The laboratories don't provide a diagnosis. The test results are sent to the doctor, who then makes the diagnosis. Payment is made for the test, not the result. The test result is not related to the payment, and it's malicious to suggest that people purchase specific test outcomes.

If we assume she means the Western blot test from IGeneX, which many have been known to request, she should know that IGeneX is an internationally recognized, tick-only lab with seven laboratory certifications. I'm also assuming she uses the term "alternative" to try to take away from the lab's credibility.

There are many studies showing the inaccuracies of the testing, but let's not forget that our provincial health minister, the Federal Framework on Lyme Disease, the Centers for Disease Control, and others now agree that there's a great level of inaccuracy in our testing as well. Isn't it time to stop making erroneous claims about other testing when ours sucks?

> AMMI: What happens, though, is that some physicians in the US—who call themselves Lyme-literate—will

diagnose patients with post-Lyme syndrome based on their symptoms. The problem is that these symptoms aren't really specific, which means that a lot of illnesses can present that way—that's why there's confusion. And that's also why when patients are being put on long-term antimicrobials—antibiotics that are often intravenous—there's no support and no way to get that treatment in Canada.

"Lyme-literate" is a general term that sufferers associate with doctors who are treating Lyme patients. These doctors, with the help of current research and clinical experience, are developing Lyme treatment plans. Every Lyme-literate doctor knows that more research and clinical information is necessary in order to combat this disease. A lack of information on the topic is no excuse to refrain from helping people.

The only instruction Canadian doctors are given is to provide no treatment at all. Would it not be productive to at least follow the solutions available in the United States? Canadian doctors should be doing research instead of ignoring this disease, doing nothing, and criticizing the Lyme-literate doctors who are saving lives on a daily basis.

"Post-treatment Lyme disease" is a common term in America because often patients get treated for Lyme or for a tick bite, and then the infection later presents itself again. What the AMMI doctor doesn't acknowledge is that many Canadians (myself included) never get any treatment, even though they present with symptoms.

> CBC: It seems to me that there's still a disconnect between the health policy and what patients are experiencing. How do we close that gap?
> AMMI: I think we need to have better research, and I think we would all agree on that.

We all do agree on that, but the question is what to do in the meantime. I would think that ignoring patients is not the most proactive interim solution.

The AMMI keeps saying there's no evidence of these issues, but then they state that more research is needed. If research is lacking, then I'd think it's more than a little negligent to keep stating that there's no evidence. Absence of evidence is not evidence of absence.

> AMMI: We need to understand and find out why these patients are having these symptoms because they're suffering. I mean, we're not saying that these patients have nothing. On the contrary, we're saying that these patients definitely have something if they're traveling to the US to seek treatment that ends up costing them their retirement savings. Now the question is, how do we figure out what is wrong?

Why not ask the patients who go to the US to find help or the doctors who are treating them? People are getting help and finding answers, so why not start there?

The AMMI may not be aware that Lyme is rarely an infection on its own. If the organization knew this, it would better understand the multitude of symptoms that patients experience. Ticks and other vectors carry many infections. As a result, numerous patients are being diagnosed with multiple infections in many different combinations. These are referred to as coinfections.

There are many studies that try to explain the multitude of symptoms that present with Lyme disease. Not only is it an infection that causes chronic inflammation, but it also breaks down the immune system, leaving patients vulnerable to other health issues. Even more complex is the exact nature of Lyme, which some suggest is more like a multisystem, neurological, post-sepsis, OspA-driven, immunosuppressive, B-cell AIDS. Some professionals suggest that the complexity of the illness and the multitude of symptoms can lead to a Lyme diagnosis.

> AMMI: And you're right—there's currently a big gap between the symptoms that are allegedly associated with chronic Lyme and what is currently being accepted as medically and scientifically relevant in the literature. Aside from doing research and studying patients—making them

enter trials or perhaps having Fentanyl clinics where these patients could be treated and tested—I don't think there's a way to actually know what's happening.

What on earth is this reference to Fentanyl clinics and clinical trials about?

CBC: On yesterday's show, we heard that it may be possible to transmit the disease in ways not previously considered or talked about—namely, that the disease may be transferred in the womb, through sexual contact, or through mosquitoes. What's your feeling about that? Can Lyme disease be transmitted in the womb, for example?

AMMI: Again, there's no evidence that this is actually happening. And in fact, animal models—mice that were infected with Lyme disease—did not transmit the illness to their offspring. So there are no animal models to support this, and there hasn't been any evidence of this in humans—at least no evidence reported in the literature. I think that—as for everything—we have peer-review journals that review articles from scientists, but as long as that data isn't available to medical literature, then there's no proof that it actually happens, either from breast milk or through sexual contact or through mosquito bites.

I could list many articles supporting alternative transmission, but it would be easier for you to listen to a presentation by Sue Faber, a registered nurse who has done countless literature searches on this topic (Faber 2017). The simple fact is that there are enough studies to suggest that other modes of transmission are possible. These studies should be examined further to seek more information, but to suggest that other modes of transmission aren't possible is false and misleading.

AMMI: Currently, Lyme is being transmitted through tick bites. The tick needs to be attached to the human for at least thirty-six hours, and so again, we go back to the prevention piece. The first step to preventing transmission is to make sure there's no ticks attached to you for longer than a day after walking through a wooded area where Lyme is present.

This is not true. There are several studies showing that transmission is possible in less than a day. Some infections found in ticks can be spread within an hour. This misinformation is causing people to assume that they're safe and that they don't need treatment. It's causing thousands to become unnecessarily infected every season (CLSA 2017).

In February 2016 the National Guidelines Clearinghouse—a national database of clinical treatment guidelines—removed the 2006 IDSA guidelines from its database. The reason for the removal was that the IDSA guidelines failed to comply with federal requirements to update guidelines according to the most current science. The only approved treatment guidelines for Lyme that exist on the national database are the ILADS guidelines, which Canada refuses to follow (Buchman 2015).

In November 2017, twenty-eight patients across twelve states filed a federal antitrust lawsuit against the Infectious Diseases Society of America, eight health insurance companies, and seven medical doctors. This lawsuit was in response to the IDSA's "bogus guidelines established by their paid consultants who falsely say the disease can always be cured with a month of antibiotics." These guidelines, established by our health minister, are still followed in Canada today (Connor 2017).

I cannot understand a system that refuses to look at all of the available science (especially more recent science), expert information, guidelines, and case studies. To insist that guidelines developed almost two decades ago—without any changes, updates, or new science—are still valid is completely irresponsible. This is especially true when talking about a very rapidly emerging epidemic. Surely over these many years, someone must have thought that something more or something new could be done to treat this disease.

Patients everywhere are demanding and pleading for potential solutions or assistance at the very least. Unfortunately, geography, finances, and policy stop them from getting the help they need. How is it possible that experts in the field, like those at AMMI can just throw their hands up and say, they don't know what these patients have, and we don't know what can be done, but what they're saying is wrong? What's worse is that those who could make a difference—top levels of government or people in positions of influence—blindly believe the IDSA and repeat what it says without verification. They turn a blind eye to the destruction and suffering happening in every inch of our country. I still don't know how it's possible that this continues to happen.

At the end of the day, CBC's questions—much like the questions of Lyme sufferers— were never actually answered by these so-called specialists in the field. Author and Lyme activist Lori Dennis answered the question better in her book, *Lyme Madness*, in saying the following: "Chronic Lyme disease is medically ignored and universally negated, forcing sufferers—for the most part, save for a few heroic doctors—to diagnose, research, treat and heal themselves. It's a do-it-yourself disease" (Dennis 2017).

AMMI's responses in this CBC interview proved Lori Dennis right without a doubt.

# CHAPTER 8

# Healing I

As I healed, I started to better understand Lyme. I started to understand how I had gotten into this mess and how we were all being misinformed. I felt passionate about bringing the right information to the people around me. I was desperate to let them know what I had learned so that I could prevent them from experiencing this tortuous illness themselves. But the more I tried to disseminate information, the more roadblocks I hit. It became glaringly obvious that this misinformation existed for a reason. And those supporting the misinformation were adamant about keeping it that way.

My meager efforts to rectify the wrongs were not enough. This battle was far beyond a single advocate like me. I knew now why patients in the past had not been able to right this wrong. The thing is that Lyme patients are very, very sick. They get much worse during the healing process before they get better. Often they have been misdiagnosed for so long that the illness has ravaged every part of their body.

As Dr. Sam Donta wrote, "if you ever want to torture someone, give them Lyme." (MacLeod, 2017) There is nothing overstated in that comment. It's so torturous. I have never been able to put my experience into words to help others understand. In short, I would do the most grueling endurance test every day if it meant I would not have to try to beat this illness. It's an overwhelming mental and physical challenge to do the most basic things, and to everyone else you look totally fine, maybe just a little tired.

The fact of the matter is that your heart is functioning as if you're a hundred years old, most of your organs are compromised, your immune system is nonexistent, latent viruses are active, your brain functions at half capacity (at best), pain circulates throughout your body, and you never know where and when your condition will be at its worst. And yet I thought I could manage all of those symptoms if not for the overwhelming fatigue. The fatigue I felt was more intense than anything I had ever experienced. Imagine your worst flu and then add every other illness you've ever had on top of that, plus the feeling of going days without sleep. After that, you might come close to understanding it. As an athlete, I had pushed my body when it was sick and worn it down to physical impossibility. This was nothing compared to the mental anguish involved in simply getting out of bed some days. There is no exaggeration here. To be honest, I still feel like this description doesn't come close to portraying the truth.

A common saying among Lyme patients is "you don't get it until you get it." And it's so true. I wouldn't wish this illness on anyone, but I know that if doctors could experience what my worst days are like—just for a day—there would be treatment, research, and solutions available. It's no coincidence that many Lyme-literate doctors have had Lyme disease themselves; that's truly the only way to know the suffering.

At first I felt my advocacy efforts were helping me heal. It was encouraging to find purpose in preventing others from experiencing my misfortune. However, I felt totally defeated after CBC's interview diminished the battle of Lyme patients everywhere.

I fell into a mild depression, which had been an obstacle throughout this illness. There are many ways that Lyme causes depression. Physiologically, I'm sure the swelling in the brain and the insane hormone imbalances play a role. On top of that, the mental abuse I felt when experts outwardly denied that I had Lyme had taken a toll on my mind. They never examined me or asked about my symptoms and treatments, yet they still denied it was Lyme disease.

The latter experience felt like the ultimate betrayal and had left me feeling somewhere between a hypochondriac, a liar, a faker, and a criminal. But in truth, I hadn't screamed or cried enough. I had let them mislead me for too long, and I was suffering because of their ignorance. It's a big hole to dig yourself out of. The professional denial and misinformation was so overwhelming that I had been forced to no longer listen to or believe my own body. Although addressing the physical symptoms of Lyme disease is a big part of the healing, there is also a long and slow emotional recovery from the turmoil that you're put through. Sometimes I wonder if the trauma of deserting and not believing in yourself can be so difficult that you might never get back to who you were. Will you ever know how to find yourself again?

On top of that, many insurance companies were denying coverage for Lyme treatment. In my case, I had to seek legal counsel to fight for the coverage I needed. It felt like the battles never ended—so much so that many times this struggle took away from my actual recovery. Many patients have used their savings for treatment and then—with no health coverage—have had to put their remaining treatments on hold.

I started to panic when these factors influenced one of the worst setbacks I would experience during my recovery. It seemed that I was once again helpless, with no way to advocate for myself when dealing with professionals. I was no longer in a position to help or fight for others either; many more were still susceptible to a situation like mine. How could I prevent them from a similar fate now?

In a letter to the members of the Institute of Medicine Committee Panel for Lyme Disease and Other Tick-Borne Diseases, Dr. Kenneth B. Liegner, who specializes in internal and critical care medicine, states, "In the fullness of time, the mainstream handling of Chronic Lyme disease will be viewed as one of the most shameful episodes in the history of medicine" (Liegner 2015, 813).

As I mentioned in my speech to members of Parliament, when my doctor finally returned from her two-year leave, she didn't even want to review what had happened while she was gone. I wanted her to know how bad my symptoms had gotten, but she didn't care. I wanted to explain that I was getting help in the US, but she simply responded by saying, "That is between you and your specialist." She didn't want to know, and she certainly didn't want to learn. All I could think was that the next person like me would undoubtedly suffer because she was not even willing to learn. She didn't even take my temperature or blood pressure—she didn't care. *What the hell is going on?* This was all I could think. Doctors are afraid to even learn about this illness because others have lost their licenses as a result of administering the intensive treatment.

I had to put my advocacy on hold because I could feel myself quickly slipping backward. I felt like there was a time crunch to get better. I also felt as though I was abandoning others, but I couldn't fight the misinformed or the ignorant if I never got better. At some point, they had to be held responsible, so I had to get better. I swore that if I ever got really well again, this was what I would do: hold them responsible. In my mind, this promise was the only way I could allow myself to be selfish and take care of myself. I could do it only if I knew that in the end others would benefit. So I went back to healing.

The thing with Lyme treatment is that there is no one preferred method. This is well explained by Professor Ying Zhang of Johns Hopkins University, a researcher in tuberculosis and the persistence of Lyme disease. He recently said, "There is no FDA approved treatment for persistent Lyme disease. It is a huge unmet medical need" (Zhang 2017).

I wish I'd known this because it is a very important fact to understand. It explains why many in the medical profession do not understand or identify Lyme. No one in the medical profession will acknowledge how hard this illness is to identify, so doctors are leading people to believe that they're not suffering from Lyme. The worst part is that they know exactly what they're doing.

The day I was diagnosed in the States, I got a dose of how oblivious professionals are to this illness. Many doctors who understand the illness have had Lyme. Some get little respect in their profession. Many couldn't get treated themselves. I'd thought that somehow my case must have fallen through the cracks in Canada until the US doctor explained that my story was not unique. At the time, I couldn't understand how that could be possible. When my primary doctor subsequently had no interest in understanding my long-overdue diagnosis and treatment, however, I knew a profound ignorance existed in the medical world. In my mind, it should be illegal for a professional to turn a blind eye to an illness that caused one of her patients to needlessly suffer for three years. Even worse, she did this and didn't learn from the experience. In my profession, I would be fired for such reckless administration of power. Yet my story is the same as thousands of others.

Dr. Neil Spector, doctor and eventual Lyme patient, was treated with a pacemaker he did not need. In his book *Gone in a Heartbeat*, he explains how difficult the experience was for him despite his medical knowledge. Spector explains, "I was largely being discounted by the medical community. If this can happen to a physician-scientist with extensive knowledge of medicine, just imagine what is happening to others who lack a medical background" (quoted in Stone 2015).

I started on antibiotics, which I would have to take for an estimated two and a half to three years. This was only a guesstimate. I would start with one antibiotic and add new ones incrementally to help my body adjust to the doses. My friends were horrified that I would eventually be on four to five antibiotics for such a long period of time. I, however, was horrified only at the measures I had to take to get the drugs. No one would support such intense prescriptions from a US doctor. How could a doctor deny me treatment and watch me suffer immensely without even trying to help me? I felt like a criminal when I was just trying to save my own life. Within a few weeks, I was seeing small glimpses of improvement. I felt as though I'd at least stopped the downward spiral. My speech had improved slightly, and my gait was a little more natural. It was enough to tell me that I was on the right path. It would be a long one, but I finally had hope where none had existed for years.

My hope would eventually transition into extreme fear as my Jarisch-Herxheimer reactions became unmanageable. I had known that the die-off would make me sick and that I had to get much worse before I would get better—that's how this illness was—but it still seemed unbearable to me. I was throwing up every day. My paralysis had intensified on my left side to the point that I was having trouble using my left arm. My speech, which had initially improved, was now much worse. I could never find the words I needed or even remember what I was saying. Walking was incredibly painful. I had to stop to catch my breath just walking up the stairs in my own house.

I felt like I could muscle through most of these intensified symptoms, but how could I get better if I couldn't keep the medicine down? Many patients are able to solve this problem by taking IV antibiotics, but I'd had to go to insane lengths just to get the pill prescriptions filled. How could I get someone to start IV antibiotics for me? I had no doctor close by who could follow my progress or help me figure this out. I was lost, beaten down, and defeated before the process even started.

A friend in the medical field helped me investigate alternative options. It seemed appealing to go away to do an intensive treatment and get over the worst of the process. I also liked the idea of incorporating alternative treatments that would build my immune system (since it's known that Lyme tears it down). The truth is that Lyme is so much more than an infectious disease. Its greatest claim to fame is how quickly it suppresses the immune system. Studies show that the illness starts tearing down and weakening the immune system within two weeks. Eventually, the disease depletes all of your system's abilities. This information made me think of the *two* times I had seen my doctor to address symptoms within the two weeks after I'd been bitten. I hadn't realized at the time how crucial treatment was within that critical time frame. I hadn't advocated for myself, and I certainly hadn't been in tune with how sick I was, nor had I realized I wasn't getting the best care. When I look back on that two-week window, I still wonder how much of this is my fault. I blindly followed the advice of one person (albeit a medical professional) with no thought about what was best for me or what I really needed.

Now, robbed of so many of my abilities, I was going to have to use my family savings to treat something that could have been easily fixed with a few weeks of antibiotics—three years ago. How could I have so blindly followed someone else's advice with no consideration of the repercussions? I didn't know how I could let my family give up so much, all so it could be lost for good at a clinic. I must be at fault here. If only I could redo those two weeks. If only I had known that not taking care of things in that two-week window would set my life in an irreversible direction. If only I had known.

As mentioned earlier, my dad had traveled to an out-of-country clinic after he was diagnosed with terminal cancer. Although they couldn't cure him, they thought they could greatly improve his quality of life until the end. I traveled with him for three weeks while he was undergoing treatment and was impressed with the quality of care, alternative information, and treatments. I always felt that it had been worth every penny. He was also able to combine his out-of-country treatments with traditional care at home. If only we could learn how to treat patients like these other countries do. Months after he left that clinic, I still consulted with the doctors on his symptoms and possible solutions. They gave as much care to the family as they did to the patient because they knew family members were often the main support. They understood mental needs as much as physical ones. This level of care was so beyond anything we experience in the Canadian system. It makes me sick to see how we are treated as patients with serious illnesses. I know that there are many benefits to our system that can't be overlooked. The simple fact that treatment is affordable to everyone is invaluable. However, for a Lyme patient, this means nothing; we're denied care in this country. The free system seems useless. And as a negligent system, it seems criminal. I was willing to pay whatever it would take to undo the damage that had been done to my mind and body. As my husband watched my decline, he more or less forced me to go elsewhere for help. He couldn't watch it any longer; it was tearing him up inside. Money no longer meant anything to him. He said he would live in a shack if it meant I would get better. So I found the most affordable clinic that offered the treatments I was looking for, and off I went.

I had no choice but to travel to the clinic alone. My husband and a few friends had agreed to join me, but the timing made it impossible for any of them to make the trip. The clinic was worried when they heard that I was traveling alone and offered to assist in any way. They greeted me that day, probably wondering what kind of crazy lady would come on her own. I had encountered danger in my life before. I had nearly been kidnapped in Pakistan, had swum with piranhas in the Amazon, and even had gotten cornered by a muskox on a cliff in the Northwest Territories. As a result, it was almost impossible for me to admit that I couldn't travel alone to a major city in the United States. Yet looking back, it was probably one of the riskiest things I had ever done. My ego was simply unwilling to accept how sick I really was.

When you have Lyme, it's not even your physical health that creates the greatest problem; it's how completely incompetent your brain is at sorting out basic, everyday situations. When the plane landed, I got a call from the clinic offering to pick me up. I told them that I had slept the whole flight and was feeling fine, so I was going to rent a car. Anyone with Lyme will tell you that you can feel fine one minute and in the next be at your weakest. Although I had slept, my fatigue was rarely cured by rest. When I got to the rental center, they explained that my car wasn't ready and asked if I could come back in an hour. I simply did not know how to respond; I stood staring at the attendant with a blank face. I knew I wouldn't last another hour. I remember wanting to lie down on the pavement right in front of the rental booth. I couldn't even form words. I couldn't figure out what time it was there, and I couldn't figure out what time it was at home. If I came back in an hour, what time would it be? I didn't answer the customer service person. I simply set my suitcase down and sat on it. I was desperate to hide my confusion.

Seconds later, the same attendant came out of the booth with a set of keys. He said, "Can I ask why you traveled here?"

I responded, "I'm visiting a medical clinic."

He then replied, "Here's an upgrade, ma'am. Good luck with everything."

Maybe this was another demonstration of divine intervention, or maybe this man just knew I needed help. To be honest, I don't have a clear perspective on how I handled that situation or how it appeared. I was just lost, confused, and not sure what step to take next.

My hotel was right beside the airport. My original plan had been to go there, get settled, and then check in with the clinic. Either I forgot the plan, or I was just desperate to get the show on the road, because I plugged the coordinates of the clinic into my phone and headed straight there. Even following the GPS was confusing. When it repeated instructions, I couldn't figure out if I'd already done that or if it was coming up. Regardless, I promised myself I wouldn't get overwhelmed while trying to get to the clinic. I had already decided that at each step I would stop, reassess, and resume only when I felt clear on what was next. It was a long drive to the clinic even though the distance wasn't very far. I stopped the car every time I got confused by the GPS instructions. I would talk myself through what I'd already done and then move on to the next instruction. When I was overwhelmed again, I stopped, got my thoughts together, and then continued on.

I felt a huge sense of relief when I arrived at the clinic. I knew this was where things would get better for me. I didn't care if I had to sleep in my car to make sure I got treated every day. What it had taken me to get there today would be my secret. This was *not* me. I was so incapable of taking care of myself that it was embarrassing. But now I was going to get better, and no one would have to know this secret. After a consultation, some baseline testing, and a review of vital records, I was introduced to some of the treatments they did at the clinic.

After the first few days, treatments started to be really hard on my body. I ceased all antibiotics while I was at the clinic because I wasn't sure if my body could handle them alongside the clinical treatments. It was the right decision at the time, but it was not enough relief. The pain throughout my body was getting stronger, and my anxiety seemed unmanageable. When anxiety came over me, I felt unrecognizable. I didn't know this person, and I refused to admit that it was becoming unbearable. I would mention my anxiety to clinic staff every day, hoping that there would be a solution. There never really was one.

Friends who had joined me at the clinic, mid-way through treatments, had researched healthy restaurants in the area that would accommodate my highly restricted diet. We had the coolest experience at one restaurant when the owner sat down with us and asked about our health issues. He'd heard a lot about Lyme and knew some of the nontraditional supplements and herbs being used to alleviate symptoms—one of the most powerful remedies being turmeric. This spice, among others, was added to my food. I figured he knew what he was talking about because he used many of the same herbs that were added to my medical smoothies (which I had four times a day) during treatment. Many people know the benefits of these ingredients but consume them only occasionally. For a person to really see the benefits, these products need to be ingested regularly and in substantial amounts. A smoothie is a great way to accomplish this.

Some beneficial ingredients include but are not limited to the following:

- Turmeric

  - Anti-inflammatory
  - Powerful antioxidant that protects cells from damage
  - Inhibits tumor growth
  - Helps rid the body of mutated cancer cells
  - Reduces flatulence, jaundice, toothaches, and chest pain

- Ginger

  - Helps with gastrointestinal symptoms
  - Anti-inflammatory

- Cinnamon
- Flax and chia seeds

  - Excellent source of omega-3s and lignans
  - Source of essential minerals

- Almonds

  - Provide healthy fats

- Kale or carrot juice

  - Provides carotenes and vitamin C

- Stevia

  - Antibiotic properties

Other valuable foods include spinach, beets, pea protein, and dulse.

Trace minerals were also added to my smoothies and given to me during hyperthermia treatment to counteract the loss from heat and sweat. Some of the minerals that I tested very low in included the following:

- Potassium and sodium (tested using hair strands)

  - Deficiencies in these minerals are linked to emotional and adrenal stress.

- Copper

  - This is an essential element in certain enzyme activity during adrenal synthesis.

- Chromium potentiates

    - An absence of this mineral can cause hyper- and hypoglycemia but also extreme fatigue and challenged stress responses. Deficiency can also increase your risk of cardiovascular disease.

- Phosphorous, iron, and manganese

Later I recreated all of my treatments at home in a desperate attempt to gain any possible benefits. Smoothies are a great way for Lyme patients to maintain nutrient levels. You can freeze portions and make large batches that last days. It's great for the days that you don't have the energy to feed yourself.

I regained most of my physical ability as my joint pain, muscle tension, and stiffness resolved. A few major symptoms still lingered, though, and it became clear that there was much more healing left to do. That's the thing with Lyme; there's no single cure. The most successful patients are those who keep doing, trying, and researching until they reach what *they* believe to be the best recovery possible. The doctor who diagnosed me said to hope for 85 percent recovery—maybe 90 percent if I was really lucky. That recovery level is something I may work toward for the rest of my life. Although the thought of battling Lyme forever was daunting, the thought of returning to 85 percent was way too exciting for me to worry about the rest.

After my clinic stay, the doctor who had originally diagnosed me was quite impressed with my physical progress. By then, I was mostly concerned with my neurological symptoms, in which I was seeing very little improvement. When my husband joined me during my last week of treatments, he had expected to see me much healthier, and I was—except for my cognitive function. It had bothered him to see me still fighting the confusion.

One day, after finishing treatments for the day, we parked in a small parking lot and took a short, five- to ten-minute walk to an observation point. When we returned, I couldn't remember the color of the car we were driving or where in the twelve- to fourteen-spot lot we had parked. This just wasn't me, and it bothered him—I could tell. It felt like he was testing me to see if I knew, and I failed miserably. I had typically been the one who was on the ball—remembering everything and anything. Now I couldn't retain anything. Nothing came to me, even when I tried really hard to remember. It was so frustrating. I tried to hide my memory issues every chance I got, but he was onto me now. He wanted to see that this problem was better, and I'm sure he felt just as bad as I did that it wasn't.

My fatigue was still pretty bad, but I had periods of high energy in the mornings that showed promise. I talked about my concerns related to fatigue and memory to the original doctor who had diagnosed me. I was assured there was still more that could be done to help me. Lyme recovery happens in stages; you can't attack everything at once—your body simply couldn't handle it. As one symptom improves, you move on to treating others. Sometimes symptoms return, and sometimes you have major setbacks for unknown reasons.

Dr. Joseph Burrascano, Lyme patient and top international Lyme doctor, explains the relationship between patient and doctor very well: "As with all Lyme treatments, specific dosing and scheduling must be tailored to the individual patient's clinical picture based upon the treating physician's best clinical judgment." (Burrascano 2008, 21).

I had been impressed when my Lyme doctor supported my going to an unknown, distant clinic to try a new treatment. It was also impressive that my doctor wanted to learn from the treatment I'd undergone. For me, regaining my mobility was a huge triumph for me physically and even more so mentally. It seemed to dramatically reduce the pain that I had been experiencing. Pain is one of the hardest lingering symptoms of Lyme. If I was managing that well, then I'd accomplished a lot. The treatment was worth it, but I was nowhere close to the end.

You have to keep trying and striving, hoping that one day you'll eventually get where you want to be. For most Lyme patients, the goal is to get back to who they were before the disease. For most of us, that's not a possibility due to more than just the damage of the disease itself. Lyme changes you emotionally and mentally. The neglect from doctors and professionals changes you as a person forever. And the battle—the battle from start to finish with every aspect of this disease—will change your outlook forever. The question is, will you change for the better, or will this disease get the best of you? It can make you so sad and bitter that you will never be you again. As much as I worked hard to show promise and hope for my recovery, this question always haunted me. Would I ever be healthy again? I didn't know what kind of mental abilities I would have, but what I feared more than anything was that this illness would wear away at my desire for a better life. I feared that bitterness and regret would be all that I could hold on to. I was fighting that fear with everything I had. Some days I was stronger than others, and sometimes I could see only a bitter and sad future ahead. But more often than not, I was determined not to let that happen. This fight was long from over, and worrying about what kind of person I would become was miles away. I still had fight in me, and that's all that was important.

# CHAPTER 9

# Healing II

As we moved into the fall, I was disappointed to realize I wasn't able to return to work. Not only could I not make it through a day without experiencing fatigue, but my neurological condition was not conducive to a multitasking management position. I had a hard time accepting this, and the only feeling that outweighed the disappointment was a sense of urgency. I needed to fix this condition, or I could be like this forever. The increase in stories of those who never recovered was overwhelming. Fear kept building in me.

I started on a strong antimicrobial drug that was available only in the States. It was prescribed to address my cognitive issues because they were more likely caused by the Babesia coinfection. Some suggest that this infection can be even harder to attack than Lyme. I wondered if my treatments so far had been combatting the Lyme but not the coinfections. Babesiosis is a malaria-like parasitic infection that is quite often transmitted by ticks along with Lyme. It now made sense that my doctor had once tested me for malaria because the initial symptoms were similar. But babesiosis was more common than malaria in this country, so why was it not even on our radar? What is even scarier is that 4 percent of the US blood supply has been infected with Babesia, but the Canadian system doesn't even test for it. In 2017, when Canadian Blood Services was questioned about this by the Standing Committee on Health (which some of my fellow advocates were involved with), the organization replied that there was no concern and that the supply was safe. Yet there's no testing for babesiosis, and we all know the testing for Lyme is useless. So for those who develop Lyme without a tick bite, there's another source to consider.

My neurological symptoms very closely mimicked the early stages of dementia. It was starting to come out in the news that some Lyme patients had originally been diagnosed with MS, dementia, or even Alzheimer's or ALS. It's always worth looking into Lyme as a diagnosis because you can often improve your symptoms with the various treatments available. Being misdiagnosed with these other illnesses often leaves patients hanging motionless (if they're lucky) or living a gradual decline—just like I was shortly before my diagnosis. And what had my Canadian doctor wanted to do? She had wanted to wait for more symptoms based on speculation that I was suffering from MS or ALS. I'm glad I didn't accept that prognosis. As hard as my recovery became, there was still opportunity to reverse most of the damage that had been done.

I'd been warned that some patients couldn't tolerate antimicrobial medications. I was told, however, that an even more intensely modified diet would help me digest the medication. Given my track record, I would still have to work hard to detox and manage my nausea. I felt stronger after my clinical treatments and really wanted this drug to work. I was determined to put in the effort because I knew exactly what was at stake: my mental health and brain function. I wanted them back.

I still didn't have a Canadian doctor to support my recovery, even though I was showing so much improvement. As a result, getting access to this drug made me feel like a criminal once again. I literally had to meet someone in a Starbucks parking lot to pay for it. It doesn't have a drug identification number in Canada, so it's not usually prescribed here, not that this would have mattered—I didn't have a doctor to prescribe it anyway. Regardless, I didn't so much as flinch at doing what I had to. I was now able to judge for myself what was best since I knew the professionals in Canada had no idea. For the first time in my life, I felt that doing something illegal was the right thing to do. No one would be able to guilt me into sacrificing my health again. I didn't care what anyone else thought.

The medication was hard on me. I had to "pulse" it—meaning that I took it only a few times each week. This is common practice for many prescriptions related to Lyme. The reason behind this method is that Lyme and other infections build up resistance to long-term antibiotics. If you pulse the dosage, however, it throws the bacteria off. Lyme is known to build cysts or morph in other ways, making antibiotics less effective. When the antibiotics are absent, the bacteria will return to its original form. It's a game. Take the antibiotics, and the bacteria will morph and build resilience; stop the antibiotics, and the bacteria returns to its vulnerable self. Resume the antibiotics, and repeat the cycle.

I would eventually dread having to resume the pills each week because I knew they would make me sick. Nonetheless, I was adamant that I had to continue them to regain control of my mind.

It was hard to judge my progress because I wasn't seeing significant improvement in my symptoms; I would see only sporadic improvement when I was on the medication. I wondered if all my abilities would come back when I finished my treatment. I wondered if the side effects and effort were worth it. I wondered if I was doing more damage than good. Most of all, I wondered if I could keep this up. I eventually talked to the Lyme-literate physician I was using, and she recommended a more potent organ and system detox. It worked brilliantly. I was so relieved. It was more or less confirmation that the drug was working. The illness I was experiencing was from parasite die-off and not the drug itself.

Next, I got a call from my family doctor's office to notify me that a new locum was replacing my doctor. Unlike the last locum, this one was paying attention to the blood work being sent from my Lyme-literate doctor and had noticed some irregularities. She asked me to make an appointment to see her. I was thrilled—maybe a fresh face and a new attitude would get me local support for my US treatments. I brought in my latest paperwork from the clinic and my American doctor and sat down to chat with her. After I provided a brief explanation of my history, she scolded me for not booking a longer appointment. In the fifteen-minute appointment, she wouldn't have time to review the paperwork, let alone my blood test results. I was so frustrated and sick of this ridiculous treatment. I told her that I was prepared to tell her all she needed to know and that I would leave the paperwork for her review.

After I quickly explained the situation, she responded by saying, "We treat Lyme with one to two weeks of doxycycline. I don't know why you're doing other treatments and taking all these other medications."

I then said, "You're talking about acute Lyme, which is an infection of less than a year. I'm talking about chronic Lyme. I had it for three years before I found out."

She had no response and no suggestions. We were then out of time.

As disgusted as I was with our conversation, the doctor redeemed herself the following week. I was called back in to see her, and it was clear that she had done some research. She was concerned about the medication I was on because—as far as she could see—it wasn't considered a Lyme treatment because it was prescribed over a longer period of time. She then encouraged me to stop taking it. As ignorant as this response was to chronic Lyme, I appreciated it more than any response I'd received from a Canadian doctor to date. She had tried; she had taken the time to research the topic in order to decide what was best for me. It wasn't her fault that she didn't have the latest information about chronic Lyme available to her. Even if she had the information, I couldn't expect her to understand chronic Lyme when even Lyme-literate doctors were constantly trying to catch up on the new research to figure out what was best for their patients. Regardless, she had made the effort. She did the best she could with the information made available to her. She cared and showed compassion; that was all I wanted when it came to this illness. She was the first one in this office who seemed to be following the Hippocratic Oath.

I contacted my primary US doctor, and she felt that I should continue because the drug was working for me. With further research, I realized she wasn't the only one who regarded this drug as a valuable option.

At this point, I was starting to get overwhelmed with all the medication again. I couldn't picture my life going forward if I was going to continue to be as sick as I was. Each day, it was a battle to get out of bed. It was a battle to keep myself from throwing up and to manage the nausea and pain. It was a constant battle to want to exist. Who wants to exist when month after month, her life of illness continues with no promise of getting better? I won't lie—I contemplated suicide many times. The only thing that saved me many times over was the thought that the next month might be better. Was I giving up too soon? I heard horror stories of people who had suffered with Lyme until their death, but I also heard about miracles, about people who had gotten back to what they loved after recovery. I so badly wanted to be one of those people, but most of the time—and for many months—it seemed like an impossibility.

I prayed daily for more help. No one close to me could understand what I was going through inside. You can't possibly explain it to anyone, and the only doctor who understands you is hours away and can help only with Lyme-related issues. I needed more help. So many things were wrong, and I didn't know if they were from the Lyme, exacerbated by the Lyme, or simply separate problems on their own. Each day brought changing symptoms—some worse and some better. I didn't know which ones to talk to the doctor about and which ones to ignore. Some could potentially be fixed, whereas others I would have to learn to live with. It was impossible to know and impossible to find someone to talk to about it. Then I got the call.

While I was sick but undiagnosed, I had applied to become a patient with many doctors. Finally, one called me; the doctor had reviewed my file and decided to take me on as a patient. I won't reveal the name of the doctor (because it would put their license at risk), but they literally saved my life. I finally had someone close by to help. This doctor had extensive experience in many areas of the medical field, and most important of all, the doctor was familiar with my Lyme-literate medical doctor in the US and was willing to work with her. On top of that, this local doctor had experience in the secondary issues that come with treating Lyme, such as immunosuppression, hormonal imbalances, chemical sensitivities, vitamin and mineral deficiencies, and viral resurgence.

After a few tests came back, I was called in for an appointment. It was just before the Christmas holidays, and I received the best gift imaginable. The doctor said that some of my blood work showed issues that would cause severe symptoms such as depression.

I indeed had been experiencing depression. I thought it was just part of Lyme (which it is), but my hormonal imbalances were so extreme that they were adding to the issue. It was possible that this was causing symptoms that could potentially be rectified.

I was told that we would have to work on healing over the next few years, but resolving this one issue was going to bring me a level of relief. I had cried leaving doctors' offices before, but this time it was for a good reason. For the first time on this journey—truly for the first time—I felt like someone was going to save me. I wasn't battling the world by myself anymore. I finally had someone knowledgeable in my corner.

I knew I had the right help when I read this quote from an interview with Dr. Kenneth Liegner: "I would have to say being in this field, if one is honest, is difficult for the most astute physicians and scientists. Because it is very complex, people are very ill, we don't have really adequate diagnostic tools to tell us clearly just what the situation is, what disease or diseases the patient is harboring" (Liegner 2017).

Over the next few years, my doctor–patient relationship developed just as a good and healthy one should. Each visit was long. We reviewed what was working and what wasn't. We discussed the symptoms that were gone and the ones that lingered. I always felt comfortable being honest and never felt ridiculed, even for the things that weren't significant. Everything I said seemed to matter, and nothing was too crazy or unimportant to share. I had known a physician–patient relationship like this was possible; I just didn't know why it had been so hard to find.

Over the years, many treatments were implemented and adjusted. All of them, however, dealt with the full scope of Lyme, including coinfections, parasites, candida, chronic fatigue, immunology, chemical sensitivities, vitamin absorption, diet, histamines, inflammation, hormonal imbalance, sleep, pain, and latent viruses. It couldn't all be dealt with at once, which made for a slow process. You have to deal with some symptoms in sequence and some as time and money allow. Slowly, you start to see progress, and you just know you're finally in the right place, at the right time, with the right people.

At this point, studies started to emerge showing parasitic relationships between Lyme and other parasites:

> In 1984, Willy Burgdorfer, PhD, who discovered Lyme itself, found nematodes in tick guts. In 2014, University of New Haven researcher Eva Sapi, PhD, found 22% of the nymphs and 30% of adult ixodes ticks carried nematodes in their systems. And in 2016, MacDonald presented on Capitol Hill, in the Rayburn House Office Building, that he found three Borrelia pathogens, including B. burgdorferi the causative agent of Lyme disease, thriving inside parasitic nematode worms, worm eggs, or larvae

in the brain tissue of nineteen deceased patients. (Patient Centered Care Advocacy Group 2016)

These microscopic worms are endosymbionts, meaning that the Borrelia bacteria dwell inside the worms. A tick bite delivers the nematode into the human body.

My antibiotic treatment was supplemented with a secondary medication due to the emerging research on Lyme's relationship to parasites.

After many months on these antibiotics, I started to see definite improvements in my cognitive function. I wasn't back to my normal self, but I was at a level where I could consider returning to work on a trial basis. At this point, I had three key concerns about my recovery:

1. My heart issues seemed worse. This might have been due to other symptoms that were restrictive at the time. As my cognitive functions improved, I tried doing more, but my heart didn't seem up to the task. I had tried to go back to jogging, but this always resulted in a horrible setback. My breathing and heart rate clearly showed signs of distress.

2. My energy still wasn't at a functional level—not even close. I crashed daily, sometimes a few times a day. When I had a setback, it would put me in bed for days, for weeks, or sometimes on and off for months. I didn't know how to cure this, but I knew didn't want to live like this forever.

3. What would happen when I stopped the antibiotics? In this situation, many people relapsed and saw symptoms return slowly. I knew the antibiotics weren't a cure-all; they worked at the infections, but eventually you had to rely on your own system to fight the infections. The key to making this possible was not clear.

I'd been getting vitamins and minerals by IV, which slightly increased my energy levels. You don't realize how low your energy is until you find something that improves it. Even still, I was able to do only 20 percent of what I could do before. This made me realize that the dozens of supplements I was taking were doing very little. This is common when you're very sick; your body is simply unable to absorb the nutrients in the supplements. Truthfully, it's also hard to find high-quality supplements. You can't expect the same benefits as you get from the natural vitamins and minerals in your food. But when you're so deficient, you have to try everything. The IV vitamins were helping, but I had to do this treatment as sparingly as possible because the cost was out-of-pocket.

I knew that if I really wanted to cure myself or be in remission—regardless of whether or not that was possible—something more had to be done. I had heard that many people had found healing in oxygen and ozone therapy. At this point, I was still doing exercise with oxygen therapy. This was where I would get my heart rate up and inhale oxygen. I assumed this treatment must have its limits because I could do it for only a few minutes a day before I would wear down my system. I had heard that ozone was beneficial especially for recovering energy. I had to try it, but it was hard to know where to go for this service. Even though it was common in other countries, it was still a controversial treatment, and I needed to know I was in the best hands.

I eventually went to a clinic in California near where one of my friends lived. I followed the guidelines outlined by the Holtorf Medical Group, which seemed to be the primary expert on ozone treatments. The doctors there explained that ozone therapy offered many benefits, many of which related to Lyme symptoms. I also was still on antibiotics; I wasn't trading in that treatment for another. I was focused on building my system where I could—increasing my chances for a greater recovery. This treatment seemed easily accessible and was definitely worth a try.

Two key benefits of ozone therapy are that it breaks down water and it is able to get high doses of oxygen into the tissue where Lyme hides and is hard to attack. But the key reason I felt this treatment would be beneficial was that ozone worked as an immune modulator. There are two sides to your immune system: the TH1, which is inside of the cell, and the TH2, which is the outside of the cell. Lyme is skilled at driving your immune system to TH2 immunity, which is very inefficient at killing intracellular infection. Lyme itself then transforms into an intracellular form, escaping the body's immune system. So the task then becomes to decrease the activity of the TH2 system, which causes the inflammation, achiness, and pains. The next step is to bring the TH1 up to eradicate the infection. Ozone treatment was a great addition to the multistep treatment approach that I was following. I had a feeling this was going to be key to getting me where I wanted to be.

I could afford only one week of treatment, but it was worth it. I wanted to see how I responded to the therapy and make sure I didn't have any adverse reactions. It's hard to say for sure after one week, but the effects seemed positive. I was really doing everything I could to recover. To some it might have seemed like I was reaching or trying too many things. They, however, will never know a Lyme patient's desperation to get better. For the first time in this process, I finally felt like things were coming together. I had a local doctor guiding my care; I had treatments for all of my symptoms. Thanks to the amazing community that surrounded me, I also had the funds to continue treatment.

I could see my future; it wasn't confusing anymore. I realized that all the doctors, lawyers, and insurance companies could no longer intimidate me. I had been right all along; I was suffering from a very serious illness. Solutions were possible, but I needed to take my time and do things right. If I did, true healing would be come at the end of this journey. This time, my path was clear, and no level of "expert" influence was going to make me deviate. My healthy future was ahead—I could almost see it.

# CHAPTER 10

# Emotions

As hard as I was working to get better, my progress was still slow. Although I knew my recovery would be a cyclical process, I was encouraged by the fact that it moved forward—even if just a tiny bit—every day. Still, I was already a year and a half into recovery, and I wanted to be at my potential best in another year or so. At this pace, I wouldn't meet that goal. I was anxious to keep pushing forward to find the key to my health.

Dealing with Lyme is a traumatic experience from start to finish (not that you're ever finished). Most patients go through a stage of denial, followed by a stage when they're neglected by professionals, and finally a recovery stage, which can be their ultimate demise. Lyme patients may endure financial loss, the loss of family or friends, and the loss of the person they once were. When you have to come to terms with the fact that you'll never again be the same, it only makes sense that there's as much emotional pain as physical.

When my dad traveled to Switzerland for cancer treatments, there was a point in his care when the doctors had done all they could for him physically and medically. They said that the rest was now up to him. His attitude and outlook were now the only factors that would determine how healthy he'd be during his final months. I remember working so hard to help him stay positive. It felt like I was clinging to positivity, hoping that it would change his outcome. Every time he complained, I tried to change his perspective. When he told others he wasn't doing well, I reminded him that the negativity wasn't helping. I tried to help him see things in a more positive light every day, and I wish I could take this back. I know now that my efforts to help him deal with his emotional challenges were misguided, and I deeply regret my approach. I didn't really understand what he was going through, and even though I truly thought I was helping, my approach was not at all what he needed.

I understand this now that I've been through a serious illness myself. When you're in the middle of fighting for your life, sometimes things just don't look bright. Some days it's nearly impossible to find anything positive in what your life has become. Sometimes you just don't have the energy or the power to fight what you're really feeling inside. If I could do it all over again, I'd just sit with my dad and ask this one question: "Dad, what does it feel like to be fighting cancer?" I'd try to understand first; I had no understanding of the mental battle he was fighting every day. I understand now, and that's how I know I didn't help him. The truth is you can't change your attitude simply by thinking positive thoughts. In fact, trying to fight your negative thoughts and constantly forcing yourself to think positively may even make it harder.

During my early recovery, I wrote daily about what was positive in my life: the improvements I'd made and the healthy life I could have in the future. I still rarely believed it. It's difficult when all day long you're living the reminder that things are falling apart: life is hard, finances are precarious, and loved ones aren't able to help or care for you. How can you possibly sum that up by saying that life is great? How can you ignore reality and pretend all is well? Quite simply, you can't.

When I realized I hadn't helped my dad with his emotional healing, it hurt. Nonetheless, I treated this realization as a gift from him. He showed me how to move forward with my own healing—a much deeper healing that I had to find for myself. I had no idea where to start. I'd always been a reflective person, and I'd done a lot of soul searching, or so I'd thought. I'd dabbled in spiritual health, where I had found many exercises that helped me and many wounds that had been neglected. I thought I'd done most of the work I needed to do to live a good life. Sadly, much of this illness went against everything I thought I'd done right.

I had thrived by eating really well. The more I learned about nutrition, the more I had enhanced my diet. I had a master's degree in natural health and had sworn by the European studies and information on healthy eating.

I had lived to exercise. I couldn't get enough of fitness programs: training people, training myself, and exercising. I loved it, but I never overdid it. It had been my passion and my therapy. I had slept, eaten, and lived so that I could go outside and do more—anything just to be active. I had taken incredible care of myself because I knew I wouldn't be able to do everything I wanted if I didn't. So where had it gone so wrong?

Looking back, I think I focused on health and fitness because deep down my greatest fear was getting sick, being physically limited, or suffering a mental decline. I couldn't imagine being unable to do the things I loved. I had always said that if I developed a physical injury or disability, I'd still find something my body could do. I admired people who had an injury or disability and still found a way to do what they loved or changed their focus to get involved in a new sport. I swore I'd be like those I admired and always make the best of any restrictions I faced. This was basically why I had done the hike. My knee injury had temporarily stopped me from doing everything but walking, so I had challenged myself with the three-hundred-kilometer trek. I wanted to be one of those people who focused on the possible and not the impossible. They were my idols, and so I had made the commitment.

To me, Lyme seemed like the ultimate failure. I just couldn't quite figure out how to make the best of it. I barely had enough energy to feed myself every day. Reading was virtually impossible for me, as it is for most Lyme patients when they're at their worst. Not only was my eyesight bad, but I couldn't retain the meaning of one sentence as I moved on to the next. I had no balance, strength, or energy. What could I do? I was often too weak to even sit and carry on a conversation. At my worst, I couldn't follow a story line on TV. Eventually, I could watch TV or surf the internet and—on a really good day—maybe do some research or write a blog post. However, even a short walk was often out of the question. For someone who lived to be active, this seemed like the worst existence possible—especially when I had no idea what I would be capable of each day. When I did plan something, more often than not, I wouldn't have the energy to go through with it.

I wasn't quite sure how I had gotten here. How had I gotten so sick if I was doing all the right things to stay healthy? As I told the members of Parliament, I remember people referring to me as the "unhealthiest healthy person" they knew. That was hard to hear, but at least it validated how hard I tried to be healthy. I blamed myself for a lot of it. I criticized myself for the small things I hadn't done well or the things I had neglected to do; they must have been the cause of my failure. I went through absolutely every detail in my medical history and considered all the things that had gone wrong that could have led me here. I felt that admitting my failures was the only way I could guarantee I wouldn't make those mistakes again. Only then could I move on with my recovery. I kept coming back to that two-week window after I was bitten and how the doctors had missed the signs—how I hadn't questioned their opinions. I hadn't known just how seriously I needed to take my health and how each step would be so crucial to my diagnosis and recovery. I'd had no idea. I hadn't done it right, and now look where I was.

A very wise psychologist told me that I needed to grieve. I was no longer going to be the person I once had been—Lyme had taken that away for good. I needed to accept that, and only then could I move on. It seemed like a rather extreme concept to me. In my head, grieving was for someone lost to death, not to disease. And I certainly didn't like the idea of accepting that I would never return to who I had been. It was like accepting defeat. I had already admitted my failures, but now I had to right my wrongs. I had been wrong to put my life in the hands of professionals who would not admit that the testing and diagnosis for Lyme were untrustworthy. I also had been wrong in not taking each and every step possible in those two weeks to give me the best chance at maintaining my health. It could have made a difference. Still, the only thing I was prepared to grieve was the opportunity I had lost in those two weeks. I planned to work very hard at my recovery so that I wouldn't have to grieve the person I had been. Come hell or high water, I was going to get that person back.

Deep inside, I knew that my stubbornness and determination wouldn't coincide with the emotional healing the doctors were referring to. Regardless, I really didn't know where else to start. After some research, I realized the glut of information made it hard to know what to do or even where to start. It became clear that there was no right place to start or right thing to do. The only key was to start where I was and simply not stop. I found myself going back to something I had relied on before my diagnosis: podcasts. Going back to podcasts for inspiration was soothing. So many times in my life, they had led me to a practice, habit, or ritual that helped me. Eventually, however, something would happen to divert my attention, and I would abandon the habit of listening regularly. I had forgotten how much the podcasts helped my focus; they kept my intentions and direction straight. Valuable advice exists if we just take the time to listen. Since reading was often still very difficult, podcasts once again became my guide.

The first lesson on my road to emotional healing was when a professional suggested you can sometimes look at an issue and ask the question "What is the one thing that you need to give yourself now that you may have denied yourself before?" Wow—that one hit home. I decided that rest was what I needed. My life had always involved a sense of urgency—like there were so many things to do and so little time. It was as though my time was limited, even more so than the time of others, and I couldn't stop until everything was done. I knew that I would likely never be done, so I just kept going and going, trying to accomplish the impossible.

I decided not to fight this illness as hard. I would try to make the most of the limited energy I had each day, and then I would rest. Then I'd do more until I fatigued again. I never rested longer than was absolutely necessary because my mind wouldn't let me. But if rest was my lesson, I would never heal unless I gave my body as much as it needed. I knew that all my energy would have to go primarily to my treatments and healing. Unless I was overflowing with energy (which never happened), I vowed to rest and let the healing happen. I became focused and intent on resting and healing and worked hard at becoming disciplined at that. It was a great idea in theory, but it didn't bring the results I wanted. I quickly became frustrated and annoyed with myself. Why was this not helping?

I hadn't yet realized that I had to go deeper than just accepting that I needed rest. The fear of not getting better was consuming me. Then I became consumed with finding the key to this whole emotional healing thing. Like everything else, it became a challenge for me. I had to figure out the solution, do it, heal, and move on. As it turns out, that's not exactly how emotional healing works.

I struggled until I had a conversation with a psychologist. This conversation would start a chain of thoughts that would lead me to an answer. I was still really struggling with fatigue, and I crashed every day—sometimes multiple times a day. I had recovered so much, but the fatigue never broke. I forced myself to push through the fatigue, which led to one of the worst setbacks in my illness. I knew then that this wasn't something I could control. Still, I just couldn't picture a life where a portion of my day—every day—was spent in bed. Why was there such little improvement? I had put everything else on hold and was focusing only on getting well. My crashing started happening even earlier in the day. I was exhausted beyond belief when all I was doing was trying to get better.

I was explaining this to the psychologist when she asked me to describe my typical day. I explained all the medicines that I took and how I took them. I explained the treatments I did daily and how I would pretend I was normal by doing small things to replicate a normal day. I explained how my crashing was happening even earlier each day. She replied, "I'm exhausted just listening to everything you're trying to do. Why do you need to heal so hard?" She told me my expectations for myself were too high. I was pushing myself like I was in a race. Regardless of how badly I wanted to be normal, to be well, I wasn't there yet. What she said seemed like common sense (and I felt a little embarrassed that I hadn't seen it myself). It seemed ridiculous to think I was pushing too hard at getting better, but I was. I was healing hard because that's what I felt I had to do to beat this stupid illness. I *was* in a race. I was racing the stupid little bastards trying to invade my body. I had given them a three-year head start, so now I couldn't waste even a day letting them take any more away from me. She was right—I wasn't normal. Maybe the way I handled my healing didn't need to be normal either. It had never occurred to me that there was any other way. Every Lyme patient I knew was fighting for his or her life. They all were fighting for any semblance of the normal life they had once known. They were trying everything imaginable to improve. Lyme patients will do some crazy shit for even the smallest possibility that their life will improve. They're referred to as warriors for good reason—they're among the toughest people I've ever met. They battle against themselves every day, and every day the battle is different. I couldn't be more proud to be among them—the strongest of the strong. I just wish I wasn't one of them.

I had to look at why I handled myself this way. Why was I going so hard? Why was I so hard on myself? During my reflection, I discovered a horrible reality about myself: I was not very nice to myself. I had never really listened to how I talked to myself. It seemed funny that I could go more than four decades without ever paying attention to how I talked to myself. When I did pay attention, I realized it was not very kind. I was hard on myself, I judged myself heavily, and I always expected more. I pushed myself to be better, to do more, and to always try harder. Even though this dialogue had helped me achieve many things (such as accomplishing challenges I had thought unattainable and surviving some pretty tough times too), it was also what had gotten me here—in this situation.

This internal harshness seemed at odds with how I talked to others who challenged themselves. When I taught boot camp fitness classes, many people were surprised by my attitude. They expected me to be more like a drill sergeant you would see on TV—yelling and challenging everyone through the exercises. I never had to be like that. I always found that women in a group setting would often push themselves beyond their limits. I never needed to push them at all. I sometimes even had to hold them back, or else they would go beyond their limits and injure or exhaust themselves. While teaching these classes, I started to realize how strong women were mentally; sometimes their mental strength exceeded their physical strength. Maybe it was the fear of being judged or the fear of failure, but women in my classes always pushed through the workout without any coercion from me. So I tried to be kind; I tried to let them know it was okay not to make the extra effort if they weren't up to it. It was better to build slowly and be proud of your progress, no matter how small it seemed. Why was it that I hadn't given myself the same consideration?

I spent a lot of time listening to my internal dialogue. I thought back to different times in my life and how I had talked myself through them. I came to the startling realization that I had overcome some of the toughest times, biggest challenges, and greatest hurdles when I spoke kindly to myself. I thought back to the hike, when I had motivated myself in a kind and gentle way. I had known the hike was going to be hard, and I couldn't push myself. I just needed to get up every day and do my best. The same went for the Ironman. My health was not the best at that time; I knew it was going to be a big challenge for me. I gently talked my way through each stage and got there—eventually. When the challenge was tough enough that quitting was an option, I knew instinctively that a kind and caring approach was best. But in everyday life or when my patience was wearing thin, I turned on myself. I was like the emotionally abusive parent who didn't realize she was doing more harm than good. I was doing more harm than good to my recovery.

It then became clear to me why I was so addicted to crazy challenges. It was in those moments that I treated myself the best; I was a kind, gentle, caring me. My mind and my body were partners—no judgment and no criticism, only kind, gentle encouragement. I needed to be that me all the time. I needed to change after forty-four years of treating myself one way and guide myself through this recovery in a caring way.

It wasn't going to be easy. There was so much I regretted and so much I was mad at myself for. There were so many facets of this illness that made me angry: the medical neglect, the financial strain, the loss of employment, passion, and ability. Those frustrations made me so angry at the doctors for dismissing me or negating my connection to my body. I had left many appointments sad and angry about what they had said or how they had said it. However, in reality, I had not been any kinder to myself. That was a harsh realization. In all the mismanagement of this disease, no one had been as cruel to me as I had been to myself. It became glaringly obvious that I couldn't expect kindness from others until I could learn to care for myself. Of all the medications I was on, that became the toughest pill to swallow. Nevertheless, it also had the most potential to provide healing.

Uncovering such a reality is difficult. It's incredible how hard you try to avoid digging that deep into your mind. Being that honest and vulnerable with yourself can be scary. I even tried convincing myself that I was looking for something that wasn't there—that emotional healing was a farce. You would probably agree that bullying, talking down to someone, and berating her at every step would be harmful to her success. Everyone knows that's not a productive way to conduct yourself. I guess I just hadn't realized what I had been doing. I never had taken the time to consider how I was helping or not helping myself. The truth is I never checked in with myself long enough to be honest about how I was feeling or where I was mentally. I watched and listened to hours and hours of self-help videos and podcasts. I completed countless exercises, wondering if any of it was worthwhile. I eventually got to a point where I uncovered this truth—an ugly one—that I thought just might help.

It's hard going to a deep, dark place in your mind, but it's even harder realizing that the work only begins there. How do you go about changing decades of mental patterns that have helped you survive and succeed but that are now hindering you? I needed to develop a whole new relationship with myself. I developed my first technique to change my internal dialogue after a conversation with a friend. When I told her about my realization, she said she found it hard to believe that I would think I was so mean because I didn't talk to my friends, clients, or kids that way (although my kids may have a different opinion on that). It was then that, with every step, I started to think, *What would I say to a friend or family member?* In most cases, I would likely try to give them gentle encouragement while accepting their struggles and letting them know that it was okay to falter now and then. I'd tell them to just keep trying. Wow—that would be an adjustment that I would have to make every day. In that moment, I could feel a pressure release, like a weight had been lifted. I had a sense that I could get through this. It would take time, patience, and most of all kindness, but I now could see the way.

It wasn't quite as simple as that. It was, and maybe always will be, a daily struggle for me to be kind to myself. There was some reassurance, however, in knowing that when I was at my worst, no one could beat me down anymore—not even me. I gained confidence knowing that I finally had my own back. When things got really tough, I knew there would always be someone I could count on: me.

I soon realized that for years I had relied on my friends and husband to keep me strong; I needed their support when things got tough. I needed them to say all the right things to pick me up and keep me going. And they did this often. I had never realized that I always looked outside of myself for support, but I knew I was lucky they always gave it to me. Even so, it's a lot to ask, especially when you are dealing with a chronic illness. People will let you down because it's impossible for them to be there to pick you up every day. With chronic illness, the need for support is daily. If I could take the burden off them and support myself, I would always have the help I needed. It took time and effort to learn to support myself like that, but in doing so, I found comfort and confidence. I, by myself, could make it through anything.

Just like I had done with my dad, I had been working so hard to remain positive throughout my recovery. Every time I had a negative thought, I tried to replace it with a positive one. It was difficult to fight the impulse to be negative. I never got better at maintaining a constant positive attitude, and after a while I understood why. If you don't dig deep enough to examine the ugliness within yourself, you can't change it. Instead, you're always fighting it. I learned that forcing myself to think positively would never work on its own. I needed to believe it, and to believe it, I needed to feel it. If I didn't feel it, I couldn't push myself to think it. I believe that to be true in all situations. If you really want something to become reality, you need to find a way to feel it. Sometimes it takes certain actions, exercises, or rituals. If you can feel it deep inside you, you can be sure it will happen. I'm sorry, Dad—if I had known better, I would have helped you in a more productive way.

I can't say for sure if this realization came at a particular time in my healing. I don't know whether or not it coincided with new medication and treatment methods that were working. I can't even say if it was part of a chain of events that showed promise and hope for a better life. What I can say is that from that day forward, I never wanted to give up, nor did I have suicidal thoughts again. Hope no longer took any effort. Sure, my hope waned and wavered now and then, but each day held a quiet knowing that things would get better. Recovery was still to come, and a better life was ahead.

For the first time in my recovery, I believed. I knew it all eventually was going to be okay. For the first time in my life, I knew that I could trust myself. I was true to myself. I could confidently be an advocate for my best interests. No longer was I vulnerable to the situations that make Lyme such a horrible disease to combat.

I had me.

# CHAPTER 11

# Exercise

For most of my life, exercise had been my therapy. Whenever I needed to sort something out, make a decision, or deal with sadness, a run usually helped. Working out made me feel like I was in control of my life and my health, and it made me feel strong. It was also a time that I felt comfortable being alone. I actually preferred being alone so that I could sort out my thoughts. When I ran, I felt relaxed and like I'd accomplished something. Running gave me a true sense of satisfaction that I rarely felt. It often could calm my anxiety like nothing else ever could. As I got sicker and couldn't run or exercise at all, I had trouble sorting out how I was doing, how my brain was processing information, and just how physically ill I was becoming.

It's hard to explain how you can get so sick with Lyme and not do more about it. How can you slowly get sicker and sicker yet still find ways to negate that there's something really wrong? But when the medical profession doesn't often detect it, it is easy for the average individual to have trouble accepting that it could be Lyme. As Lyme slowly takes away all of your normal coping mechanisms, figuring out what is going on and how serious it is can be challenging.

When you keep asking for help and are told you are fine, and when the disease stops you from doing what you'd normally do to deal with issues and sort out problems, it is amazing that *any* Lyme patients are ever able to find help. Eventually, the disease becomes undeniable, maybe not undeniable to medicine but undeniable to the person living in the body that he or she doesn't know or have control of anymore. Actually, "undeniable" may be too mild of a word—because eventually the disease ravages every single part of who you are forcing you to decide whether you even exist or want to exist. And if you do want to exist, you have to do something major to make that happen.

I had fought losing my physical abilities with everything I had. I remember having to give up personal training. I could no longer balance all that was happening in my life. I gave up long-distance running and eventually found myself unable to catch my breath after just ten minutes of any exercise. I remember doing some short videos to share on my fitness Facebook page. Within minutes I could hear my breath and had trouble speaking. I still posted them, but to this day I cannot watch them. I don't want to relive how I couldn't maintain my breath in a short video when I used to do several fitness classes in a row and never have trouble speaking. I had always been a big advocate of doing ten minutes of exercise daily, and now I couldn't do it—I was a fraud.

I saw several doctors early on, when the illness was really only affecting my fitness goals. And I appreciate how they advised me. It was due diligence. My doctor warned me of overtraining, and another doctor commended me for being supersensitive to my symptoms. He said hypersensitivity to what was going on in our bodies was a common trait of endurance athletes. He felt it was a good idea to watch things so closely, but in truth, he was suggesting I was overreacting. I respect that these opinions were natural and proper when I initially told these doctors about my symptoms. However, what makes me so sad thinking back is that I could never convince them that I wasn't overtraining or being hypersensitive. I was actually declining at, what felt to me, a rapid rate, no matter how I tried to carefully, gently, and cautiously improve my fitness. I knew there was much more going on inside of me, and I had absolutely no ability to convince anyone of it.

It's possible that I was hypersensitive, and that's why I sensed a problem and an illness early on. If not for my fitness interests, I wouldn't have picked up on the symptoms so quickly. That's because fitness activities challenge your body in such a way that symptoms of Lyme can be revealed more quickly than normal. But they also help fight them, somewhat tamping them down. One Lyme-literate doctor explained to me that they've seen athletes who seem to have an ability to control the symptoms for a long time, but when the symptoms eventually eliminate their ability to exercise, the Lyme takes over at a rapid rate. That is exactly what happened to me.

I fought the loss of my ability to be physically active. I tried everything. It got to the point where I was trying to do a two-minute workout twice a day so that I could recover a little in between. It is amazing what little exercise is required to keep you fit if you do it wisely and consistently. Now I believe that staying in shape as much as I was able to also worked against me when I was examined by doctors. They did not believe me when I told them how sick I felt. I couldn't possibly be sick if I was still so fit.

Eventually, I got frustrated with trying to convince the professionals that I was not overtraining. Yes, even when I told them it was just two minutes a day, I could not convince them I was not overdoing it. I probably sounded like a liar when I said I did only two minutes of exercise a day, but it was the truth. And even those two minutes were getting harder and more painful to do. I finally threw my hands up in the air and said to myself, *Fine, I won't do a damn thing.*

That decision was the beginning of the end. I can see now that that was the point when the Lyme had the ability to completely take over. Within a few months, I was having trouble walking.

I have often wondered if stopping exercise completely was the right thing to do. If exercise was helping me fight the disease, then the best decision would have been to keep trying. If I am honest, though, I knew I was not going to be able to do it for much longer anyway. I think I really threw my hands up because it was just too hard and exhausting to keep trying. For the first time in my life, I was relieved to just say I was not going to exercise anymore. I've wondered if that's what the experience feels like to people taking up exercise for the first time. It's hard. You keep trying to make it a habit, to love it, and to feel motivated to do it, but when it doesn't happen and you give up, there is a sense of relief. Knowing that it was just too hard trying and now you don't have to fight it anymore—I get that now, I really do.

As I reflect now, I can see a pattern early on in my illness. Exercise was helping me fight the infection and boost my immune system. I would go for what had become a short run, and it would feel okay but never as good as it used to. I never got a runner's high anymore. I figured it was because I wasn't running long distances. I used to love the days when I would go for a run and feel like I could go forever. That never happened anymore, but I was at least happy to go for a run at all. There was some satisfaction in that. But then the next day, I would feel like I was getting sick, like a flu or cold was coming on. Then the day after that, I would be fatigued and not feel up to doing any exercise. It would take me a week to recover enough to exercise again. I would automatically think I had overdone it with the run, so I would do a little less the next time. Yet the same thing would happen after each run. And so began the loss of my physical abilities.

What I didn't realize until I started being treated for Lyme was that the exercise actually had been fighting the Lyme. I was getting sick because the exercise was killing off Lyme and causing the Jarisch-Herxheimer reaction; this is the reaction your body has when the toxins from the Lyme dying off are released. However, by that point my adrenal glands were likely also depleted, my hormones were a mess, and my vitamins and minerals were alarmingly low, so the exercise might have helped me fight the infection, but my body was not able to recover. I often wonder about all the things I could have done to help myself if I'd just understood the disease better. I could have been taking natural supplements to boost my immune system. I could have changed my fitness program to deal with my issues, and I could have been doing a million things to help my adrenals. But no one, including me, knew what was going on. So we did nothing. Nothing was suggested, tried, or encouraged. It was just me struggling, denying, and hoping that something would change, but it never did.

It all made sense after my diagnosis, but then it was too late. I had given up on exercise altogether and was going to have to build myself back up. The doctors stressed that although I would get much sicker with treatment, I had to try my hardest to exercise every day. They were honest in telling me that some days it would not be possible, but to go for a walk whenever I could. This advice was music to my ears, and I swore I'd go for a walk every day. I never imagined how hard it would be to keep that promise. I felt that as long as I could get the smallest bit better, walking would not be an issue. Once again, I couldn't have been more wrong.

In all my training days, I'd never had any sympathy for those who would not at least go for a walk. I truly believed everyone could walk, even if it was for just ten minutes. If they could get up, they could walk. I never considered for a second that there were situations in which weakness could be so profound that walking was close to impossible. Maybe this was my karma for being ignorant of others' struggles, or maybe I was having this experience so I could speak the truth, but I was to spend many, many months in a reality where a short walk would be one of the toughest challenges I would face and on many days would be completely impossible.

One night in particular will forever be engrained in my memory. I want to always remember this struggle because it is a perfect example of how sometimes mind over matter is not the solution. Sometimes, you can literally be so sick that even when all your effort is there and your mind is more motivated than at any other time in your life, something as simple as walking can bring you to your knees. That happened to me many times over, but this particular night was a glaring reminder.

I had spent the day swearing to myself that I would get out for a walk no matter how I felt. It was one of those recovery days when I was not particularly sick, but I was weak beyond explanation. It's hard to explain. You can't exactly point to the problem, yet you just have no ability or strength to do anything for more than a few seconds. You try to force yourself, but overwhelming fatigue sets in instantly, and you feel close to being crippled, unable to hold yourself up. I tried all day to get out for a walk, and it just never happened.

Two months before, I had broken down and gotten a new puppy. It was hard to look after a puppy when I was so weak, but the company saved me in so many more ways that it was necessary. We'd had to euthanize our fifteen-year-old border collie a year and a half before, and I initially had been too sad to consider a new dog. But the loneliness of this illness was overwhelming me, and I typically had participated in all my favorite outdoor activities with my other dog. I missed the company. My new puppy was a laid-back and obedient dog, so getting her proved to be a good decision, except for the guilt I felt on the days I couldn't take her for a walk.

On the one day I remember so well, I had spent most of the day browbeating myself for not getting out for a walk, and I finally tried around seven that night. It was the start of winter, so I had to bundle up, and I turned on all the outside house lights because it was dark. I was still struggling, but I had decided to try the old philosophy, which had worked on the healthy me, of just getting myself there, believing that then the

115

feeling would come. That strategy does not work with chronic illness, but clearly, I hadn't accepted this yet. Because I didn't really know how the attempt would go, I planned to walk around my house, right around my house. There were three doors I could go in if I started really struggling. I almost feel too pathetic to write this, to admit I was that weak, but I had to be sure I could make it to the next door in my house.

I started to walk. I am not sure if I set my goal before I started walking or shortly after, when I realized I was not going to make it far. At some point, I decided to strive for three trips around my small 1,500-square-foot, two-story home. At one and a half trips, I stopped. As I tried to catch my breath, I prayed for more strength to come into my body. As I stood there, my legs proceeded to get weaker. I wanted to rest, but it was early winter, and we'd had one small snowfall already, so things were cold. The ground was cold, and I felt frozen, not knowing what to do next. I knew I couldn't do it. Energy was draining from my body as I stood there, so I started to cry. I couldn't believe what had become of me. It wasn't even possible that I was the woman who three years earlier had completed an Ironman. We must be two different people. I couldn't believe how weak and pathetic I felt—and not just physically; I felt weak and pathetic in my mind. How could I not get around my house one more time? But I couldn't. I stood frozen at my back door, knowing I had to go in, or I would be caught outside without help. I couldn't believe there was no way to push my body around one more time. I could not believe it. I wasn't sure if the issue was my physical abilities or my mental abilities, but I just knew my body was unable. I fell to my knees, cried a little, and then knew for sure that I had to go inside. I was pathetic and seemingly worse than ever, even after being in treatment for six months. I decided I was never going to recover. This was my new reality. "Depressed" was a grossly understated description of how I felt.

I had originally thought the guilt over not taking my dog for a walk was the motivation I needed. I quickly accepted that motivation had nothing to do with it. I felt a deep dread that I was never going to be physically active again. I swore in that moment that if I ever became well again, I would dedicate my time and experience to those with chronic illness. It is so misunderstood. I felt so much regret about not having understood those who really struggled with energy that I felt I must deserve this pain and struggle. After a long period of sadness, I made that commitment. It felt less selfish that I no longer wanted strength and health for myself, but rather wanted it so I could help others. This allowed a new desire to burn in me. It was going to be a long road. But I felt a strong sense of purpose about getting to the other side. I had struggled with the fear of giving up and now hoped this would give me motivation to keep trying and striving for the other side.

I learned a lot about fitness during those tough days. I learned much more than in all my previous years of fitness and training. Many people think walking is the place to start; nothing is easier than walking. Well, that's not true. Certain factors can be problematic, like cardiovascular issues or time and endurance. My blood oxygen levels would drop within minutes of exercise. Ironically, that had happened several times in my doctor's office. She had noted it but often felt it was an anomaly. Doctors, take note: if you have an endurance athlete who is complaining about lack of endurance and who keeps showing a low blood oxygen level while sitting in a chair, something is wrong. It's not that my doctor thought the levels were okay; she sent me to a specialist for further testing. But when nothing came of the testing, it was forgotten. Oh, how I wish I had stomped my feet and yelled and screamed. Yet I don't think that would have mattered. The doctors I was seeing knew of no other way to help me. They had exhausted all of the medical options they had been taught in school.

At one clinic, I quickly learned the right way to exercise with a debilitating illness, and believe it or not, it involved weights. You see, with an illness like this, your blood oxygen will drop within minutes, and it takes nothing to skyrocket your heart rate. So the fitness strategy has to be high-impact activity in an incredibly short amount of time, or else your system will start to shut down, and you will not see the benefits of the exercise at all. Exercise is necessary for a person to recover well. It boosts the immune system, improves circulation, gets more oxygen in and out, builds muscle strength, and most of all improves mood. However, if it does more damage than good, it can't continue. The key to fitness for healing is knowing how to do more good than damage. And short, quick, intense actions were the key to that in my situation.

Initially, my trainers focused on the largest muscle groups. These muscles would have the biggest impact and recover the easiest. I would do one or two exercises for one set only. I was done in seconds, but with just those simple exercises, I boosted my nitric oxide levels (which would help with circulation and blood oxygen levels) better than I could have with anything else. There was a fine line between boosting my blood oxygen and depleting it. This method helped without the risk of depletion. In my mind, it was brilliant. I could feel my body getting stronger within weeks.

Cardio was added, but at an even more minuscule level—literally ten seconds of high cardio. Of course, a slight warm-up was necessary. But after a ten-second sprint on a bike, my heart rate spiked. Afterward, I had to inhale oxygen to help my oxygen recovery, but I was practicing improving my heart rate, without any side effects. It was difficult, but until you can start to improve muscle and heart strength, your body cannot help itself. It was amazing to me that some workouts totaled only thirty seconds of work. And yet the approach was helping. I realized how wrong all the literature was when talking about fitness for chronic fatigue and other chronic illnesses. There the advice was all about walking and other cardio-type exercise and building time and pace. Oh, how awful. That was a recipe for disaster. Once again, "the professionals" were writing these articles as though their advice was the only way. I had to wonder if people with chronic illness all over the world were feeling defeated and hopeless because the information being shared was the worst they could be given and most likely was only working against them. And as with many other facets of a chronic illness diagnosis and recovery process, these same people were probably being led to believe *they* were failing themselves, not that the system that was failing them.

The more I followed this process and saw the results, the more committed I was to sharing this knowledge with others when I was better. The truth was that I always felt like people were being misled by the fitness industry. Fitness is big business. I sometimes thought it was trendier than fashion. There was always some new equipment or program or workout style. And it was always marketed as good for everyone: the newest trend would solve all of your problems. Very rarely is one single program right for a lot of people. We often train as if we are competing in one type of event, and that isn't always necessary. To be a runner, you don't need to follow a five- or six-day-a-week running program. Running can be one thing you do, once a week. Just because you want to lift weights doesn't mean you need to be in the gym every morning, building your capacity like a weightlifter. You can do a little bit of all of those things and more.

I have often found that people want to put themselves in a category, and I was guilty of that too. What are you? Do you love Zumba and belong to a Zumba gym? Are you an endurance athlete who runs marathons or triathlons? Are you a boot camper, weightlifter, or CrossFit competitor? The fact of the matter is that people tend to find something they like and figure out how to be good only at that. Then if they experience injury or failure or simply no longer enjoy it, they feel lost, with nowhere to turn to fulfill their fitness needs. Maybe they give up on fitness for a while, feeling a sense of failure, and then eventually return when the next thing piques their interest. Or maybe they return to their original activity for a while, only to fall into the same cycle again. Why? Because they don't focus on doing what they love first. There's so much focus on results, such as weight loss, that we forget to figure out what we enjoy doing—what we could look forward to doing for the rest of our lives. Exercise is not a means to an end; it is a part of life that your body needs for circulation, organ rejuvenation, digestion, muscle health, bone health, and most importantly, mental health. We must first start with what we love and build from there to develop into our own type of athlete, whatever the combination might be.

In my last years of fitness training before becoming ill, I had been doing a lot of research on hormones. I'm not sure what originally piqued my interest, but I was training a lot of women near my own age, in their forties, and seeing some of the same issues I was experiencing. Many women were telling me that they were having trouble keeping weight off when this hadn't been an issue before, and their moods were going up and down when exercise normally helped balance them. And even though they were trying harder, going longer, and adding more, things only seemed to be getting worse. I knew what was going on: their hormones were out of whack. It's almost impossible not to mess up your hormone balances these days. We are exposed to so many things that affect our hormones: food additives and modifications, stress, bad news, lack of sleep, and mostly women pushing themselves beyond their limits and still feeling like they are failing. All these influences wreak havoc on our hormones, and then in defense, the hormones make it worse. It's a vicious cycle with no end unless something major happens.

I also started to think about all the women who were stressed by even going to an exercise program. I taught exercise classes and yet still found it extremely intimidating to try anything new, go to a new facility, or join new people. Now the experience of not knowing what my body was capable of, what side effects I might experience, and whether I was going to cause myself a setback caused me so much more stress. It made me think of all the women attending boot camp for the first time and what the stress of just showing up was doing to them.

When we're stressed, our body releases cortisol, and cortisol signals our body to hang on to calories. It is an old survival mechanism that assumes stress is danger, and in danger we need to reserve calories in case we need them. And that is just the start of the hormonal unbalances that are created. I thought about all the women in my classes who might have worried they couldn't keep up or couldn't do an exercise, or even the women who were not comfortable in their clothes or how they looked or felt. I had known that everyone experienced this on some level; I just hadn't known how much damage it might have been doing to hinder their efforts. In some cases it might have been overriding what they were there to accomplish in the first place. I wished I had done more to make them feel comfortable, to find a way to eliminate the stress and promote finding enjoyment in the process.

Lyme also wreaks havoc on your hormones. I had completed some of this research earlier on, probably because I suspected problems with my hormones, even though all of my testing showed no issues. It wasn't until long after my diagnosis that I found a doctor who was well educated in hormones and who explained to me the inaccuracies of hormone testing and analysis—just another test and diagnosis that had failed me and probably many others. It wasn't until this doctor started treating me that I realized how miserable life is with messed-up hormones and how little we do to help ourselves. I discovered that stress was a key component, yet I previously had thought I thrived on stress. Stress is doing so much more damage than we know, and we put very little effort into decreasing it. Rather, we feed it every day, and it only increases with time. It became obvious to me that if we can't learn to decrease our stress, exercise is going to do very little for us. Hormones will always override any progress. And if we continue to do things that we don't enjoy, that are extremely hard and that we dread each day, we will only feed the problem.

I had always tried to encourage others to focus on doing what they love first. I wanted people to take pride in themselves and their efforts and always feel a sense of accomplishment, no matter what they were doing, as long as they were doing something. So I had to admit I felt cheated. If I had been doing the right thing all along, why was it all being taken away from me? I wanted to do something I loved, but most days I could barely walk. I missed running so much, and all I heard from other Lyme patients were stories of how they had never returned to running. I felt like I was being punished for doing something wrong. I had sworn I would always be physically active no matter what challenges were thrown my way, but I had never imagined a day when nothing would be possible but thirty seconds of exercise.

I had lost most of what identified me, such as being extremely active and working as a fitness instructor and park manager, and I had even failed as a mom and a wife during recovery. What was left? Who was I? Who would I become?

I knew there were only two options in front of me: I could become bitter, mad, and depressed, or I could find purpose in all of this, purpose that would bring good to the world, not bad. I felt like this illness had ruined my life, having taken most of what I loved and loved to do. I felt the only thing that would be big enough to overcome that loss would be something that would help many more people than just me. If what I had lost would help others, then it would be worth it. I just had to figure out what that something was that would help.

I knew I could help those with chronic illness work with their abilities and incorporate some exercises that would help, not hinder, their recovery and future health. I also knew that I could help those who dealt with chronic fatigue improve their energy, not decrease it. I wanted to help people find things that they loved to do, not that they felt obligated to do. I wanted to see people accomplish what they had never thought they could. I wanted to do all of that, but I knew it had to be more than that too.

I wanted people to learn to listen to themselves—to learn what they loved, when they were not strong enough, and when they were tired and needed rest. I wanted to help them realize when they were doing something out of obligation and not because they wanted to, when they were doing something because the experts said so and not because it felt right for them. I wanted people to know when they needed help and to ask for it, to know when their body was out of whack and what would help it, to enjoy doing something and change it when they didn't. I wanted to empower people to know what was right for them, what felt true, and to have the confidence to say so when it wasn't. I believed that with exercise and fitness, all of this could be achieved and would only overflow into other aspects of people's lives. Maybe that was my purpose. Maybe that was what all of this was about. I started to look at my struggles in a new way. If they had purpose—if I struggled so that I could understand others' struggles better—then I could accept them.

I would try new things that would set back my healing immensely, for sometimes weeks, even months. Lyme patients are called warriors because they become masters at falling and getting back up. The whole recovery is all about getting worse, then getting better, and not giving up. Every day there are more questions than answers, and what works one day won't necessarily work another. You never know if you are succeeding or failing. You just keep trying. I had a horrible time finding my limits when I was feeling better and paid for overdoing it immensely. I found the setbacks severely depressing. I would have a brief feeling of accomplishment, quickly followed by regret and self-berating because I had lost progress. I hated the cycle and wanted to give up on all of it so many times. I might have except for the quiet, lingering whisper: "But what if you can help someone else?"

# CHAPTER 12

# Eating

I thought the changes I needed to make to my diet were going to be the easiest changes of all. I had already made changes recommended by the US doctor for other reasons such as sugar, dairy and gluten elimination. I had learned much about nutrition when my dad was treated in Europe and the rest while I was studying for my master's in environmental health. I had once sworn by these nutritional health changes and taught most of them in my health and fitness programs. Many of the nutritional recommendations were not typical of what you'd find in Canada. But they were starting to become more mainstream as nutritionists were emerging who understood health and nutrition beyond the farce that is Canada's food guide.

I had to be completely honest with the doctor who diagnosed me because months before, when I was at my worst, I had let go of all the nutritional habits I had preached about and adopted. I'd continued gluten-free because I was guaranteed to be in bed for days if I ate gluten. But beyond that, I had abandoned all the other vitally important nutritional practices. It was as if I knew nothing about eating well. The doctor said she saw this happen all the time. Your body becomes so sick and depleted that nothing you eat helps it. When the health practices you've followed no longer serve you, you turn to all the wrong things to get through. I had seen it happening in myself and had known it was all wrong, but the only way I could seem to get through a day was by consuming sugar and caffeine. When I did eat, I wanted to curl up in a corner and pass out. Everything I had spent decades trying to avoid as much as possible, I was now surviving on. But it was literally the only way I could get through a day.

Part of me questioned what I had been taught about nutrition, and I wondered why it had worked for so long but now seemed to fail me. I sensed it was happening because something was really wrong with me. I had no idea where to turn because I knew the right thing to do (eat well), but it wasn't working, and I knew the wrong things I was doing (consuming sugar and caffeine) were eventually going to hurt me. I was caught, and I was a little embarrassed that I was not following my own rules. I knew I was going to pay for these decisions, but I just did not know what else to do.

It was when I was diagnosed that I realized what had been going on. The sugar was feeding the Lyme, as it does with all infections, and although it made the situation worse for me in the end, it seemed to give my body a small reprieve or some sort of temporary boost. This was not surprising to me because my dad's clinic had shared the link between cancer and sugar. Heck, even one of the tests we do to find cancer here includes sugar because it quickly travels to and helps identify it. The truth is that sugar is killing us at an alarming rate. It's feeding all the wrong things in our bodies and providing a false sense of satisfaction. And we have absolutely no idea how harmful it is.

Sugar is in everything, so even if we try to avoid it, we can still become addicted to it. Some scientists believe sugar is more addictive than cocaine. I believe it. I had worked for many years at reducing my sugar intake, but in the last few months before diagnosis, I had given in to my cravings, and my sugar levels had spiked to an all-time high. I knew I was going to be miserable for a while as I was getting off sugar, but like every other part of this process, I was ready to address it head on in order to recover. I experienced the harsh realization that even when I thought I was eating low sugar, I wasn't. It is in absolutely everything, and it takes extreme measures to eliminate it from your life.

Removing sugar, especially refined or processed sugar, is worth the struggle for so many reasons. I learned not only that sugars feed the overgrowth of candida in your body, but also that candida is where Lyme hides and makes it hard for antibiotics to attack. Just the health issues that can be caused by excessive candida itself will blow your mind. Sugar also increases stress and stress responses, which we know can also affect our hormone balances and adrenal loads. And simply the fact that sugar accelerates the aging process should be a clue that a lot of damage is happening with its consumption. If you are eating refined sugar, you are dying at a faster rate than you can imagine. It's hard to believe we would voluntarily do that to ourselves.

I would have to eliminate all sugars, even natural sugars, for some time to try to decrease the candida load and get my sugar levels down. I also took prescription medication to try to kill off the candida and other medications to try to regulate my blood sugar levels. I took it all very seriously and followed everything faithfully, only to find out how hard it was to undo the damage. Aside from how hard it was to actually fix the sugar issue, that was only a very small piece of the nutrition puzzle. There was so much more wrong and so much more that needed to be done.

For years I had been faithfully gluten-free. It had been a hard change at first, but I had no choice. I had celiac disease. It had been determined that I had both genes, meaning both my parents carried the genes. My dad died of esophageal cancer. He initially had been diagnosed with ulcers, and after fifteen years of ulcer medication, he had coincidently developed tumors in the same location. No one could be sure if gluten had caused the cancer or exacerbated it. But while he was still alive, I was having similar troubles and had developed the same ulcers, and the doctors wanted to put me on similar medications. My dad told me not to accept that answer. I didn't and eventually found out I was celiac. I have never had a stomach issue since. My dad saved me from his demise. I wish I could have saved him from his.

For years, though, I would notice mild gluten symptoms even when I ate gluten-free bread. I'd feel a wave of fatigue and weakness, not as strong as with gluten products, but not good either. I wondered for a while if I was just paranoid or had some weird association with bread and the symptoms in general. I ignored it for years and continued to eat gluten-free breads. The part I question now is why someone (me) would continue to eat something that she knew didn't serve her best interests consistently. But I did, and now I realize that as a society, we do this every day. We don't listen to our own bodies. We don't ever consider what food fuels us or works against us—as individuals. We are so focused on what the news says about a certain food or what the latest diet fad is that we never actually consider what is uniquely right for us. I was as guilty as anybody. As much as I knew and had learned about nutrition, I was as guilty as anybody else of never considering what was right for me.

As I moved further into treatment, it would all make sense to me; I was craving energy that just wasn't coming. As much as I was recovering and seeing symptoms start to recede, even disappear, I could not gain my energy back. I was a year and a half into recovery, and the fatigue was still profound, so I feared this was how I would have to live forever. What kind of life was it when anytime, or anywhere, fatigue could overtake me? I knew I would crash a minimum of once a day, and that was if it was a really good day. The exhaustion affected every aspect of my life. I worked so hard to reserve my energy at all costs, but it never helped. Nothing made a difference until I spoke with one doctor who suggested I needed to look deeper into the food I was eating, one issue being that grains of any kind could be wearing my system down. There are a few reasons for this that can be argued one way or the other, but I believe the focus should be on whether these foods work for our own individual bodies.

Some believe that as long as you eat items that have less than twenty parts per million (ppm) of gluten, your body will not react. But what if your system is weak? What if you are more sensitive than that? What if you ate a lot of items with just less than 20 ppm, and then they added up and overwhelmed your system? I learned that all grains have some gluten in them; we just consider some to have gluten content so low that they are essentially gluten-free. I wish someone had told me that. Somedays, I just might have had too much, or I was not at my best and probably unable to have any at all. Now I was fighting Lyme, and no amount of gluten was going to be okay. I needed every ounce of energy I could muster, and even the tiniest part per million of gluten could take that away.

It's no wonder gluten is an issue for so many people. Our foods are just overloaded with gluten and fillers. Over the years it finally has become too much for our bodies to handle. I believe that has to be a factor, especially when you realize how much wheat is used as a filler in processed foods. I remember when I was a student, and a chain of grocery stores developed a generic brand name that made all of the other brand-name products at a cheaper price. The products were very similar to all of the brand name's items, so we all thought it was a great deal. What we didn't realize at the time was that wheat and flour products were added as fillers in order to make more product for less, adding wheat to everything we ate all day. It still happens. There are many products that are gluten-free as long as you eat the original-brand product and not the generic version. Can you imagine what your body would tell you if you ate the same thing all day long? Well, basically that's what happened.

While doing my master's, I studied a lot about enzymes in food. In my earlier days of school, experts thought that enzymes were catalysts for biological reactions. I never knew what that meant, and it certainly didn't seem important. By the time I was working on my later degree, it was known that enzymes were more than catalysts; they were a primary factor in digestion. Enzymes exist in raw foods naturally, and sometimes a certain amount of heat can increase them. However, there is a fine line because after a certain point heat can kill enzymes. In fact, overly processed and prepared foods have no enzymes at all. This means our body receives no enzymes to aid digestion and therefore must use all of its own resources to digest food, thus depleting energy.

Issues with gluten made sense to me when I learned about how wheat is processed in the fields. Originally, wheat was cut and stacked in the field. Sun and moisture would increase enzyme production, even after the wheat was cut. During the day or two it was left to dry before being collected, the wheat was exposed to the morning dew and the daily sun, thus increasing enzyme production. Now the wheat is cut and processed in one step, a very efficient process, but not good for enzyme production. It is possible that this lack of enzymes is why our bodies are having so much trouble processing wheat.

Even when we think we are eating a lot of raw foods, upon closer examination people are often astonished at how much food is actually cooked and prepared. It's very rare for people to just eat something without a dip, sauce, dressing, or spices. We've lost our taste for the original versions of food. Food marketing is all about adding items, combining items, or changing the taste. We always feel the need to make each piece of food more than it is. The baby carrots that so many people buy every week (mostly because they work well with dips) are an example. If you compare the taste of a baby carrot to that of a regular carrot fresh out of the garden, you realize the baby carrots have no taste. The rich, true carrot taste is missing.

Regarding gluten sensitivities, some will argue it's not gluten but a reaction to the chemical applications to our food or genetic modification that causes digestion issues. The truth is we don't know. No one can conclusively tell us what might or might not be hurting us, no one except our own bodies. I ate gluten-free products for years because everyone insisted they should be fine. Now that I am honest with myself and taking a closer look, it's obvious these foods were not fueling me.

Years before Lyme, when I had so much trouble with my stomach, my doctor thought she had tested me for celiac disease, but somehow it was missed. When another specialist finally did have me tested, I was clearly positive, and I found some relief right away when I stopped eating gluten altogether. It takes some time to repair the damage caused by celiac disease. So when I returned to my doctor with the test results, the doctor wanted to retest using the Canadian system to confirm. I would have been fine with that, except it meant I would have to eat gluten again for a month. I knew at that moment the doctors had no understanding of what gluten actually does to the body of a person with celiac, or else they never would have asked me or any other celiac sufferer to do that. There was no way I was going to go back to the pain and discomfort after just starting to feel this good. This was when I realized patient feedback meant nothing. I was feeling so much better, and yet they wanted to do another test. I simply said, "I don't care if the other doctors are wrong. I am feeling so much relief that I am doing something right, and I believe the gluten is the key." All of this made me doubt my own assessment of my health; maybe I hadn't considered what other foods might not be serving me either. The system gives such little weight to a patient's self-assessment that a patient's ability to serve herself is crippled.

Later on during my recovery from Lyme, I eliminated most grains from my diet and started to notice a difference. That was enough to confirm for me that there was an issue with gluten in other grains. People often tell me they don't want to admit what foods bother them. They don't want to do testing or acknowledge the truth. My advice now is that information is power. It doesn't mean you can't indulge once in a while, but if you know your body needs to be in top form, or you are fighting something that needs all your body's healing power, then that information will be golden to you. People are often hesitant to do allergy testing, but I would encourage it. The information could be very important to you someday. I was always encouraged by the program my dad followed while in treatment, even though it was very restrictive. And even though the plan was part of treatment for people who were fighting for their lives, the doctors still had realistic expectations. They told him that the recommendation was to never eat some of these things, but to interpret that as almost never.

That realism always stuck with me because even when a nutrition plan is intended for a life-and-death matter, we can't white-knuckle our way through it. I saw my dad work very hard to strictly adhere to his plan, and even though he felt that each day he faltered was maybe one less day he'd be alive, he understood that we are human and heavily influenced by indulgences. Once in a while, we all have to indulge.

When I was newly diagnosed with Lyme, I fought hard not to falter on anything. Initially, I eliminated all sugar, even natural sugars, all dairy, and all grains, and I ate limited meat and only select fruits. Even some vegetables were forbidden. But I had to do it. The feeling you have when diagnosed belatedly with Lyme is that so much time has been lost in misdiagnosis. My body had been ravaged by this and other infections, and full recovery would be almost impossible, but I had to try. I felt obligated to follow the recommended plan exactly as it is laid out because it is your only hope to give your body the best possible opportunity to deal with the medications and treatments as effectively as possible. You are white-knuckling it. You are making sure to do everything in your power to get better. It feels like every second, every actions, every effort will be the difference between long term chronic illness or any hope for health.

In the first stages you are really detoxing more than following a nutrition plan. Something in health and fitness that has always frustrated me is when people adopt a diet plan off the internet or from a new book. Sure, they feel results because they have completely altered the type of foods going into their body. If anything, they're detoxifying, and that is no way to live. The chance for success long-term is zero. I have seen it, many times, with chronic and critically ill patients. Realistically, they can't maintain strict adherence to these plans even though their lives depend on it.

I had great resources in doctors after diagnosis, and they guided me really well through my nutrition plan. At first I didn't understand that when I changed medications, I might handle them better if I followed a particular diet. I was having trouble adhering to a plan and was told not to follow a plan from the internet but to simply use the plan as a guide: take from it what you can apply easily to your life, use the recipes to replicate some of your favorite meals, and build from there. Following a strict plan based on someone else's diet is doomed to fail. What are the chances that everyone who follows this diet will like the same things, do the same activities, and feel the same way? Impossible. To be successful we need to gather ideas and information from other sources and build our own eating plans. We should develop these plans slowly over time, incorporating healthier versions of foods we enjoy, and should not dwell on what we can't have. It does work if you eat according to your own likes and dislikes, knowing that it won't always be perfect. Every new change or new recipe you enjoy is one step closer to living the life you want.

I eventually saw one doctor after another who raised other possible nutritional and allergen issues, suggesting I might benefit from further elimination of foods or even explaining histamines to me. When all is said and done, you will have actually tweaked your diet more than changed it. So it doesn't feel like you have lost that much. Now you just know what feeds and fuels you and what holds you back. Like they say, knowledge is power. The biggest difference I have noticed is that because I make most of my favorite foods from scratch, they have so much more taste and texture to them, and I love them more. I use spices more than sauces, and wow, the food is amazing. I have replaced many grains with vegetables, and amazingly, you start to taste all of the ingredients more. It doesn't happen overnight. It's been years, and I still have so many things to improve on. But it no longer feels like I am being denied anything. It's actually fun to find better ways to enjoy the foods I've always loved.

An eating plan certainly doesn't solve all your problems with Lyme because there is no way to explain how little energy someone has while fighting Lyme. I know I sound like a broken record saying that. But it is so profound, so immense, and so indescribable that I can only keep saying it to try to get the point across. I have done so many things to push my body to its breaking point, and all of those things don't hold a candle to the overwhelming and crippling fatigue of fighting Lyme. That's why you are willing to do literally anything and everything for the smallest chance that it will restore even the slightest bit of energy back into your life. Although there is so much energy lost in Lyme due to other health issues caused by the illness, I found that assessing my food intake was the most effective tool in regaining some energy until my healing started to progress. No one can calculate his or her level of energy, every minute, every hour, or every day like a Lyme patient can. You analyze every thought, movement, and ounce of nutrition and assess whether it helped or hindered your day, and because your body is so weak, you can tell very quickly and very easily. If you imagine your body operating at 5 percent of its normal ability, then adding .02 percent to that is vital. And that's exactly what's it like. Every .01 percent of energy you gain is like gold. I would almost declare that a Lyme patient could scrutinize every human action or activity for how it will serve their level of energy, like no other human could.

So you can also imagine how a Lyme patient would be mystified as to why every patient is not equipped and supported to make every possible change in her life to support her health and boost her energy. It seems like attention to diseases and illnesses is much more focused on medical solutions and less on all the abilities a person has to make lifestyle changes that could build and support the person through his or her medical journey. Food is your fuel. It impacts every part of your body. Sure, patients are told to exercise and eat right. But that can mean so many different things to different people. The advice is rarely tailored to a specific person's illness or unique issues. People need to be empowered to make very detailed changes that pertain to them alone and their specific needs. I experienced this process with a very knowledgeable Lyme-literate doctor—a few, actually. It is a very different process than our system incorporates now for patients.

The real truth is that we as a society are suffering from extensive inflammation in our bodies. Some think that it is simply weight gain, and I can tell you from experience that looking at inflammation and its causes is a much more valuable indicator of weight fluctuation than calories. If you are one of those people who feels you do everything right and still can't lose a pound, there are a few factors you should look at: medical issues, hormone imbalances, and mental factors, and without a doubt, the most significant factor you should look at is inflammation.

There are so many things that cause inflammation that it is a complicated process to sort out what might be the cause, or if there are many reasons for it. Inflammation can cause so much pain, especially in your joints. Some believe this is part of aging and arthritis, but many times, decreasing inflammation significantly or eliminating it altogether can relieve the chronic pain. Inflammation is also responsible for many cognitive symptoms (memory, processing, etc.). It can even affect your eyesight. Inflammation is responsible for so many Lyme-related symptoms because infection gets into your tissues, and sufferers see the effects all day long, every day, though the symptoms can wax and wane. The average individual sees the effects too, daily, although at a more moderate level. It's just that people don't realize it's happening because the inflammation continues and builds, never breaking the cycle. It isn't until you see a break or improvement in it that you realize what it is doing to you.

Decreasing inflammation in your body is a complicated process because there are so many factors. Until you see a significant decrease in these factors, you won't realize how much inflammation your body is fighting. Toxins in our environment and our food are a huge factor, but one that is very hard to quantify. It takes a lot of effort to decrease enough of these factors in order to see significant improvement. But once you do, it will be worth it. So much improves as you improve inflammation. Food is the first and easiest place to look. Some of the sources are obvious, such as sugars, artificial sweeteners, fried foods, fast food, artificial additives, trans fats, processed meats, saturated fats, refined flours, and synthetic oils. Traditionally, these are found in more fake foods— foods made synthetically or heavily processed—so it makes sense that our bodies would not handle them well. I think we overlook how exceptionally hard these foods are on our bodies. It is difficult to associate problems or side effects with certain foods because they don't happen the second the food is in our mouths. We simply don't process them well because our bodies are working really hard to deal with something they were not meant to deal with, and there have to be repercussions. Inflammation is one of the repercussions.

The funny thing about inflammation is that it, much like many other defense mechanisms in our body, aims to help us. Inflammation has a purpose in healing us, much like a swollen ankle after we twist it. The inflammation is how the body not only supports the injury but also heals it. So if our bodies are chronically inflamed, does that not suggest that we are constantly doing something to injure it? It's true—our bodies' chronic inflammation is a sign that much of what we are putting in our bodies is causing our bodies to try to protect us against it.

The emerging science that has been most significant in my wellness has been the understanding of histamines in food. We often think of histamines only in terms of allergies. But experts are starting to realize that foods themselves have a certain histamine level, regardless of whether or not you are allergic. The histamine level in your body alone—whether from a high histamine level or your body's own histamine reaction to that food—can have a significant impact on your health and energy. In my effort to hang on to every .01 percent of energy, I started to take this information seriously. And although it would never bring me back to 100 percent, I started to find the small improvements vital to working on the rest of my healing.

The histamine bucket was one of the most valuable examples I was given as a way to monitor what saves you and what doesn't give your body the best chance to thrive. We think of histamine as something released in an allergic reaction. But histamine is not only in our foods; it also is released by our cells to aid in the digestion process and healing. It is good for us, but too much can be bad for us. The key here: don't overload the bucket.

If you are stressed or not doing well, your body will not deal with histamines properly, and the bucket will fill faster. If you eat a lot of foods high in histamines, the bucket can overflow. Or if you have sensitivities to certain foods, eating them can fill up your bucket faster. Sometimes the reaction will be worse, and you will have to let your bucket empty and your body regain balance before you'll feel better. But if you can intermittently allow time for your bucket to empty and recharge, then you can usually eat a certain amount of these foods as long as you don't overdo it and put your body in a compromised position. This certainly made clear to me why certain foods affected me worse on some occasions versus others and why so many foods seemed so bad for me while fighting Lyme. I also learned that it is not always necessary to eliminate an entire food group just because you seem to have a sensitivity to certain items in that group. Maybe you can't eat cheese, but other dairy might be fine. It's a process you need to learn yourself by gauging your own feelings when eating certain foods.

At the end of the day, there is so much to learn about food and how it affects us. It is the one thing that we ingest every day. We need it to survive. I believe we need to take our food intake far more seriously, and the easiest way to do that is to monitor how we react to certain foods. It's not okay to just say something gives you a headache or makes you feel tired because if that is the case, it is doing far more damage to you than you are aware of. Plus, there are many foods whose effects on us we may not even notice, especially if we are not in good health. People really believe they are eating fairly healthfully. But the foods that are marketed to us are meant to fool us into believing that. These foods are not as healthy as the corporations would lead you to believe, and how would they know anyway? They don't know you. They don't know what serves you. The only person who can really be sure what is right for you is you. We need to stop giving our power to others and letting them tell us what is right. We need to start focusing on deciding for ourselves what is in our best interest.

Improving your nutrition plan should take a lot of time. It should not happen overnight or in one grocery order. The best approach is to decide on one change at a time, meaning one new purchase at the grocery store. Eat or cook that item, and see if it works for you. Subtle changes over time really add up and will stick if you follow through properly: buy the foods, try them, and see how they feel for you. Don't be swayed by what the news says or what the latest diet fad is. These things are focused on profits, not your health. No one who doesn't know you can possibly have an opinion on what food is right for you to eat. Even all the doctors who advised me only gave me suggestions to try. Even they, who knew everything about my symptoms, didn't know for sure what was right for me. You know yourself best. So take care of yourself, feed and fuel yourself the best you can, and trust yourself to always try to make the best decisions based on what you know at the time.

Eating should become something new to enjoy for all the right reasons, not something we indulge in and then feel guilty about after, not something we bash ourselves for afterward because we didn't have willpower to say no to the treats or the extra helpings. It's a gentle process where you add and look forward to small adjustments here and there, where you can discover what you enjoy. It also includes the occasional indulgence that does not make you feel guilty because you have made so many other valuable decisions, so you deserve it. And above all else, food should be something that best fuels you, gives you more energy, and makes your life better. Food is life, and that's what it should give you.

# CHAPTER 13

# Detox

It was getting hard to explain to people why I wasn't better. They were very compassionate, but it was so hard to explain how this process works that I really didn't even want to answer the questions. It was hard even for me to understand the process, so how could I possibly explain it to someone else?

I had never stopped getting better and seeing symptoms fade or disappear. It just felt like I should be all better by now. Why I was not back to my old self yet? I didn't know if I would ever be better. I had good days and bad days, but I rarely knew which it was until the day was over. Well, actually, a bad day could be pretty obvious sometimes. But some days, you'd white-knuckle through what had started as a good day, praying for things not to go downhill. Yet even a good day was nowhere near as good as your life used to be. It is not even proper to call them good days, but they're so much better than the worst days that they're good. What I could never explain were the bad periods that lasted weeks and sometimes months. Recovery would stall, and I could not even feel the progress I thought I had made. These periods usually followed what seemed to be healing, but they felt worse than ever. They made me think maybe I would never get better.

I called these periods setbacks because that made me feel like they were temporary, and therefore I could overcome them. And usually they were. But sometimes they lasted so long that I would eventually convince myself that this was how the rest of my life was going to be. They played horrible games with my mind. And if I'd been trying to do normal things, people assumed I was better, so they didn't understand why then I was all of a sudden so sick again. My husband could see the patterns. There wasn't actually a true pattern, but he seemed to know what was going on and didn't question how I could be so good and then so bad. What he didn't know was the extreme guilt and depression that accompanied every setback. As a Lyme patient, during these periods you feel like you should just be as you were. You feel like you're a burden again to your family and friends. You wonder, if it stays this way, can you keep doing this?

If I had to give it a number, I would say that after more than a year of recovery, at my best, I was between 60 and 70 percent better. But when I had setbacks, I could go back to somewhere between 20 and 40 percent. And even within those setbacks, there were good and bad days. But most days were bad. In such circumstances, how can someone else understand how to help you? How, as a patient, are you supposed to plan your life and try to get better? I was constantly trying to figure out what I had done that made me feel better and what I had done to cause a setback. My doctor eventually told me to quit driving myself nuts. It was the illness, the disease. It was cyclical, and sometimes there was no explanation; there was no way I could control it.

I so badly wanted to understand it so that I could make plans and know when I would fail and when I would thrive. But that became impossible. My efforts to be kind to myself really failed because I would try to do things and then blame myself when I couldn't follow through. Many times I didn't fail; I was just not able to even try in the first place. The old me could talk herself through anything, but now I could not talk myself through a damn thing, no matter how badly I wanted it. Many evenings, I would find myself showered and dressed and yet still not able to go to what I'd prepared for. I'd have to watch my husband go ahead without me. Then I'd cry alone at home, frustrated and furious with myself. I was sure this was how I was going to have to live from now on.

One day I decided that I must be crashing each day out of habit, so I was going to spend the next few days forcing myself to keep going without a nap and without rest to try to break the pattern. I thought that if I knew someone with this illness, that was the strategy I would offer them, so I should try it. It was one of the worst strategies I ever came up with during my recovery.

I became dizzy and nauseous. My heart issues and chest pain became so intense that I had to go to the emergency room. I couldn't think straight and often couldn't see well. My balance was off, and I probably shouldn't have been alone. I depleted my body, and I spiraled into a horrible setback that I was sure I would never recover from. I hated myself for derailing my recovery like that. I knew that if I never came out of this hell that I had put myself in, someday I would give up for good. I just knew it.

I started to tell my husband and close friends about my morbid thoughts, mostly because I wanted to let them know I no longer trusted myself. I had promised myself all along that I would never give up. But giving up sounded so good now. My husband said he knew I would not give up. Not only was it not in my nature, but I also would never do that to my family. Normally, he would have been right, except that I felt I had become a horrible burden on my family. I was not bringing in any income, and I was spending money by the thousands to get better—yet I was not getting better. I could rarely do social things, and if I did, it took so much effort for me and my husband or friends to accommodate my needs, such as having to go home early or go to an event early. I missed calls from my kids when they needed me because I was sleeping, and they could rarely count on me to help them. I hated being this person. I absolutely hated it.

It was during these times that I was so grateful to have a doctor who had been through the illness because never in a million years could I have made a medical professional understand this. It sounds very psychological, but it is not in the least. She could talk me through these periods. Some visits, I would be on top of the world, sure I was going to conquer this illness, and during the next I would be devastated that it was going backward. During one visit I was frustrated because progress seemed to have halted, and I wanted to try something new. I had planned to go to the US again for IV ozone. She was very familiar with the treatment, but very few doctors in Canada could get approval to do it, and it was rather controversial in the medical community. I knew of many patients who suggested it, and it was also recommended by a friend in the medical field who'd had a loved one do it while battling cancer. My doctor offered to refer me to another doctor in Canada who could provide the treatment, but of course the waiting list was months, maybe years, long. So off to the US I went—again.

At the same time my doctor changed my protocol because she thought it might support the ozone well. I was suffering immensely with cardiac symptoms, and she knew of a protocol recommended by a Lyme-literate doctor who had recovered from Lyme carditis. It would require strong antibiotics again and a parasite accompaniment. Every time I learned of a new Lyme treatment, I read up on it, and this gave me confidence that my doctor knew what she was doing—well, as much as any doctor could know because Lyme treatment is a matter of trial and error. We were always revisiting and tweaking, trying to deal with my worst symptoms one at a time. The doctor felt I was making great progress as far as Lyme treatment progress goes. She was also considering all the other aspects of treatment, such as candida, parasites, blood sugar, hormones, other infections, immune building, adrenal issues, and inflammation, plus cardiac and neurological damage. It was all factored in, but we just couldn't deal with all of it at once. I needed to be patient, but patience was not my strength. I had been building my patience muscle as much as I could, but it was wearing very thin.

I also knew that if I was going to start a new protocol, my usual challenge of detox was going to haunt me again. The Herxheimer reactions seemed to hit me hard, and I had finally accepted that my body did not detox very well, even with help. So I began a protocol of extensive detox rituals that I hoped would help. I also began extensive research into detoxing that would lead me to very interesting, intense, boring, and insane areas. But I was ready. I was done being frustrated, and I was done not seeing major progress. I wanted something major to happen, and I was willing to do almost anything to make it happen.

I found in my detox research some key messages I received were from published doctors that many of the organs in the body need support not only to detoxify them so they are as healthy as can be, but also, as infections such as Lyme and babesiosis are killed off, the body needs assistance getting rid of them. That was the part of the process that my body just was not doing well, so that when I took strong medications to kill off the infection, even with detoxification efforts, I still got sicker and sicker. I knew I was going to have to do more.

Detoxification is actually a chronic issue in our society that few are looking at from a medical perspective. Our bodies are exposed not only to a multitude of chemicals each day but also to electromagnetic frequencies from Wi-Fi and cell phones. These unnatural influences are proving to impact not only our bodies' ability to heal but also our ability to detoxify, which should be a natural process for our systems. So if this was an issue for healthy people, then it made sense that it would be an issue for someone weakened by Lyme.

When you read more, you realize that parasites now play a role in average individuals' health as well. Ironically, parasites can play a supportive role in that they often absorb chemical toxins in our body. You can think of them as trying to help us out by consuming toxins. The only problem is that if our immune systems are weakened and our detox pathways are not functioning well, there's no way to get rid of the parasites. We hang on to them until they overrun our system, and then they harbor the infections and chemical toxins they were trying to help us get rid of. Then our bodies become overburdened with parasites, infection, and chemicals, so it's no wonder we feel sick. Some studies suggest that increased parasitic infections correlate to toxicity.

I ended up adopting a multitude of methods in my efforts to relieve my body of all the things wearing me down and making it harder to fight Lyme. Since new studies had shown that some parasites showed signs of Lyme within them, it was clear they had to go.

Dr. Davidson, who wrote the book *5 Steps to Restoring Health Protocol*, also explains in a great article on natural cleanse solutions that "around 85% of Americans are estimated to be infected with some manner of parasite" (Davidson 2017).

This doesn't mean all parasites are a cause for concern. It can be accepted that some parasites in some cases might do more good than harm. But I think we need to acknowledge that, as with other infections, a blood test can't tell the whole story and that as developed countries we overlook parasites as the potential health issue they can sometimes be. And with the environment we live in now, our bodies may not detox parasites like they once did, and we may have to consider assisting our systems to do so—in a guided-by-experts kind of way, of course. So we are lucky that there are emerging experts doing a lot of research on the topic and doctors who are sharing these protocols. Parasites are always worth looking into if a mysterious health issue is of concern.

Trying to detox these things is a bit of a dance. Admittedly, I got anxious sometimes and tried crazy things. I don't recommend some of the things I tried. But I would say, on the other side of it all, the efforts made a difference. I really started to delve into the area of detox when I started doing ozone treatments, based on the premise that detoxing can support how effective the ozone and other treatments are. Then I learned more about the Gerson Therapy, which included juicing and coffee enemas. I was quite familiar with juicing—I had been doing it for years—but a coffee enema was well out of my comfort zone. I eventually had to get over that, and it's a good thing I did. I also started to use some of the herbals recommended by Dr. Jay Davidson and other experts from the parasite summit, and they proved to help a lot.

Following that, I eventually fell into the controversial world of Dr. Hulda Clark, who wrote the book *The Cure for All Cancers.* and has a huge website with extensive health information, quite beyond the norm (Clarke, 2006). It started to make me realize that with all my travel and exposures, it was crazy to assume I was parasite-free, virus-free, and bacteria-free. It made me aware of my assumption that if I didn't drink from unreliable water sources, I was likely free of worry. I know I am not the only one who thought this because it was one of the first questions I was asked when I was so sick after my hike—had I drunk any untreated water along the way?

Detoxing is one of many recommendations Dr. Clark lists in her book, and she gives tons of detox suggestions at that. She delved into this world deeper than anyone else of her time and was scrutinized heavily for it. History tells us that forms of detoxing have been some of the longest-standing remedies of our time, but they are rarely mentioned today.

She wasn't the only doctor I researched who swore by sometimes-ancient detox remedies. I found one who studied old native practices that removed candida. I knew there was validity to all of these situations because I was not only being treated for parasites (of which Babesia is one) but was also on a medication to cut down the candida in my body. But the problem was that the medications were treating those issues in a body that was too weak to remove or detox the issues once the medications killed them off. I truly believe that as I moved further and further into detox, all of the other treatments I was doing started to work much more effectively. And when I say detox, I mean the ability to flush toxins out of my body, not just kill them but get them out completely.

I will always encourage people to consider how well they are detoxing in their daily life. We like to think of detoxification as this extreme effort we make to starve ourselves and completely wipe everything out of our system. But a simple example that many apply is lemon juice. I have suggested lemon juice to many people, and some see benefits right away; for others it's not enough. Another doctor told me to just keep trying mild detox systems that could be purchased at local health food stores. Some recommended charcoal tablets and other herbs. I wouldn't say that any one solution was the key for me, but I did many detoxes, and they all did something positive. Detox is the kind of thing where you will know if it is working and if you need to keep going. Personally, I may never stop.

After months of extensive detoxification protocols—which can be really hard, by the way—the line between not noticing anything and being in extreme discomfort, pain, and illness can be a fine one. I really recommend following an expert on your detoxification journey. Go slow and be gentle on your body, making sure that you have a plan to nourish and cleanse your body through exercise, clean diet, and hydration. The truth is there is little point in detoxifying your body from something you did not permanently eliminate from your diet or exposure. Sometimes it may make your system more vulnerable.

In addition to heavier detox, I added in some more gentle physical treatments such as Epsom salt baths, dry brushing, and lymph massage. With chronic illness it is quite common for the lymph system to get blocked or backed up. I initially went to a massage therapist who specialized in lymph massage. At first it made me sick, and then some of the best days followed. I eventually adopted lymph massage as an almost daily practice, and I will likely continue it forever.

The one area that really piqued my interest was one of the key reasons our bodies no longer detox very well: movement. Of course, diet is a huge factor too. We eat so much food that it is hard for our bodies to process and eliminate properly. But movement, not necessarily exercise, is not a daily activity for us. Even if we are active people who work out, we often have heavy workout days and then more sedentary days as a rest. But our bodies need movement, real movement, every day. It gets the circulation going, pushes things through our system, and keeps things flowing and moving. It's how we are naturally meant to operate.

One piece of information that took me a while to absorb and understand—and now that I do, I feel it's vital for everyone to understand—is how electromagnetic frequencies, or EMFs, are affecting our bodies. They are actually making it difficult for our bodies to detox and heal. Three doctors that I know have done extensive research on this topic and have found that our exposure to EMFs, such as from cordless technology or Wi-Fi, disables our body's ability to detox and hinders the good bacteria that support our bodily processes. Our bodies have had no chance to adapt to such intense and continual exposure, and maybe they never will.

One doctor promptly had me remove my Fitbit (another doctor had recommended it to watch my sleep patterns). It's a tough call, but I was really struggling with anxiety during treatments. Many treatments would cause extreme anxiety for no reason, which some days felt intolerable. I had to do anything I could to alleviate it, and the doctor explained that EMF signals can exacerbate such symptoms. I couldn't believe what I was hearing and wondered why I had never heard anything about this before.

My research would take me further into finding out that not only do EMFs inhibit detoxification and increase anxiety, but they also have the ability to encourage infections to thrive. I learned this after coming across a presentation by one of my old university professors, Magda Havis, who explained that in studies, "Wi-Fi is shown to reduce the immune system and allows mold to take over."

It is impossible to escape. Wi-Fi and cell phones are everywhere. Even if you don't have it in your home, Wi-Fi is everywhere, and in our case we gave up our landline for our cell phones, so there was no turning off the EMFs. Most homes now have "smart" power meters too, so they are exposed to EMFs even if they don't want to be. I took this information seriously enough to put a manual timer on our Wi-Fi so that it would at least be off while I was trying to sleep, except eventually that cheap timer would drive everyone and me in the house crazy with its ticking. However, I had found that I was sleeping better with the Wi-Fi off, so I decided to invest in a better-quality, digitally controlled version. I thought my problem was solved until the timer fried my modem. I felt defeated by stupid electronic signals but was still consumed with trying to alleviate the side effects they might be causing.

Researchers were stating that current evidence indicates that chronic exposure to electromagnetic signals, at levels that are found in the environment, may affect not only the immune and nervous systems but possibly also the cardiovascular and reproductive systems.

So doctors were suggesting removing cordless phones, which I had with the removal of our landline. They also suggested such things as turning off fuses at night or using timers, which clearly had not gone well for me. But then I came across information and recommendations that talked about grounding. I recognized the term because many Lyme patients had been using grounding mats and bands and had reported benefits. I had to decide for myself whether it was all a hoax or had some truth to it. The documentaries were convincing, so I had to try.

Some doctors or scientists refer to the practice as "earthing," and watching documentaries on either topic will make you curious. I can easily proclaim that a grounding mat on my bed, layering my whole body, made a significant difference. I noticed a decrease in inflammation. I certainly noticed improved sleep. This also came at a time when I was making significant improvement with treatment, detox, and ozone, so it's hard to say what percentage or role the grounding played. But I will say, without a doubt, it will have a valuable impact on your health. Quite simply, my husband stopped snoring—is that not proof enough?

If you really go back to the root of grounding, you'll find that it is about the electrons in the earth. We always hear how getting outside is beneficial to our health, and this is one among many of the reasons. The original form of grounding is literally putting your bare feet on the natural ground. It's healing in the sense that we absorb the electrons that balance the energy within us, so it only makes sense that the more we do that, the more we counteract the unnatural electrical signals from Wi-Fi, for example. It helps our cells combat the unhealthy signals that destruct them. But it's rare to see someone barefoot on the ground, so it's unlikely we are receiving the benefit.

We have lost a connection with the earth; many of us will agree with that. My fitness programs were a novelty when I did them because they were outside. The concept of being fit and active outside should not be such a strange concept, but it has become so. If most of our life is spent inside and influenced by electronic waves that do not match the waves that support our bodily functions, and we rarely spend time outside where our body has the ability to rebalance, then it makes sense that our systems can't function properly. I decided it was worth the investment to help counter electronic influences indoors, and as I got better, I was able to get outdoors more, where I always knew I was healthiest and happiest, except for one factor; those damn ticks.

Ironically, many Lyme patients are outdoor advocates. Before their illness, they were active and outdoorsy most of the time. They believed in the benefits of natural environments and the health perks of spending as much time in nature as possible. I know this because I was part of a university study where the researcher explained that many of the people participating in the study on Lyme still said that they found help and healing in being outdoors, even though that was where they were infected. I wouldn't say that is the case for all. It's very scary to venture back into the world that caused such horrible pain and suffering. But for some of us, we needed to find a way back, whether or not it was the right thing to do.

It's hard to explain it. You know that the bug infected you—you could even say it tried to ruin your life—but somehow, being outside still feels like the right thing. I knew, even when I was sickest, I felt better outside. I feel like connection with nature is what has brought me balance and insight all of my life. I believe it has saved me more times than it has hurt me. I can't explain why ticks have taken over our world, because without a doubt they have. They have instilled more fear than many terrorists. They are taking us away from who we truly are. I hate them, I really do. But as with terrorism, we must find a way for this horror to bring us together. Doctors, nurses, researchers, patients, and politicians must find a way to come together as one, or the ticks win, and right now the ticks are winning. I don't know why so many doctors have to treat patients like they don't know what they are talking about or like they are overreacting. Why is it that politicians feel that a fluffy document will cure what has become a pandemic? I can promise them the guilt will be overwhelming if they ever have to watch their child suffer. I have been confronted with health officials and even one researcher who have said we as patients are inaccurate in some of what we say. To that I say, "I dare you to walk a day in my shoes and then say that." I know these people don't know better; I know they don't understand. But I have full faith that one day all the truth will come out. It always does, and the test for me is to keep the faith that it will. I know it will.

And maybe that is why nature has always been a refuge for me. Nature can be vicious, but it doesn't judge what it doesn't know. The ravages of nature occur purely for survival, not for power, fame, or money. In nature everyone is just trying their best to get through life. As much as I completely despise ticks and certainly maintain a great fear of them and the illnesses they carry, that tick did not deceive me. It bit me and infected me. It was the health system that told me I was okay because the tick was not attached for twenty-four hours. It was the blood test that said I was okay when I was not. It was the doctors who believed other doctors that my symptoms were not Lyme-related, when they were. The tick revealed itself to me; it bit me and attached and fought hard to stay attached. If not for all the other influencing human factors, everything about my experience would lead you to believe I had Lyme. If only we had all believed that during my two-week window, I would not be suffering as I do today. So maybe it is understandable why nature still felt like a safe place to me, despite what happened.

Feeling better outside also made sense because one of my key treatments was exercise with oxygen therapy. I would try to spike my heart rate and then inhale concentrated oxygen, trying to overwhelm my body with oxygen. I watched my blood oxygen levels and saw them fall and rise as I did each portion of the treatment. What was extremely interesting was that when I replicated the exercise outside, it took a lot longer for my blood oxygen level to fall. This suggested to me that my blood maintained a higher level of oxygen simply because I was breathing outdoor air. I live in a very rural, natural setting, and I am sure that helps as well, but this fact was consistent throughout all of my healing.

I had seen similar results especially with the "learn to run" people I had trained in the past. If they had been training indoors, they could rapidly improve their progress and breathing simply by taking their training outside. I was never able to do a formal study on this, but I was sure that if I did, my findings would be similar to the results I experienced. People seem to relax better outside. You will often hear people who are stressed say, "I just need to step outside." Instinctively, we know it helps; it's just hard for us to see.

For a while I was quite confused about my position on the outdoors. I had always been a huge advocate of getting outside. I had pushed the benefits and felt conflicted when it was just that advice that took all of my pleasures, accomplishments, and characteristics away. So the question I kept asking myself was, how could I now confidently push getting outdoors as a health benefit? The answer to that is "cautiously." I still believe the health benefits of the outdoors far outweigh the downfalls. We need to be careful. Mother Nature has known to be fierce and cruel at times. But as a daily part of regular life, there is so much more healing offered in the outdoors than not.

If saturated oxygen was a big part of my healing, then of course the outdoors were vital. Detoxing through our skin, our lungs, our cells, and our tissues is necessary, so we must get outdoors. If feeling the right balance of electrons through our body is vital to immune health, then we must get outdoors. If stress is killing us, then we must get outdoors. The easiest and best way to destress is to get outside. We also better absorb vital minerals and vitamins that we know we are deficient in by being outdoors. There are so many things that happen to help our bodies when we are outside. I could write a book on that topic alone. So I can't let that tick take that away from me. I will always use every prevention method at my disposal to keep myself safe, but I will never, ever let that bastard of a thing take away from me my favorite place, a place I love and belong, the place where I did find healing. It has already taken too much.

# CHAPTER 14

# Stress

I have blamed and battered myself many times over about how I got sick, how I treated myself, how I let myself be manipulated by a faulty system. I know now it was not my fault. But I still won't let it happen again. The one area for which I will continue to take responsibility and that I now realize is a hugely important factor to everyone's health is how I managed my stress.

Stress responses are among our most important survival tactics. Stress responses are designed to save us from danger, and without them we would not survive. We have heard so much about the "flight or fight" response and how it works in our body. Yet that information doesn't seem to change anything in our lives. I talked about stress in many of my fitness presentations. I understood what stress did to our bodies and had also been treated for adrenal fatigue in the past, so I thought I was handling it, but I wasn't.

I think many people believe they are handling stress well. But in truth, we just become so accustomed to operating with stress that we don't notice the rise and fall of our stress hormones. In some cases they rarely fall, so we don't notice anything. We can't operate like that for a long time. If we don't take the time to recover from high-stress situations, all the reserves in our body eventually (although very slowly, over a long period of time) deplete altogether, and it is almost impossible for the body to recover on its own.

Truthfully, stress is a really good thing that we've turned into a bad thing. In the case of our ancestors, those with the best stress reactions were the ones most likely to survive and reproduce, proving Charles Darwin's theory of the "survival of the fittest." But now we don't manage stress properly, so it's working against us. In fact, it's turning stress addicts into the most vulnerable of our species.

Just think about it. Our stress response is meant to save us in highly dangerous situations, such as when a bear is chasing us or a hurricane is coming. It heightens our senses and quickens our reactions. We run on instinct and don't need to take the time to think things through. It tells us whether to fight the situation or flee (flight), and in most cases, it saves our lives because we get rid of or get out of the danger. Of course, that is a good characteristic to have. But the fact of the matter is, today we operate in stress mode most of the time. We wear down that system, and we deplete the adrenal glands, leaving nothing for when we are actually in high-stress situations.

The problem is for a while you function at a higher level when stressed, or at least it feels that way. So when I was stressed, I was able to push through things I didn't like or want to do. Eventually, you subconsciously create stress so that you can use that adrenaline push to get you through. You then start to use that system for most things in your life because it seems easier, until eventually you don't know how to operate without stress. So you seek out stress wherever you can—for example, interpreting the actions of a coworker in a meeting and then going back to your office angry and frustrated (stressed) yet feeling determined to shed some energy. Sometimes you get a lot done. But you start to learn that it's not an effective way to work and even harmful long-term. It's just a matter of whether you realize it too late.

So what happens biologically when we are stressed? Simply put, much more than we can imagine. Adrenaline and cortisol are released in high amounts, which causes increased blood flow and increased breathing, and of course, our heart pumps faster to make both of those things happen. This heightens our reaction, but it also sends numerous signals to the rest of our body to do other things to protect us, such as subdue digestion and especially our immune system function—the reason being that those activities are less important for the short time period that we are stressed and will resume when the stress is gone. But what if the stress is never gone?

The problem is we never release what has built up or recover from the reaction that was created. Our body doesn't have a chance to return to its original state and rebalance all of the systems so that it can take time to heal and rebuild reserves of adrenaline and cortisol. When your body doesn't recover adrenaline and cortisol, eventually they are depleted and unable to restore themselves. It's not that we don't want stress reactions ever. It's probably better to overreact to a particular situation than underreact. But we must have the opportunity to expel the buildup and/or rebuild the reserves. We need proper rest and relaxation to do so. But these days, there is so much going on, so much stimulation and outside influence on our bodies, that the rest and recovery never happen if we don't consciously do it for ourselves.

That was me. I operated at a low level of constant stress, and I didn't recognize what it was doing to me. I had worked on decreasing my high anxiety and avoiding intensely stressful situations. But I always operated best with a little bit of background stress, so I would find it or create it whenever I could. It came in simple ways such as creating long to-do lists, engaging in constant multitasking, and always doing just a little more than my energy levels suggested I should. Generally, you can get away with that for a very long time, unless something major happens in your life or an illness uses the opportunity to take over your immune system, as happened with me.

It is very rare to find individuals who do take proper care of themselves and provide for proper recovery from stress. The standard we set for ourselves does wear off on the people around us. It really is just a matter of time before it all becomes too much and we wear down. If we do take downtime when we need to rest or recover, it's rarely proper downtime. Watching TV is relaxing to many, but it's still hugely stimulating to our bodies. A computer involves both the influence of the screen and whatever activity we're using it for. We think it's relaxing, but it's just proof that we don't really know what it feels like to restore and recover our systems because we rarely feel that. We never allow ourselves to actually get to that place where our body is totally calm and able to rejuvenate all of its systems.

One value in Lyme is that your body is so broken down and weak that all of a sudden you truly experience exactly how each activity, thought, and feel in your life affects you, such as how you react to certain foods, how stretching and exercises make your body feel, how the things you read and see feel, what people say to you, and most of all, how stress makes you feel. It's like a heightened ability to sense what feeds you and what tears you down. And I can promise you that even a stressful thought can bring a body down in a split second, and it can take a long time to recover. We greatly underestimate how the smallest stresses break down our system.

I think if we realized that one of the key things stress does is drastically increase the aging process, we'd pay more as attention to it. We all work so hard to do things that defy time and aging, yet we don't spend a lot of time dealing with the one thing that ages us the most, every day. Stress also decreases our brain power; it's not meant to improve our thinking processes, just help us run faster. It muddles messages and assumes we are operating on instinct, but sometimes we really need to be clearheaded to figure something out. When you feeling like you aren't able to sort out an issue, try to find a way to decrease your stress, and you'll be shocked to find how easily the solution may come to you then.

I taught on this issue regularly in my health and fitness classes, especially to those who wanted to lose weight. If people are having an issue with weight loss and they are regularly stressed (even low-grade stress), they will not lose weight; it's impossible. When stressed, your body wants to hang on to calories because it thinks danger is near and calories may become scarce. Then everything you put in your mouth, your body will hold on to and convert to fat or reserves so that there will be enough energy when it's needed. This means your body will not process and use the energy from your food as it normally would.

You need to get your body to a place where it is secure in knowing that no major situations are going to happen. When you're in this relaxed state, your body can use and process your food in a way that's in your best interest at that time.

I truly believe that people need to make this first important step before they try to lose weight or even get healthy, or it's a losing battle. Once you are stressed and your body is reacting to that stress, your body uses hormones in an inefficient and ineffective way. They become unbalanced, and hormonal imbalances can be a huge factor in troubles with weight loss and a million other health issues too. So much is happening in a stress situation that will work against any efforts to feel better; the key is getting stress under control first.

For me, an issue was that I didn't realize how stress damages your immune system. When your body is stressed and cortisol is produced, the body reacts by producing fewer proteins, proteins that usually signal the immune cells (lymphocytes, which are B and T cells) to produce. The basic concept is that your body does not want to waste energy right now on immunity or healing; it will get back to that once the stress is over. But if the stress is never over, then your immune system never really functions properly. If your immune system is not functioning properly and is low on the cells that would normally recognize harmful things introduced to the body, it becomes susceptible to illness.

Two doctors who regularly deal with Lyme patients and chronic illnesses hear this story regularly. They told me they often ask people, "What intense stress or long-term chronic stress did you experience as you noticed your illness increase or intensify?" Many, including me, can identify the stress each time symptoms progress, plus the long-term, low-grade stress that was there when the infection took over. I basically allowed Lyme to invade my body. I crippled my immune system when I needed it the most and continued to hinder it the whole time my body was trying, with all it had, to fight the Lyme and coinfections. I had no idea. If only I had realized what a role stress played at the time, would things be different?

I wasn't going to make that mistake again. I needed to find better and more consistent ways to deal with my stress if I was to get better, to make sure I never got this sick again. The funny thing about decreasing stress is that one of the easiest, cheapest, and always-available-to-us ways to do it is simply breathe. I know that everyone knows that, yet we never or rarely take the time to pay attention to our breathing. I taught proper breathing in running yet never practiced it when I wasn't running. It's been demonstrated that people rarely take a proper breath throughout the day, and if you think about it, you'd probably admit that it is true for yourself too. I admit that I never took a second to stop and take some deep breaths. But yet we will go for a massage or see a therapist or say we need a drink to relax, without even taking a second to stop a take some deep breaths.

Many of the self-care methods we employ, whether time at a spa or time with friends, have a purpose and benefit, and I am not suggesting otherwise. What is amazing for me is looking back and thinking of all the time I spent trying to decrease my stress, when really I needed to first stop, sit, and take some nice deep breaths. Maybe I needed to do that many times throughout the day. But how did I expect the one or two activities I did each month to relax to make up for all the high-stress situations I created all day long, every day? I needed regular efforts, all day long, to counteract all the stress I was creating, but it never happened.

I could blame Lyme for the intense anxiety I was experiencing, but truthfully, I had done little to manage it before getting sick. Yes, anxiety is heightened when you have an illness that affects your nervous system, cardiovascular system, and brain. But I needed to take some of the responsibility. The problem is that when anxiety reaches the level it did with me, it definitely becomes more than a mind-over-matter situation. Your thoughts can do only so much at this point because you have trained your body to be a certain way. Your systems are habitually reacting in a certain way, and it's all enhanced and intensified when your body is sick and weak.

I remember standing in the middle of my house, not able to figure out which way to go, what to do, or whether to lie down, sit up, stand up, cry, scream, fall, pull my hair out or, call for help. I was standing there for no reason, and my whole body was vibrating inside and out. I looked at my arm and saw it shaking slightly, but this was not even close to representing the tremor I could feel overwhelming my whole body. I don't think you can ever truly give others a sense of what this feels like unless they have been through it themselves. I can't express how helpless you feel. It's like your body has been hijacked or tied up, and you are completely unable to break free and solve the situation.

I don't think all anxiety is the same, and I don't even know where this feeling would rank on the levels of anxiety. I just know it felt very crippling. I also know that it was certainly more intense than any level of anxiety or nervousness I'd had before. And trying to figure out ways to alleviate it, manage it, or possibly cure it was one of the most mysterious processes for me as well as every expert I ever talked to. As a result, I now admire professionals who help people with extreme anxiety because I don't know how they do it—finding a way to help despite not being able to feel what their patient is going through, especially when the patient struggles to explain what the experience is like.

I completely understand why people become reclusive. I was someone who barely stayed at home and was constantly active and social, and I too became more reclusive. Social events seemed to be way too much to handle every time I went out. Eventually, the thought of how much effort it would take to go out and deal with tons of people or activity was overwhelming, so I stayed home. My body was so sick and weak that even the thought of doing some things took way more energy than I thought it was worth. And sometimes even if I was excited to do a particular thing, I would regret it as soon as I arrived—or if not when I arrived, then shortly after, when my body grew tired. It was a mental roller coaster that kept me completely unsure of how I felt in the moment or would feel in a short amount of time. It then became so exhausting that I gave it all up.

I decided that I really didn't know how much was Lyme- and illness-related and how much was my tendency toward anxiety, but in either case, I was going to have to try to find ways to manage it. I like to think I mostly used natural methods to treat myself, but to be honest, I did end up doing hormone therapy, which I know helped. But before the hormone therapy, my savior was gamma-aminobutyric acid, or GABA. GABA is a natural supplement that our brain produces. It is a neurotransmitter that sends messages between the brain and the nervous system. It is thought to have a natural calming effect on the body, reducing anxiety and excitement. I found GABA very subtle, so it did not make me tired or drowsy (more than I was anyway). It took the edge off the intensity of the anxiety I was feeling. It was also a nice safety blanket because I could take it with me and have some only if and when I needed it. I didn't need to take it daily, just when the anxiety hit. Even though it did take about thirty minutes to notice a difference in my mood, once it took effect, all of a sudden I would realize the anxiety had lessened. GABA is produced by vitamins in the body, so it could be that my mineral deficiency was causing the heightened anxiety. But Lyme too has an amazing ability to attack the nervous system, so I knew it could be more than that.

Even though there was a solution to the intensity, I knew that in order to recover and especially preserve energy, I needed to eliminate as much anxiety as possible, or I would be completely drained. Breathing helps and is necessary to help with anxiety, but at this point it was not enough on its own. I did realize that regardless of the other techniques I employed, I needed to make sure I practiced and improved my breathing. Nothing else

I did to recover would be as effective if I didn't breathe well. I had been trained in Level 1 yoga. I was never very good at it but was well aware of its value when I did practice it. I was not a very good stretcher, even though it improved my flexibility and muscle tension a lot. But I struggled to stay focused and keep the commitment with yoga. When my anxiety was at an all-time high, I knew that yoga would be good for me, but I couldn't do it. It forced me to feel my anxiety all too intensely.

I eventually stumbled upon qigong. I knew I was terrible at it, but it sure filled a need and seemed to be more doable even when my mind and body were racing all over the place. I really don't know a lot about the practice. I know it is similar to, but not the same as, tai chi. Regardless of the fundamentals, it was something that suited me because I could continue to move while trying to quiet my mind. I won't say I was overly committed to it either, but practicing for a few minutes while I was unable to do anything else was helpful. I had always used long-distance running or a heavy workout as an anxiety buster, but my body was simply too weak to consider those activities now. Qigong is worth considering because there is something very calming about it while it still uses muscle power. For someone like me, that is an extremely powerful motivator. I eventually reached a point where even on my worst days, I could do two minutes, and I learned two minutes could change the course of a day.

I would eventually learn that I needed to retrain my body signals. Once I better understood the imbalance I had created between my parasympathetic and sympathetic nervous systems, I knew this would play a role in my healing. I think now that what I didn't realize, like many others who feed off of stress, was that we create a system whereby we stimulate our sympathetic nervous system (the fight-or-flight response) so much that eventually it becomes dominant and can almost deactivate our parasympathetic system.

And so I fell into the world of "tapping" with the Emotional Freedom Technique (EFT). In the article "Basic Steps to Emotional Freedom," Dr. Mercola, a *New York Times* best-selling author, describes EFT as "the psychological acupressure technique [he] routinely use[s] in [his] practice and most highly recommend[s] to optimize your emotional health" (Mercola 2018). The truth is that we focus so much on healthy eating and exercise that we believe that's all that is required to maintain a healthy lifestyle. Hell, I believed that. That is precisely the mistake I made. We think that as long as we have stressful periods and then no stressful periods, we are recovered, but the truth is we are not recovering enough before the next stress hits, and the problem mounts instead of cycling.

Stress is incredible at helping us avoid our deepest feelings. Stress, business, and multitasking keep us focused so intently on whatever it is we are dealing with that we easily lose sight of ourselves. Stress manages to successfully take us away from who we are and our own feelings. And when I broke it all down to the core of most things I did, I was desperately trying to avoid my deepest emotions, present and past. It works brilliantly. If we always stay busy, operating at a high intensity, overly stressed, we can manage to never stop long enough to check in with ourselves to ask, "How am I doing?" Because at the end of the day, we can be pretty sure we won't like the answer. I knew I had spent most of my life not taking care of myself, especially my feelings. I knew that I had pushed things down for years, telling myself to move past it. There was nothing really ugly, just years of things I didn't want to deal with. So to imagine stopping and checking in after forty years was scary. After forty years of living, could I actually check in and see how I was feeling and how I felt about myself, my life, and my hurt? Wow, that was a scary place to go. I could only imagine the mess I might find.

Here's how tapping was explained to me: stress (e.g., due to illness) overstimulates our sympathetic (fight-or-flight) nervous system so much that the latter is unbalanced with our parasympathetic system (rest/recovery, etc.). So many things cause an automatic sympathetic reaction in our bodies. EFT stimulates our parasympathetic nervous system and teaches us to relax as we work through emotions and stresses. And then with time those issues or thoughts no longer create a stress reaction in our bodies; rather they create a relaxation response. It is a tactile action you do (tapping acupressure points on your body) while working through the emotions that you have, eventually creating a lesser or a better physical response to those emotions. For Lyme patients this is huge because you are no longer wasting badly needed energy on stress responses. As you get better, some of your body's responses will be a habit from when you were really sick. So EFT can break old patterns that once served you, such as worrying about tiring from doing too much. Your body can actually get tired without doing anything, simply because it is so used to fatiguing.

We need to start challenging every belief we have about situations because many of these beliefs cause unwarranted negative responses in our body. We may have a negative association, past troubles and experiences, or even truly a bad situation, but regardless we can still retrain our body to have a different belief about the situation. EFT helps retrain our physiological responses to situations, but we can also use all kinds of tools to help change our beliefs. Of course, meditation is a useful practice, and I like to think of meditation as a way to actually release the belief and allow a new one to enter. But sometimes, for people like me, who are not very skilled or practiced at meditation, it does not work well right away for the beliefs we want to fix quickly. I still believe it is beneficial to continue the practice. I used EFT to physically help replace beliefs, but I will always work on meditation as a tool and hope that, with time, it will become as useful to me. I was once told to consider meditation as a muscle: the more you use it, the more it strengthens.

But mostly for me, taking the time to practice meditation has served the purpose of forcing me to stop, give my body a rest, and get a sense of how I am doing. I really have always sucked at it, so I am sure it will take a lot of time. Being quiet, still, and contemplative is one of my weakest abilities. But I know that the fact that I thought I didn't need to ever try was one of the reasons my whole life spun out of control on me, and I really had no idea until it was all too late. If all we do with meditation is take a minute to stop, take a big breath, and rest our mind, I believe we will gain the most important benefits from it. Sometimes we make it so complicated that we feel we fail every time we try. It's not that complicated. It's just a pause, just two minutes a day to stop and breathe and ask yourself, "How are you doing?" Then just sit for a minute to see what you have to say. I believe you will be more in tune with who you are than you have ever been in your life. Can you imagine how supported you'd feel if someone asked you every day how you were doing and really listened? Why can't that someone be you?

I really made a commitment to meditation when I was struggling for energy. I just could not imagine how I could live a life where my body would crash several times a day. What kind of job can you hold when you can crash at any time? How do you plan events or activities when you can never depend on your body to make it through? I was eventually told that meditation was the next best state, after sleep, for restoring body function and energy. I thought maybe I could make a life for myself if I could periodically meditate and rest so I could make it through. It never really worked that way for me. And I still struggle with being effective at it, but I believe I owe it to myself to keep working on it. In health and sickness, I have always expected so much of myself that I think I owe it to my body and mind to be much kinder this time around. I believe meditation to be one of the most effective tools I can use to do that. I recommend people just play around with it. Don't take it too seriously. You don't need to act like a yogi to make it effective. Just take time with yourself, for yourself. I learned from qigong that you also don't need to be still. For some, sitting still is half the battle. So if that poses a problem for you, move; just do it in a relaxing way. Take deep breaths and clear your mind. Sometimes moving helps that relaxing feeling if you do it in the right way. Just find what feels right for you. You don't need a special mat or special music or a special room. You just need quiet and you and a little bit of your time.

Truly, I believe all health, healing, and fitness starts with managing our stress. And even more importantly, happiness starts there too. But it takes commitment and daily effort to make a difference. It takes time with yourself, figuring out your thoughts, worries, and fears and working through them. Ignoring these issues provides no opportunity to overcome them. You must feel them, work through them, and try to find ways to help yourself manage them. Quite often people will discover the feeling and peace that comes from working through stress and can become quite addicted to it. Sometimes we like it so much the pendulum swings to the opposite side, where we avoid stress and drama on all accounts and avoid much of our normal life because of it. I had to do that for a while, and I think it's okay. Sometimes we have to go to the other extreme to find our balance point. Eventually, we slowly come back from one side or the other and find a place that represents what we love, but also that we love ourselves enough to take care of our health. I think dealing with stress is the most important place to start.

I think I will always battle stress, or more accurately, I will always battle battling stress. In other words, I will always be inclined to push myself to that point where stress kicks in. It's an old habit that will die hard. But I think I care for myself enough to now try to do my best to stop short of that point. I know the damage it can do, and I know that living under those conditions is not living my best life. Stress does not bring out the best in you, unless you are trying to survive a life-and-death situation.

All the things I put in place to deal with stress are valuable, healthful practices that with time become a very comfortable place to be. But it may always take effort to make sure I am practicing them. Or maybe eventually they will become easy habits that happen every day. I don't know; I haven't been committed long enough to be sure. Even when I start to have periods of healing that are really good, I see signs of reverting back to that overachiever, high-intensity, push-yourself-to-the-limits person. So I try to remind myself that that approach is not overachieving; it just feels that way. I am not accomplishing more or doing better. I am just hurting myself.

The other incentive I have for managing my stress better is the impact it has on sleep. Many think they may not be sleeping well because they are just worried about something, and yes, stress can play a role that way. But over time the mismanagement of cortisol levels can cause them to spike at all the wrong times. And when I was told that there is some healing that happens in your sleep that science is unable to replicate any other way, I gave it a whole new value. In other words, some health issues can be fixed only while sleeping. There is no medicine or treatment that can help it without sleep. We need to be serious about good sleep. Dealing with stress is the first step to improving sleep. But don't stop there. Just like dealing with stress, improving your sleep may take many solutions, daily practice, and tons of continued effort. But just like managing our stress, managing your sleep will be well worth the effort.

At the end of the day, we don't give our bodies enough credit for the natural instincts and practices that they put in place to protect and heal us. We tend, more than anything, to do things that counteract or abuse these natural processes. We need to understand our bodies more, appreciate all the natural abilities our bodies have to help us survive, and work with those. Our bodies really are engineering marvels, and we rarely look at them that way. If we can feed, support, and understand our bodies better than we do, we have the ability to help our bodies thrive like they never have before. If we can start to look at the human body as the amazing machine that it is, then we can start to operate it more effectively and efficiently than we have.

Although I feel Lyme and infection overtook my body, the disease lost. I have to look at how amazing it is that my body fought the illness for almost three years before it really wore me down. And if I am to be honest, it was largely my human ignorance, my unhealthy practices, and my lack of appreciation for my body that caused my final demise. If I knew earlier what I know now, I could have supported my body better, and just maybe the Lyme might not have done so much damage. There are a lot of what-ifs in this game. So I choose to look forward and just know that I have the ability to treat my body with care, to manage stress in such a way that gives my body a chance to recover, and to allow my body the proper time it needs, such as with sleep, to heal. Our bodies have an amazing ability to heal themselves; we just need to be sure we are allowing them to do so—and even better, are supporting them along the way.

# CHAPTER 15

# Hope

Although I was hopeful for the opportunity to continue ozone treatments, I couldn't afford the travel or treatment costs. I was on a waiting list for a clinic in Canada, but I had no idea when a spot might open up. So I had to review my situation with my doctor and plan the next strategy from there.

My last antibiotic protocol had run its course, and I had regained a lot of cognitive function from it, and for that I was very grateful. I still battled with short-term memory, but not as intensely as before. I could now remember information I needed to retain for some time, whether it was something I needed to process or a task I needed to do. Although I wasn't losing thoughts immediately, as I had been, I still had to employ many of the memory techniques I had adopted, especially if any time was going to pass. So I wrote things down and set timers on the stove to remind me. Often, if I thought of something I needed to do soon but not right away, I would set something out on the counter as a reminder because if too much time passed, I would simply just not have that thought again. However, I could do some work and carry on conversations, which felt so much better.

What was most concerning was that most of my cardiac and chest-pain issues were not improving at all. I had backed off some of the exercise with oxygen training because I just could not get my energy back, but it seemed my cardiac and anxiety issues were intensifying.

It was hard to know why my cardiac symptoms were not improving and sometimes seemed to be getting worse. My doctor said it was common in Lyme patients who might conquer one issue, only to have another return as they tried to conquer the next problem. I guess that is why a person is never really cured of Lyme. It's always there, lingering, waiting for a way to take over again. And depending on what treatment you are doing, Lyme looks for other opportunities to attack where you may not notice. It certainly is opportunistic in its nature. So although I could accept the fact that many issues and symptoms would never truly be gone, there was some comfort in knowing that something you had done had improved it at least once. But my cardiac issues had been there since early on in my illness, and so far no treatments had helped.

Adrian Baranchuk made a presentation at the Lyme Disease Association, Inc. Conference in which he stated the following: "Lyme carditis poses a challenge to physicians given dramatic clinical presentations. Very little information is available on how to handle these particular cases" (Baranchuk 2017b).

My doctor and I decided that I would try a new treatment of a well-known Lyme antibiotic protocol and once again pair it with other microbial cyst busters and a series of other supplements to support the detox. The regimen would also build my immune system and add vitamins and minerals to my body while balancing my hormones. I would pulse the key antibiotics for many months (meaning there would be breaks within the time period I was taking them). Many can be quick to judge long-term antibiotic use, and at first I found it hard to decide the right direction to take. It felt like there were so many options out there and no way to know what the right one was. Some "experts" will tell you there is only one solution, and usually it is the one they are trying to sell you. But by this point I had learned a very important lesson about recovery: there is no one way to go and no one treatment for all.

I felt for everyone I met who was struggling to figure out what to do and what not to do with their recovery. Sufferers felt a need to figure out the right treatment for themselves before they even started, to make sure they didn't make a mistake. I thought the same way at the beginning, and truthfully, you just keep trying. You keep whittling away at the problems, improving what you can. Some say antibiotics won't cure Lyme because it becomes much more than a bacterial infection, and they are right. Others will say that you shouldn't take antibiotics for that long, and in one sense they are right too. But I challenge any critic to be in my shoes and not try everything in their power to get their life back, whether or not it's frowned upon. No one ever criticizes a cancer patient for doing chemotherapy, which is immensely hard on the system. And no one criticizes cancer patients for trying something new when the first treatment doesn't work. In my world, it seemed the same: you are just trying your best to get well using the information you have at the time. The only thing I would ever criticize myself for would be not trying at all. And that wasn't going to happen.

I would eventually return to antibiotic protocols in combination with all the other treatments I was doing, to try to manage the infections. Dr. Burrascano explains why you must do combinations of antibiotics, because not only are you dealing with a multitude of types of infections, but also within those are many forms and places they hide. If you weigh the drawbacks versus the benefits, there is really no debate for the average person dealing with chronic Lyme. Although some people were horrified to hear about the antibiotics I was on, more horrifying to me was the idea of getting as ill as I had with Lyme and not doing anything about it.

> Using two or more dissimilar antibiotics simultaneously for antibiotic synergism, to better compensate for differing killing profiles and sites of action of the individual medications, and to cover the three known forms of Bb … Note that GI intolerance and yeast superinfections are the biggest drawbacks to this type of treatment. However, these complications can often be prevented or easily treated, and the clinically observed benefits of this type of regimen clearly have outweighed these problems in selected patients. (Burrascano 2008)

But you cannot just do antibiotics on their own. Your immune system is completely paralyzed by the Lyme and coinfections. Within two weeks of infection, they start to tear down your defenses until your immune system is completely depleted and unable to fend off the infection any longer. It is critical to boost your system and try to kickstart it so it's working properly. This sounds much easier than it is. For some, it can happen slowly over time, yet for many, it never happens. The system is too broken. I so badly did not want to think that that much damage had been done, so I tried everything suggested to me to recover.

I was amazed at how much IV vitamins and minerals helped. Even when most of the oral supplements I took were similar, my body was functioning at such a low level that it didn't have the ability to absorb the vitamins and minerals to help itself. I tried to buy the highest-quality supplements possible, but the cost can break the bank. I continued to do IV vitamins when I needed to and when I could afford it, but I was told to continue on oral, with the hope that my body was getting something and that as it repaired itself, it might be able to use more and more. It seemed futile. The supplements cost so much. I finally told my doctor I would rather pay for IV vitamins and decrease my oral. Then at least I would be spending money on what was working. We worked together to determine what I could decrease in order to save money to do more IV. It wasn't the best scenario, but it was the best under the circumstances.

There were so many supplements to take because although I was doing antibiotic protocols, the treatments were always accompanied by natural and homeopathic supplements. Some people find success just following a homeopathic route (Cowden and Buhner protocols were the most popular protocols I'd heard of). But in my case, I always had to work with my doctor to see what was working and what wasn't, and that generally guided my decisions. At every point during my healing, there was some natural element in the mix, the most obvious one being a probiotic to help alleviate any adverse effects from the antibiotic. Most doctors who deal with supplements will tell you that pretty much everyone should consider a probiotic. It is a complicated world out there when you delve into probiotics, or even natural healing in general, so it is worthwhile to seek a naturopath to follow your journey. I really believe, after what my dad went through with cancer treatments and my journey with Lyme, that any illness treatment would benefit from both a knowledgeable medical doctor *and* a naturopathic doctor. If one doctor refuses to work with the other, that should be a clue that you need to seek another medical professional. Once I was on the path of proper medical care, I was supported by a medical doctor who also treated with natural supplements, or a doctor who was happy to work alongside a naturopath in my treatment. That scenario happens more with Lyme patients because there is no cure, and treatment is uniquely individual, but shouldn't it be something we all consider for whatever our medical needs are?

One area of healing that was becoming better-known was what happens when the immune system is broken down. Often latent viruses emerge because there is no system to keep them at bay. I had contracted mononucleosis (mono) while in university. A lot of people get mono, and it comes and eventually goes without too much thought. But there should be more thought given to its prevalence. Mono is brought on by the Epstein-Barr virus. I remember being diagnosed with it during my holiday break. I knew something was coming on, but I already tended to get sick when the break finally came. Our bodies are amazing that way—they hang on and hang on until we finally stop, and then they try to recover. We often wonder why we get sick during the holidays or when we finally have some time off, and it's because our bodies don't give in when they know they need to function. Then when we finally stop, our bodies crash and try to rebuild. The truth is we should have stopped long before and recovered, but we didn't. Our bodies don't fail us until they know it's okay to crash. Our bodies are amazing when you think of it that way.

After I returned to school, my doctor asked the health center at the school to retest me to see how I was doing. I remember getting an emergency call from the health center telling me to come in right away. I started to panic and wondered what they possibly could have found. I had to laugh when, in all seriousness, they said, "We're sorry to tell you this, but you have mono." Apparently, someone had forgotten to tell them that that had already been determined months before. I was better in my mind, so I actually laughed. What I wish I had paid attention to is the fact that the test was for Epstein-Barr virus, and the result was proof that it was always there. It had been triggered and would always sit and wait for the opportunity to take over. Anything that suppressed my immune system would give it opportunity. So when Lyme came on board, I am pretty sure Epstein-Barr said, "Right on, it's time to party."

I had some friends from the guys' rugby team who bought supplements from a small health food store downtown. It was owned by an older European lady and wasn't really the type of store you could browse through. It was so small and jam-packed with stuff that you always had to ask her for what you wanted. There was no semblance of order, but she always seemed to know exactly where everything was. One of my friends who shopped there had also had mono, and the store's owner had sent him away with a mix of vitamins that had helped him get better. When he told me about it, off I went to see her. I often think of that trip and realize how much everything makes sense now. If only I had understood better then.

I walked into the store and said, "I am told you have a cure for mono." She replied, "No," and that was it.

I was a little stunned for a moment. Then I said, "Well, I have a friend who came here, and you gave him something for mono."

She paid a little more attention to me, but not too much. She explained, "There is no cure." But, she continued, if I wanted something to help my immune system, she could maybe suggest some things. I was rather confused at the time, so I just kept asking questions until I got somewhere. I eventually ended up with some sort of B complex vitamins and vitamin C, but I can't remember what else. It seemed rather simple to me, and she didn't seem overly enthusiastic to help.

Now I look back and realize there was so much going on there. I think the biggest part of it was that I had walked in looking for a one-time cure. I had already been making the mistake of pushing myself too hard. I had been playing rugby, working out, and cramming for exams, all the time knowing my body was getting sick, but I had nothing to help it. I also think she was trying to tell me I would always have Epstein-Barr and that these vitamins would help, but I needed to take care of myself. At minimum, I needed to know that when my body wore down, it needed protection, and the least I could do was make sure I took the vitamins I was prone to be deficient in, but I never did. Once those bottles were done and I was feeling much better, I never thought of them again. I wonder how many people like me she saw regularly. I am sure she could tell my story that day, the same story I repeated most of my life, over and over. The more I was down, the more I would push, until one day there was no more push in me. I guess it was bound to happen.

As I read more and more about latent Epstein-Barr and how it, along with many other viruses, is triggered once Lyme does its damage, I knew Epstein-Barr would be a key in my recovery. I had read a few studies about prescriptions that helped some, and I remember taking one of those studies to my doctors—apprehensively, of course. I was so desperate to get my energy back that I couldn't wait to try something that might help, anything really. Viruses are those tricky entities that many doctors say you cannot do anything about. But I already believed that to be wrong because vitamins had helped once before. I was taking those vitamins now, but I had also let this virus do much more damage, so it only made sense to me that I might have to do more.

It is amazing when you take a piece of information to a doctor who listens to you—when even though they already knew all about it, they tell you why and when it would be a good idea and suggest a better idea in the meantime and even suggest that you can revisit the idea *together* if it doesn't work. That is a fucking doctor. They don't have to shut you down right away just because you are trying to help yourself. They don't have to dismiss you because you might not understand the idea at the level they do. They are compassionate and understand that you are desperate to get your health back. They admire you for trying, for constantly trying, to do what's best with their guidance. Now that is a doctor. I was told I was rushing things. Some of the recommendations for dealing with viruses do not mix well with some of the prescriptions I was on. It was a process, and I was a few steps in, with a few more to take. That was why it took time to recover.

It was clear that my panic and fear of never recovering my energy were consuming me, so my doctor and I had a long talk about that. I was showing signs—like my mitochondria trying to spark—that suggested I could still recover, and I found comfort in that. I just had to do my best to not wear down my system every time it showed a glimpse of renewed energy, and that was hard for me. Dr. Michael Lam, MD, international best-selling author of seven health-related books, explains in an article that "treatment of Lyme disease once the infection is well established and has spread throughout the body is more challenging" (Lam 2017).

At the end of the day, I was doing a lot, and things were always improving. There was not much I hadn't tried and not a lot that I didn't think helped. It was hard to know exactly what helped and how much, because many times treatments worked together. I thought, *As long as things keep improving, I can't just stop trying.* By this point I had done the following for the following purposes:

Microbial attacks

- Long-term antibiotics
- Herbal protocols
- Exercise with oxygen therapy
- Pulse electromagnetic frequency
- Hyperthermy
- Stevia (diet)
- Hydrogen peroxide IV
- Diet—no sugar, gluten, or dairy

Detox

- Supplements
- Gerson Therapy
- Enemas
- Parasite protocols
- Candida protocols
- Epsom salts and hyperthermy baths
- Lymphatic massage
- Glutathione
- High-dose vitamin C
- Saunas
- Coconut oil and baking soda for health products
- Heavy metal testing

Immune support

- Low-dose naltrexone
- GCMAF (with vitamin D)
- IV ozone

Inflammation

- Serrapeptase
- Diet (paleo/keto)
- Earthing sheet

Gut repair

- Restore
- Probiotics
- Diet
- Supplements

Hormone therapy and energy

- Replacement therapies (progesterone, testosterone, and thyroid)
- Herbal supplements
- Stress management
- Exercise
- Reiki and qigong

I am not sure where it fits on this list, but the research into cannabidiol hemp oil (CBD) was starting to build as well, and the patients who were seeing benefits seemed to be building.

I am sure there are things I am missing, and there are a million other options people have found success with. That's why I strongly believe that you must find a Lyme-literate doctor or naturopath. The only true way to find help is with someone who has some clinical experience with the disease. People often ask me about my time at the clinic, and I believe strongly that it restored so much of my physical abilities that I will never regret the time and money spent. Even more so, because it restored my physical abilities, it also restored a lot of my hope and improved my mental state. But it never replaced my need for a doctor who understood this illness to follow me through my recovery. That is mandatory. If your doctor knows Lyme, he or she will guide you and also be open to trying things *you* want to try, unless the doctor has experience suggesting otherwise. It's a long, slow road recovering from Lyme. Many doctors told me that repeatedly, but it took me a long time to truly accept that reality.

I know I am not at the end either. I believe that in some fashion I will continue many of the habits and treatments I adopted, though over time I'll do many of them less and less. But there is some comfort in knowing the options are there. I still have some cardiac and cardio recovery to do. And still, most of all, I want to regain my energy. But all of those issues continue to improve, so I am well on my way. Will I get to where I was before? No one knows. It's rare, but some do, so it is possible. One doctor said the hope is always for 75 percent or better. Another thought 85 to 90 percent is possible. All of that sounds pretty good to me, and one can always hold out hope for the best. According to one doctor, once a patient can stay in remission for three years, the chance of relapse is pretty low. I like that idea a lot. But that means a few more years of recovery and a few years past that of being extra careful to maintain what I have gained. In the end, the journey will be a decade long and may be lifelong.

I just have to believe that options will continue to be available to me to improve my health. If they ever run out, then I will have to believe I am where I am supposed to be. This illness will always make taking care of myself my priority. And maybe that's the way it should have been all along. Sometimes you have to wonder if the most healing comes from the lessons you learn. There have been many lessons in Lyme, as any patient will tell you. You can't have a disease that affects every aspect of your body, mind, and soul—and consumes every aspect of your life and the lives of those around you—and not experience many, many lessons. During my treatments I learned the power of these three words: faith, hope, and love.

I had to believe there was a power greater than me guiding me, or I never would have found the path and the help I did. Many times I was lost, scared, and confused, and the right person, professional, or opportunity would then present itself. It wasn't until I gave up and gave in that things started to happen for the better. I tried to control the situation for so long. I tried to hide my illness from others and force myself to be well, but it never worked. When I gave in, prayed to God to help me, and begged for something to change, it did. Faith was the only thing that turned this situation around.

It was then that I learned the power of hope. That to me is the greatest gift anyone can give someone going through a tough time. Whether it be a doctor, a friend, or a family member, everyone has the ability to give hope. And that is one of the awful things about this illness—when the professionals shoot you down and say it can't be Lyme yet offer nothing else, leaving you to believe it's all in your head (something not treatable and progressive) or it's nothing at all. In all of these cases, they offer little to no hope. If they don't know what it is, they should not have the right to say it is not Lyme. That is what AMMI did in the CBC interview. The experts, without examining me or any other patients, say our disease is not Lyme but have no idea what it is. That offers nothing—certainly not hope.

In fact, the first doctor who saw me who was open to treating Lyme offered me hope. And can you imagine where I would be had I not ventured toward the possibility of recovery? All the Canadian system offered me was the option to get worse, to see if it was a terminal illness. There is no hope in that. Now look at me, well on my way to being better and maybe a full recovery. That is hope.

The only times along my journey when I have wanted to give in or give up have been when I lost hope. I might have felt that a treatment plan had run its course or that there were no other options out there for me. Sometimes, I would feel like I had lost ground in my recovery, and this was as good as it was going to get. It was only then when I lost hope, when I was at my lowest and wanted to give in. Hope comes from many places in many ways. It comes from a success story, a quote that inspires you, a message from a loved one, or just a gentle hand that reminds you things will get better. Hope is free. We all have the ability to offer it, and almost nothing feels better than gaining hope.

The only thing that could possibly be more powerful than hope is love. I have experienced it from so many directions the last little while. Before, I had no idea how many different forms love came in. Love too is free. And I have also learned that the times we want to give love the least are sometimes the times we should give it the most. Many people did not understand why I did the things I did, why I seemed to back out of and not fulfill my promises. This had not been in my nature before, so I believe it bothered people even more. But there were those who did not understand yet still offered me love and lifted me when I needed it the most—those who could have judged me for what I was saying or what I was doing or not doing and instead gave me love at a time I needed it the most. Sometimes when someone is at their most unlovable, that is when they need love the most. I have decided, after being on both sides of love, that the less I understand someone's struggle, the more I might need to offer love.

# CHAPTER 16

# Self-Care

I have always believed in the philosophy that life tries to teach us lessons, and if we ignore them or fight them long enough, they will eventually hit us so hard that we have no option but to stop and learn from them. Maybe that's what Lyme was for me. I don't know. I have tried, many times, to look back and find where I missed the messages on how to live my life better, fuller, happier... There certainly had been signs, but I didn't think I was completely oblivious to trying to improve things for myself, or live a better life. And I certainly felt I was always striving to do better. Maybe that was the part of the problem. I never stopped to just accept what was, in myself, in others, in life. I was always striving for better.

I believe my biggest lesson in this journey was self-care, not in the way we typically think of self-care, but rather self-love, acceptance, kindness, and genuine belief in knowing who I am and loving myself always. Self-care is not taking time for a massage now and then. It is loving yourself in many ways, in all actions and in daily ventures, so that a massage or whatever other care mechanism you use is an indulgence, not a fundamental part of your self-care. Self-care is when you take the best care of yourself always, in every way possible. You trust yourself, you believe in yourself, you stand up for yourself, and you genuinely care about what's right for you. I believe it to be the best way to make sure you are always there for yourself and never succumb to the mistreatment or judgment of others. I also now realize that it is the best way we can give to others.

I believe Lyme to be the greatest test of your self-care, self-worth, and self-love. Everything about Lyme challenges you to see what you are really willing to do to support yourself, stand up for yourself, and heal. It changes every aspect of self-care there is. Dr. Ralph Hawkins, one of very few Lyme-literate medical doctors in Canada, shared a perfect example of this. I served as a patient witness while he served as an expert witness in the House of Commons on the Federal Framework on Lyme Disease. He also served as an expert witness to the Federal Health Committee on Lyme, where he had this to say:

> Lyme disease sufferers are an identifiable group who are being systematically wronged by a system not responsive to their plight. We are in the midst of a tragedy of our own making … Wrongdoing is not always deliberate … I would recognize the hardship of Lyme disease sufferers in Canada exists today as the result of systemic institutionalized wrongdoing … As a private citizen, I would suggest to this committee that a formal inquiry would be the appropriate remedy. (Hawkins 2017)

It's amazing to me that a system such as Canada's can leave people struggling, in pain, broke, lonely, and without hope, but it has. When you are strapped with Lyme, you quickly realize that you must be there for yourself, in every possible aspect. Without your participation in your healing, there is not much that can be done. As much as the system wronged me—as it does thousands daily—I also was not there for myself, and if I was going to heal, I needed to make sure that would not happen again.

During my healing journey I experienced a huge realization about my lack of self-care and trust in myself. This was during my battle for disability while I was in treatment. I had to prove my case, and I was encouraged to seek out character references to share with the insurance company. I asked for help from the same people who had supported me along the way: my friends, certain family members, even some of the organizations and businesses that had helped me. It's a lot to ask of people to take time to write a detailed letter such as this, so I asked only those who had time. The letters that came back to me shocked me in many ways.

Not only did so many people take the time to help me, but the things they said in their letters were a surprise for many reasons. You don't realize what people notice about you or what you're quietly doing. You sometimes don't realize the impact you might be having on them. It also struck me that sometimes we say these things about one another only in a eulogy at that person's funeral—how tragic, for a few reasons.

I started to see how people thought about me. It struck me that they thought more highly of me on a regular basis than I thought of myself on my best day. The experience was timely too, because fighting with insurance companies when you are ill is not the best activity for your physical and mental state. These letters served as pick-me-ups at a rather low time. But the experience also made me wonder why I could never be satisfied with my own efforts or see what others saw in me. It made me sad that I could never say these considerate, thoughtful things to myself, especially when I realized the powerful effect reading these letters had on me. It made me sad to realize how much all of us probably tear ourselves down, when it does no good at all, instead of trying to always pick ourselves up. How good would it be for all of us to hear the positive aspects of ourselves from people we've impacted?

The letters touched me beyond words, and I thought that if ever someone were struggling, probably the best gift we could give them would be a letter, a letter to tell them what we admire about them, why we know they are going to win this fight, and how much they deserve all the love and support they are getting and the health and healing that are to come. How powerful. Simple but so powerful.

A few weeks later, I received a letter from my husband. He'd decided to write a character reference as well. He had been so strong during this journey. He was always such a positive person. He believed the best in everyone. It was not natural for him to judge anyone. He always just wanted everyone to be happy, so much so that as I was getting sicker, I didn't think he believed me. He tried to talk me out of any thoughts I had. I knew this was just his personality, but I was getting scared. Yet when it came to treatment and spending money, he never hesitated. He always did what he could to help and never once, not once, made me feel bad for not being myself. So when I say I am blessed, I am so blessed to have this kind of man by my side every day. I'm sharing his letter here:

If asked to write down some simple facts regarding Kristy, it would be very simple: she is my wife of over 20 years, mother of 2 of the most incredible kids and a friend to all.

Nobody is as stubborn, hardworking, motivated or caring as my wife. She has always busted her ass from the time her feet hit the ground in the morning till it was time to rest at night, doing everything mother nature could throw at her: skiing, biking, swimming, boot camps, running, hiking, hockey, and list goes on and on. She held a great job that brought her a lot of satisfaction which was a huge bonus for her, as well as her being a very valued employee.

I guess what I'm trying to say is that everything in our life was going along perfectly until she began to notice a few symptoms that just wouldn't go away, nagging at her and eventually impeding on her everyday activities. I remember very clearly one evening she asked me if I had noticed any changes in her at all. I murmured, "It's just nice to see you slow down a little." I was just trying to make light of the situation, but I had noticed things were changing. I began to watch her stand up after sitting for a period of time, and she would limp along for the first 10 steps or so until things felt better. This certainly wasn't normal, especially for the most in-shape health nut I have ever known.

Some who don't know us may think my comments are very one-sided, like I'm putting this lady on a pedestal because she is my wife. However, those who do know us would completely agree with me on everything I am writing (so yes, I guess I am putting her on a pedestal). But getting back to the symptoms: my father had called Kristy and me to walk over to his house to help out with a few computer issues he was having. The walk to his house entails at most 400 yds. After this walk I had seen enough. I couldn't believe what I was witnessing. My wife arrived to the house in complete exhaustion, like she had just completed one of her triathlon adventures. She was so completely exhausted and worn out from a short walk! We needed answers, and we needed them quick ... yeah, good luck with that!

She was struggling at work, slurring her words once in a while and going downhill quick. After a complete waste of time dealing with our health care personnel here in the Ottawa area, we had no choice but to start pulling our savings out to send Kristy to the States, where we could get some answers. At this point she was no longer able to work or participate in any of the things she held so dearly to her heart, which was devastating to both of us. After [Kristy's] being diagnosed with this brutal disease, it has been an uphill battle the whole way, but we remain optimistic she will eventually gain strength with her many, many treatments and once again enjoy life.

She has sacrificed so much over the past few years—her family, job, activities, financial stress, etc.—but she is beyond strong, and we will continue to fight this together. I will wrap this up by saying once again, if this letter makes Kristy sound like she is too good to be true, well, just ask anyone in our community, and they will be more than happy to tell you about Kristy and her character. She really is one of a kind!

I wanted to share this letter because sometimes as we battle an illness, it feels like no one understands or believes us. I did feel that way for a while. I tried explaining my symptoms to my husband, and he always made excuses for why I was probably feeling a certain way. He would often make light of what I was saying or say he was experiencing the same thing. I realize now that such reactions aren't always lack of support. Sometimes loved ones don't want to believe that you may be getting ill. Sometimes the thought of you getting really sick or having something serious is too painful, so denial is their best defense.

I wondered for a while why he would not support me but now I realize he was hoping for the best. How he helped when it all came to light is what was most important. How he never stopped hoping for a solution or a treatment or the money to do whatever it took shows the real support. With loved ones we are counting on for support, I think it's important to realize that it may not always be easy for them to support us how we need them to and that they are hurting too. Suddenly losing the wife you married and not knowing if she will ever come back is painful to accept. And if denying the possibility for as long as possible was holding off the pain for my husband, then that was only natural. As selfish as it is, I must admit that for quite a while I didn't consider his feelings in the whole process.

This lack of consideration may come from the fact that many Lyme patients experience a period of disassociation. I don't know if that is a proper medical term, but when it was explained to me, I realized that was exactly what I had been experiencing. I had developed a lack of emotion in response to most things I normally held dear. Maybe it was a bit of a defense mechanism, but I also believe it to be somewhat biological too. I just kind of stopped feeling many things. So considering how my husband was doing and feeling during my diagnosis was not top on my list. I was also so focused on healing and doing it quickly that I figured there was nothing for anyone to get upset about; it would be over in no time at all. But of course, that was not reality either. It all came to light when I was finally being treated and discussing some alternative therapies with another doctor, who turned to my husband and said, "I am going to get you your wife back." My husband just nodded because he couldn't talk; tears were streaming down his face. I had felt bad for him because this illness had hurt our lifestyle in so many ways, but I had never considered how much pain he was in.

I also realized that he had hidden that pain because he didn't want me to feel bad. He knew I was already feeling bad enough for what I was taking away from our family. The guilt over not having my own income any longer, not helping provide for my family as I'd always done, and not helping around the house was intense. Then add to that the fact that my husband no longer had a companion. I could do very little with him and nothing for him, and all of our conversations were about what symptoms were bad and which ones weren't too bad. Some days the conversation was closer to my wanting to give up and him explaining why I couldn't. This is not a fun existence for a spouse, and it can last years, even decades, for many. He made the best of the situation all the time. I had to wonder when he would wear down, but he never gave up. This gave me confidence many days— if he wasn't going to give in, then how could I possibly give in? It also made me wonder, if he, my friends, and my supporters could take care of, think highly of, and do anything to help me, then what the hell was wrong with me? Why couldn't I do all of those things for myself even better? Learning to love, care for, and trust myself more than anyone else became my only mission.

Self-care became one of the greatest lessons I learned on this journey. And as I said before, I mean real self-care, not a massage now and then or attempts to exercise and eat better. I mean self-love, self-kindness, and putting yourself first—despite what others say or think. That is big to Lyme patients because traditionally they are judged by many, unlike people with other illnesses. They are judged by researchers, doctors, and nurses who may not believe, by health educators who don't always agree, and by many people who don't understand Lyme, especially chronic Lyme. So learning to stand tall despite what others think they know about you is huge. It is about being genuinely who you are despite the circumstances or what others expect. There is so much peace and freedom in that place that it feels as though nothing and no one can ever hurt you again.

Yet I believe I learned another level of self-care far beyond anything else I could have learned: eliminating self-judgment. I was always so hard on myself that self-judgment was the core of my motivation. Not realizing how insanely unhealthy it was, I continued to think I thrived on it. Although I always strived to be less judgmental of others, I never realized that was impossible until I stopped judging myself. It's a really hard lesson to learn, one I am sure I will always grapple with. But ultimately, I believe Lyme was the biggest teacher and will be a consistent reminder.

The main reason I believe Lyme to be one of the greatest teachers about reserving judgment is that it is one of the most mysterious, untested, minimally researched, misunderstood, and rarely believed illness you could possibly get. Add on to that a lot of misinformation, conspiracy, and just seemingly impossible reasoning for why the illness is so dismissed. And the icing on the cake is that you don't even look sick. Some of my friends and family won't necessarily agree with the last part because they often saw me at my worst. But to the average individual who sees you on the rare occasions when you are doing okay or have made the effort to get out, you look absolutely fine. No one wants to look sick. I would go to great lengths to look as healthy as I could when I went out. But you do have to wonder how much better the care would be if the signs of illness were more obvious.

It makes me reflect on what I would have thought of someone battling Lyme from the outside. And what makes me most ashamed is the judgments I most likely would have had. I would not have believed that someone could literally not be able to get out of bed day after day, if she or he really tried. I would not have believed that dozens of medical professionals would not be able to find the person's problem. I certainly would not have thought people with such a condition would need tens of thousands of dollars to help themselves with something that couldn't even be seen. And I know for sure, I would have believed they needed to change their mindset to improve. I believed anybody could help him or herself if the person really wanted to, and yes, eventually I would. But for years I couldn't, no matter how hard I tried.

It makes me incredibly sad to think of how I might have judged someone in my position without knowing anything. Well, actually, I did judge someone in my position: me. I was very hard on myself. I was disgusted that I didn't do better, stay more committed, or resolve my issue. I thought many times that it was all in my head. I just have to be grateful that I at least felt inclined to pray and beg for help. And I believe that eventually, the universe or God helped me because I don't think there was any other way out. I really don't know how it all came together, how I found solutions, help, and recovery, but I did, and for that I am grateful.

I promised myself that no longer would I hold judgment over anyone, including myself. I have no idea what anyone is truly going through, even though I think I might. I can't feel what they feel, experience what they experience, or know the history, trauma, or exposure they have had. In truth, I will never know exactly what someone else is going through; therefore, how could I possibly have any thoughts on the matter? Even one Lyme patient's experience is very different from that of another. I couldn't know about another Lyme patient's struggle even though I have been through my own. It's not an easy process to reserve judgment; it's in our nature to analyze. It is also a way to make ourselves feel strong, as we think about how we would handle a situation better than another. I learned the hard way that I had no idea, even sometimes about myself. So I had to strive for better from myself and for the benefit of others.

If nothing else, I hope this book provides some better understanding of what goes on in the mind of a Lyme patient. I feel for those struggling, because when family and friends can't understand, it is an incredibly lonely place to be. Even when they do try to understand, it's hard because it's close to impossible to explain, in short or at all. Many times Lyme patients don't know what they are experiencing until they get to the other side of a bad spell, a setback, or healing in general. Sometimes reflection is the only time we understand ourselves at all. So for those reading this book, I want to thank you. Thank you for taking the time to listen and try to understand because maybe it will help you understand another's struggles in life. If nothing else, I hope it gives you the ability to opt for empathy before anything else. Empathy is healing you can offer someone else—because even when we don't understand, we always have the ability to offer empathy.

Two remaining aspects I had to get perspective on were living in the past and fearing the future. Both are easy to do with Lyme. I kept reliving the two weeks after the bite, wanting to redo it all differently. I kept looking toward the day when I would be better, having moved on from Lyme. Both of these notions were impossible. I couldn't go back and change anything, and never would I know a life without Lyme. It was here to stay, so I had to replace both ideas with something else. There was only one thing, and that was happiness in whatever was in the present moment.

I had to find a way to reflect on my journey in a healthy way and look to my future in an even healthier way. It was hard because in a small way I felt like I had been here before. The hike that was supposed to have healed me had created an illness so severe in me that I was sure it was trying to take my life away. At a minimum, it had tried to ruin my life when all I was doing was trying to grieve and get better. At some point I had to believe that this was part of the plan. I had asked for healing, and to truly find it, I was going to have to go deeper than I thought survivable, to a place I thought I would never return from. It would take me to the depths of despair, where I would just wish I was gone. It took me to that ugly place where I had to face all the ugliness in my life.

But at the end of that path was me, like I had never known me—a freedom in me more profound than I could have found any other way; a healing so intense it crossed body, mind, and soul; a peace in trusting myself more than I ever could have imagined possible; a life almost as good as I ever could have dreamed. What I had been searching for from the very beginning was finally revealing itself to me. It just hadn't happened how I had imagined it would take place.

I will never forget that day, looking in the dimly lit mirror at the campsite, horrified to see so many ticks on my back. My first reaction had been to swipe and grab every single one that I could, as quickly as I could. There had been instant panic until I said to myself, "Don't worry, you know what to do." But unfortunately, I thought I did, and I thought others did, but they didn't. Those vital few weeks after the bite were my chance to save myself, and I assumed everyone knew better. I let myself down.

But no more, not again. I now had to be there for myself. I had to know when I was okay and when I wasn't, and if I didn't know, then I was not keeping the promise I had made to myself. It was a feeling like I had never known, a comfort that I would always be there for myself. I knew that if at any point again I felt as though I was not okay, I would have the courage to stand up for myself. I will never let someone try to convince me I am okay when I know I am not. And if no one listens, then I will move on to find someone who will. I will no longer think I deserve less. No one deserves less. We all deserve proper care, from ourselves and from those in the professions that give care. Can you imagine what it would be like to be treated as though everyone cared?

That is what I have worked on so hard through my healing. Yes, a lot of it has been for myself, but greater than that, when I reach wherever I am supposed to get on this journey, I want to be there for others who aren't able to say, "I'm okay." It's a scary place to be, when you know you can't say that, and yet there seems to be nowhere to turn.

We all have struggles in this world. It is not an easy adventure to navigate. Many of us spend most of our lives lost and struggling to make it look like anything else. The experience is not easy; it's full of turmoil, drama, tragedy, hurt, and evil. We all have pain, loneliness, and uncertainty. And I would dare say many of us have wanted to give in, give up, or check out. So we have to be there for one another, whether we know about each other's pain or not, whether we can see it or not. We can be certain of one thing: if we are not struggling now, then we will be, or we have. It's just the way life is. But if we can use our strength to help others when they are weak, then we are serving a purpose. And if we don't know whether someone is struggling, let's just assume they are and offer them kindness. When we know they are, offer them hope.

But we must remember that we can give away only what we have to give ourselves. I plan to care for, love, and trust myself—more than I ever have—so that I can do the same for others. I ache when I think of others struggling, feeling lost, or confused. I wish I could take that away from the whole world. I don't know if we must go through these things to understand. Maybe it's the old saying ringing true: "If it weren't for the rain, we would never appreciate the sun." I so appreciate the sun now, and even when it's raining, I have faith that the sun will shine again. I want to be able to help others see that too.

# CHAPTER 17

# **Animals**

I would be remiss if I didn't share with you the story of my dog—well, my puppy to be exact. She became my hero because she literally saved my life in many ways. Mostly, she helped me through the extreme loneliness I felt with Lyme and in Lyme treatments. But because I also in turn was able to save her life when at six months she was clearly battling Lyme, she gave my illness purpose. I know I would not have been able to stand up for her and insist on treatment had I not experienced what I had. I had missed the signs in my last border collie when they said it was genetic hip problems when it was Lyme. But I did not miss the signs this time, because I had experienced them myself.

While I was being treated for Lyme, I fought the thought of getting a puppy. I worried I was too ill to properly care for one. But when the opportunity to get a border collie mixed with a Great Pyrenees came around, I had to consider it. I thought the mix would be ideal for what my new life was going to become, and after a year and a half of missing my last amazing pet, I was starting to feel it was time for a new dog. I truly missed the companionship of a dog when I was walking or doing things outdoors. I hoped the puppy would give me an incentive to find that old part of myself. I looked forward to the day I would be healthy enough to do those things again. So my son and I headed off to pick up our new puppy, Aggie, and we have never looked back.

She was great company and would just hang out beside me when I was too ill to do much else. One day following a hike, I discovered an engorged black-legged tick on her. Unfortunately, it was days before her three-month appointment, where she would have started preventive tick treatment. I saved the tick to show my vet, and she felt it was not a concern because it was not engorged (although it had seemed so when it was attached). I think there is a lot of misunderstanding with humans and animals. A tick can seem engorged while attached and deflate or appear less engorged once removed. But that doesn't mean it wasn't. It could actually mean that it spewed into the host and infected it. But different levels of engorgement can appear quite different once the tick is removed. Trust me—I have removed many. Regardless, it was too early to test, and I was sent back home with preventive meds and the tick.

It's true that the testing will likely not be positive for many weeks after a bite because the testing looks for antibodies. The test shows whether antibodies have been developed by the immune system to fight off the Lyme. The test does not actually detect Lyme, just the signs that your body is fighting Lyme. This is also why people and animals will not get a positive test many months after they have been infected with Lyme: Lyme attacks the immune system, and after a while, the immune system may stop developing antibodies as it wears down from the Lyme attack. Therefore, there are no antibodies to be detected. That's why Lyme has such a great ability to overtake your body and why so many chronic Lyme patients will not produce a positive test result; there are no longer antibodies.

After a month of keeping an eye on things, I became concerned with her loose stool and called the vet, thinking it might be Lyme. The amazing thing about vets is that they have the best understanding of Lyme out of any medical professionals. The treatment animals receive from the veterinarian community is far superior to what any human receives from the medical community. While I was serving as a Lyme patient witness to the federal government, one MP asked the expert doctor if he was trying to suggest that the data and treatments animals receive are better than what humans receive, to which the medical doctor responded, "I am not suggesting; I am telling you it is a fact."

That's why when the vet told me loose stool wasn't necessarily an indicator of Lyme, I let it go, even though I was a little surprised. It can be a common symptom in humans, especially since fever and flu-like symptoms are early symptoms of Lyme. And remember, with Lyme the immune system is under attack, which means a symptom of it is that you catch many illnesses and viruses going around—not exactly Lyme but caused by Lyme. Aggie was a young puppy, eating many new things and new to me, so it was hard to determine what was out of character for her. I also knew I was probably hypersensitive because I didn't want anyone or any animal to struggle as I had with this disease.

A few months later, I knew it was getting to be too much. I called the vet and insisted she test Aggie for Lyme. After a quick in-clinic test, she reported, "I guess your instincts were right—she is positive for Lyme." And here comes the most important part of this story. The veterinarian then stated, "Typically, we would not treat her with anything since she is not showing symptoms, just the presence of Lyme in her system. So I have to ask, why were you so adamant she be tested for Lyme?"

I said it was because she was symptomatic for Lyme. Aggie was showing many of the same symptoms of Lyme that were missed when I first started to get sick, such as the following:

1. She was panting and breathing heavily.
2. She was often feverish. Some nights she would get me up to let her outside to just sit in the cold.
3. She was happy to go for a long walk and play hard but seemed to be very lethargic the following day or two.
4. She drank more water than any dog I had ever known.
5. Her shedding increased.
6. Her eyes were regularly bloodshot.
7. She appeared clumsy and would trip once in a while.
8. Even though she might want to jump up on a couch or something, she seemed hesitant, and it looked like she had to coax herself to push off to get up.
9. Her loose stool would seem like it was getting better, and then it would return.

The one thing I remember clearly with this illness is that just as you think you are getting better, all of a sudden sickness returns, and it may be even worse. It's a cycle that makes you think you are better and then sick with something else. And in a dog it is even harder to detect because the cycles make you think the issues are unrelated, and sadly, our furry friends can't tell us how much they are suffering. A dog's natural instinct for survival is to hide suffering, to avoid being vulnerable in the wild. So you can never expect to know how bad it really is, and well, Lyme is called the invisible disease for a reason.

The vet explained to me that the symptoms she was looking for were limping, stiff joints, and loss of appetite. And that was right, but for me, as a human, that had happened three years into my diagnosis. It is chronic by that time, which means recovery is much tougher. We want to get to a point where we catch this disease early so that it is treatable and responds to antibiotics. I was adamant that Aggie receive treatment. I was confident the signs were early Lyme, and I never wanted what comes next in the progression of this illness for anyone, human or animal.

I share this because Lyme is still a very misunderstood disease. As they say with Lyme, you don't get it until you get it. Humans are treated for Lyme at a lesser level than animals in Canada, and once it's chronic, you cannot get treatment here at all. That's why we are not learning a lot about the illness here. Our pets can't speak and tell us what's going on, and the humans who can share their struggles are usually dismissed. And so the medical community is not learning about the illness from any angle. Our veterinarians know the most about Lyme, so what does that tell you? We could learn from humans, but not many in the medical world will listen. Vets would be able to learn so much more if doctors were more open to learning from Lyme patients. But for some, the negative implications for their practice—if they were to treat a Lyme patient (with long-term prescriptions)—are too big. I guess we can't blame them.

Even though I was sure Aggie had Lyme, it was hard for me to feel I wasn't overreacting. I felt so sure, yet the lingering doubt made me wonder if I was just too petrified of someone else suffering. She also had Great Pyrenees in her, and I was less familiar with that breed. Some of the symptoms, at first, could have been attributed to her breeding. But they progressed and seemed more extensive than they should be. So having been there myself and knowing that passing off my many symptoms for too long had led to my chronic Lyme diagnosis, I was not going to let the same thing happen to my new best friend.

The other thing I know with Lyme is that many of the symptoms seem minor on their own. Then they start to build and add up, and you need to keep a running list of what is happening. As minor symptom after minor symptom starts to add up over time, you may have a valid concern for Lyme. My Lyme symptoms were very hard for me to explain to my doctor for years, and so it would be close to impossible for a dog to let us know what is happening and have us understand before it's too late.

If your dog tests positive for Lyme, please don't assume he or she is not symptomatic. It is a horrible, hidden disease. Vets not only are better diagnosticians than doctors; they also are very willing to properly treat animals for the illness. Yet it is still complex and sometimes a misunderstood illness. Just be aware. You don't want your pet to suffer silently.

One other note about Lyme: don't assume that because your dog was treated with an antibiotic, the illness is gone. The vet told me that day that she'd had a dog who was treated but in whom the illness returned. She wasn't sure whether the dog had been bitten again or not. I explained to her that there are many scientific studies proving the persistence of the Lyme bacteria. Treatment can attempt to kill it all but can fall short, and the longer someone has the illness, the harder it is to treat. It is possible for someone to recover with antibiotic treatment and have the illness return, which just means not all of the bacteria were killed off. So to be safe, monitor for symptoms long after treatment.

You should also consider the possibility that the animal's immune system will still be compromised several weeks after a bite. This is hard to treat in humans, so I am not sure where you begin with animals. But it's worth knowing and talking to your vet about. I added probiotics and supplements as I learned about them. I do think the symptoms came back many months later, and I treated her again. But now it seems they have all disappeared. So it's really hard to say, and as much as I hate the thought of treating my dog with unnecessary antibiotics, the thought of her suffering with Lyme is a far worse option. It's not even a close comparison or reason for debate: a few extra weeks of antibiotics is nothing when you consider the smallest possibility of the alternative, trust me.

And since I know she was infected, I will always be hypersensitive to her health. I am always looking into better-quality foods and learning about supplements that will build up her system, just like I do for myself and my family. I drive them all nuts analyzing symptoms and concerns. I really don't want anyone I love to suffer, even just a little bit. A very tiny part of me feels there is some blessing in knowing Lyme so well. I hope that it means I can prevent infection of or at least get treatment to the ones I love as soon as possible. I see the signs all the time, and I won't ever again make the same mistake I did with myself.

I am grateful to my dog for being there with me through some pretty rough years. She took on a lot of responsibility for such a young dog, and she thrived on it. In fact, I had her certified as a therapy dog. She is so sweet, gentle, and kind that it's like she was meant to come into my life when I needed those traits the most. She kept me company when the whole world kept spinning but my world had stopped. Oh, and in case you are wondering if I have learned something new, shedding may be a symptom of Lyme, but apparently, it is also a significant characteristic of a Great Pyrenees! Mind you, shedding seems pretty minute when you consider she saved a life.

# CHAPTER 18

# Gratitude

I knew deep down inside that my true emotional healing on this journey would come when I could find gratitude in all of it; the illness, pain, loss and challenge. It does seem like an impossible task, especially when you are talking about Lyme. It is probably the most insulting thing you could say to a Lyme patient: that she must find gratitude in it all. I would never say that to someone else, because it may not be that person's truth, but for me, I knew it was what I had to do.

It may be hard to imagine how you could overlook the dismissal of tons of doctors, which had led to a life of a chronic, debilitating illness, or how you could get past the fact that your country neglected your needs so badly that you had to use all of your retirement savings and your kids' school tuitions to travel out of country to get help. It's hard to digest the fact that after doing all of that, you still have to spend years of recovery to maybe get to 75 percent and have to give up that promotion you worked your whole life for. And then, just when you think it couldn't get any worse, the insurance company you have invested in your whole working career denies your coverage. And you know that all of the physical and mental activities you love to do are not possible and may never be. How does one find gratitude in all of that?

Jenna Luché-Thayer, human rights expert and former senior advisor to the United Nations and US government, stated the following in a presentation at the 2017 International Lyme and Associated Diseases

Society Conference, about the treatment of Lyme patients around the world:

> These are very extreme and gross human rights violations. I have worked across the globe on human rights ... I've seen some horrible situations and ... you just want to cry. I can tell you since I have become a member of the Lyme tribe, I have certainly seen as many in this situation as others.
>
> Almost all UN member countries have ratified health human rights. Yet many Lyme patients are desperately marginalized and suffer gross human rights abuse by the hands of state actors and intergovernmental bodies such as World Health Organization, the [US] Centers for Disease Control and Prevention and the National Institute of Health. These violations by our public institutions indicate corruption and undermine our trust. (Luché-Thayer 2017)

So the question becomes, how do you possibly find gratitude when you are suffering from one of the world's greatest health human rights violations right now? I don't think that is what you find gratitude in, exactly. I couldn't possibly, because I was dedicated to changing the treatment of Lyme for the sake of others, in any way I knew how. I knew I would never give up on that challenge, so I wasn't going to be grateful for what I knew so badly had to change. But remaining with a bitter heart would always sap my energy and potentially hinder my healing. So I had to change how I saw it all and how it made me feel and turn it into something good. That is where the blessings of where I live, the friends I have, my close family, and the people in my community became the most important factor to my recovery. I almost felt a little guilty to be so blessed because the people in my life were so amazing that without a doubt, I had the greatest chance of recovery, simply because of them and all they did for me.

I realized something very important for me, someone who had always wondered what was the right thing to do for someone who had become ill or experienced a loss or a trauma. The answer of what to do became very clear: you do anything that will create a sense of gratitude in the person in pain. I realize that is the main purpose in why we do things for those who are suffering. Gratitude can be a very healing and very powerful emotion. If you can, for a few minutes, override the pain someone is experiencing and fill that person with gratitude, you create healing, comfort, and warmth. It may be a short break from the pain, but it is a break. That gesture has more power than we know. It really is so much more than bringing them food when they don't feel like cooking or flowers to brighten their day. It is about filling them with a sense of gratitude to help them heal. It is as simple as that.

During the years of my recovery, I had friends who would shoot me a text occasionally just to say hi or ask how I was doing. This meant the world to me because with Lyme, when you have to opt out of or cancel plans constantly, you become very disconnected from the world around you. It might have seemed like nothing to the person sending the message, or sometimes, I know some of them felt bad that they hadn't touched base sooner. But that was never the point or important at all. That instant connection often would come on a bad day or just when I needed it the most. It would be just enough to make me smile. Actually, if I am honest, it often made me cry—a cry of gratitude, I guess you could say. The messages really were often timely, and I'm sure the senders never knew how timely, but they made the effort, and that was so valuable. The same goes for all the people who sent me inspirational quotes and messages. Ironically, they would often be the inspirational messages I needed exactly at that time. I will never underestimate the power of sending someone a note just to say I am thinking of them.

People often ask, "What can I do for you?" and although the question comes with the best of intentions, I have come to realize that the person who is ill or suffering may have no idea what he or she needs or wants. I think that is especially true for a Lyme patient. The sicker you are, the more difficulty you have sorting out your thoughts and organizing your needs. You really have no idea what you need or want. Your memory is so bad that even if you did know at one point something you needed, by the time someone asks, it might be forgotten.

My suggestion is to just do anything. Follow your instincts, and as strange as your idea or thought may be, it could quite possibly be the most important thing you could do. For example, one of my friends gave me a brush. I had borrowed a similar one many months before I was diagnosed. I had known I was sick at the time, but I hadn't understood why or with what. I had borrowed the brush and realized it didn't hurt or give me a burning sense on my head. It was also really light and brushed through tangled hair very well. I didn't think about it much at the time, except I commented on how nice it was. She gave me a new brush just like that one. I am sure she didn't think much of it at the time. But as I recovered, I realized why I liked it so much. My arms were weak, and my hair was so unhealthy that it was dry and tangled even after a shower. And Lyme had attacked my nervous system, so all my receptors were ultra-sensitive. That brush was one of the best gifts I could have been given, but I didn't even know or understand it at the time. Had that friend asked me what I needed, I never would have said a brush, but it was the perfect gift.

The big thing with asking for help when you are ill or struggling is that you don't want to do it until you need the help the most. But how do you decide when you need it the most? The fact is, the fear of needing help more another time always holds you back from asking for something. I would think, *I don't want to waste an "ask" on something because tomorrow I could be worse.* People would offer to make food, but I never knew day to day whether I was going to be well enough to make something. If there was any chance that I would be able to prepare food that day, I didn't want to have someone make me anything, in case tomorrow I couldn't do it. I swore I would ask only when I really had no choice but to ask. However, once you need help the most, it's too late to ask. Even when you have a bad day, you think there is always the chance that you will feel better and be able to make some food.

Many days, making supper for my family was all I could muster the energy to do. It was my first priority, and I tried hard every day to make it the one thing I did for sure. Some days, though, it was impossible, and to me it was the ultimate failure to accept the fact that on those days, I was so weak, so sick, and so useless that I couldn't even feed my family.

The situation was made worse because people knew I was on a very strict diet, so of course they wanted to find out what I could eat before they made anything. I felt horrible that they would have to go to that trouble and/or pay extra for specialized foods, so I would tell them not to worry about it. Some close friends didn't listen and just figured out what I could eat and made it anyway. For that I was extremely grateful. On those occasions, I knew I would not have to stress and worry that I wouldn't succeed that day.

I always worried that I would have a day so bad that I couldn't feed my family. I felt like they were all out at school or working, and I was at home wasting time and space, so if I could not even feed them, what was my purpose? I felt that if supper was available at the end of the day, no one would have to know that I had been unable to do anything else throughout the day. It felt like the ultimate facade. But it was the only way I could maintain some dignity. I just felt so horrible about myself. I was just a waste of time, money, and space. I was crippling my family financially with my treatments, and I was not able to contribute to our income and was barely able to help with chores around the house. Why was I even there?

Later in my recovery, I thought I should have just told friends not to worry about my diet. I could have dealt with that. Any meal that would have fed my kids and husband when they came home at the end of the day would have been just as much help and relief, without anyone trying to accommodate my crazy diet. Afterward, I thought that any food would be of help in a situation such as mine and someone would enjoy it. Maybe it would even be shared with a visitor. It would still be a burden off the person it was given to because it would be something they didn't have to make for someone else.

It really always is hard to know what to do to help others. It's something I have grappled with forever. I always felt like I didn't want to do or give something that a person really didn't want, or I felt that if it turned out to be something the person did have or could do herself, then it would have been of no value. I soon came to realize that was far from the truth. Our neighbors plowed our laneway even though we had our own plow to do it. This meant that my husband didn't have to do it after a long day at work, and it was always a relief for him and me to know it was done. They never asked; they just did it. Many times when they came in the laneway, I was filled with emotion.

Local businesses would ask about my needs that related to their products and about what they could do to accommodate me. To them it might have felt like part of what they did, but it meant the world to me. Another local businessman helped me one day at the grocery store. At the cash register, I realized I had lost my wallet and would have to leave my groceries and go home to hopefully find it, but that effort would have proven useless because (1) it might not be at home (I had no idea where I had left it), and (2) I would have been so exhausted by the time I got home that returning would have been impossible. The businessman followed me out of the store and told me that he would pay for the groceries and I could repay him when I was able. Jokingly, we talked about how he knew where I lived and could hunt me down for repayment. And when I did repay him, we joked about how awful I had looked that day and how he had just known I was not at my best. He was right; it had been all I could do to get in there, and trying to figure out where my wallet was was more than my brain could handle. The healthy version of me would have been so embarrassed that this had even happened. But the sick me, she was only grateful. I was operating at a minimum, and anything anyone did that could lighten the load meant the world to me.

Local organizations such as the fire department and organized clubs found ways to support me, often more ways than one. After I shared my story in my hometown, with the hope of sharing a lot of preventive information, it was like they took me under their wing. I had grown up in a small town. When I was young, there were about three hundred people there. My dad owned the trucking company on the main street, and my best friend lived a few blocks away. That was pretty much the town. After marriage I had moved to the next town, and now it felt like I had two hometowns rallying to do anything possible to help me. One of the speakers who joined me to talk about Lyme described me like Lorelai Gilmore of Stars Hollow. In a sense it was a perfect analogy. Lorelai was a well-intentioned person who sometimes went off-track, but at the end of the day, the town loved her for who she was, and she loved them. That's exactly how I felt. Not many can say they have experienced a whole town rallying around them when they are down, but I sure did.

Maybe it's a result of living and growing up in small towns, but my friends have always been like family to me. Some of my close friends really and truly are family. One of them would often stop by unannounced or send me a text, wondering if I wanted to go somewhere for an hour or two. She would always promise to bring me home as soon as it was too much. Some days she would stop in, and it would be clear to her that I was not doing well. So she wouldn't mention her plans on those days. Of course, I wouldn't know that until much later. But once in a while it would work out, and it felt really good to get out of the house on those days.

What is beautiful about this gesture for a Lyme patient is that quite often the effort to get ready to go out takes all the energy you have. Many times, I would shower and get dressed and then lie down in tears because there was no chance of making it out. I remember the day it happened before a friend's memorial. I had been really careful with my energy the day leading up to it, and I had taken my time getting ready. I thought I was out of energy, so I lay down, hoping the episode would pass, but it just got worse. I was dizzy and nauseated. I couldn't hold my head up, and sitting made me feel like I would throw up. It took some time for me to admit it, but I had to tell my husband I couldn't go. I badly wanted to pay my respects, and I just lay there crying while he went. It wasn't the first time that had happened, and it certainly wouldn't be the last. I just didn't know if it would keep happening forever.

When my friend would just stop in, I was rarely ready or showered, but I would just throw on a hat and deodorant and go if I could. She was someone I was incredibly comfortable with, so I didn't care. It felt safe because if things started to go badly, she was quick to take me home. I never felt like she didn't understand, even though there was absolutely no way she could understand. The fact that I didn't have to worry about planning an excursion and not being able to make it took all of the pre-activity stress away. So I had as much energy as possible to go out.

I would never say, "Stop in and surprise me with an outing." The thought of that would cause too much worry. But when it did work, I felt like a normal human being for a short time. When I did have to go home early, she would always give me a reason why she too had to go home early. These may have been lies, but anything that made me feel like I was on the same wavelength as others made me feel good. For that short time, I felt a little more like myself, a little more like my life was normal, even though nothing was. It's amazing—when you are in that place, the simple, normal things about your life really are what you miss so much. Anything anyone can do to make you feel those experiences again, in any capacity, is an amazing gift. What Winnie the Pooh said is so true: "Sometimes the smallest thing can take the most room in your heart."

But of course, it didn't stop there. Friends shared their air miles to help me travel for treatment and eventually a vacation. Others shared products from their family businesses that I was able to give as thank-you gifts to medical staff and others who had helped me. Companies and organizations came together and funded some of my treatments, and friends, family, and even coworkers took me to appointments. Others shared their services such as spa treatments for free. My coworkers had a "Lymeade" station at work and shared the proceeds with me. It just never ended; people gave and helped in every way.

At first I had a really hard time accepting this help. Many offers, I turned down for a while, until I heard an explanation about abundance that made me look at all of this in a new way. It basically suggested that we continue to ask for help and abundance in our lives, yet when it comes, or if it doesn't come in the way we expect, we pass it up. How are we supposed to ask the universe to continue to bring more good in our lives if we constantly say no to anything that is offered? It made me think of the Drowning Man story:

> A fellow was stuck on his rooftop in a flood. He was praying to God for help.
>
> Soon a man in a rowboat came by, and he shouted to the man on the roof, "Jump in! I can save you!"
>
> The stranded fellow shouted back, "No, it's okay. I'm praying to God, and he is going to save me."
>
> So the rowboat went on.
>
> Then a motorboat came by. The fellow in the motorboat shouted, "Jump in! I can save you!"
>
> To this the stranded man said, "No, thanks. I'm praying to God, and he is going to save me. I have faith."
>
> So the motorboat went on.
>
> Then a helicopter came by, and the pilot shouted down, "Grab this rope, and I will lift you to safety."
>
> To this the stranded man again replied, "No, thanks. I'm praying to God, and he is going to save me. I have faith."
>
> So the pilot reluctantly flew away.

Soon the water rose above the rooftop, and the man drowned. He went to Heaven. He finally got his chance to discuss this situation with God, at which point he exclaimed, "I had faith in you, but you didn't save me—you let me drown. I don't understand why!"

To this God replied, "I sent you a rowboat and a motorboat and a helicopter. What more did you expect?"

I knew I was going to have to put my pride aside through all of this and accept help, wherever it came from. This battle was bigger, longer, and harder than anything I had ever been through, and many days I just wasn't sure that getting through it was possible. I had amazing people in my life, and I was going to learn to graciously accept their help. It wasn't in my nature to accept help from anyone. I had spent my whole life trying to prove that I could do things on my own, that I was tougher and stronger than people knew, and that my survival instincts were strong. One of the goals of my hike had been to prove I could survive all on my own with just the supplies on my back. Man, had that ever gone wrong. Because of that hike I was now physically disabled, mentally struggling, and more dependent on everyone in my life than I ever could have imagined being. My ego was shot. It had to be set aside. I needed everyone and anything they could do to help me through this. And everyone was showing up, bigger and better than I ever could have asked of them, way beyond my greatest expectations.

For months, my friends begged me to let them do a fundraiser. I just couldn't do it. I had been part of a committee that organized fundraisers for twelve years. I knew the amount of work that went into them. I kept saying, "No, but thank you." It was kind that they were offering. Eventually, coworkers asked my friends why nothing was happening, to which my friends replied, "You try to get her to agree"—which they did.

Eventually, they won us over. My husband and I worried about how hard it would be to accept this kind of help, but when we showed up that night, it was unlike anything I could have imagined. It's quite an experience to walk into a room full of people who are there to support you. People I hadn't seen in ages, including not only present but also past coworkers, had come, and there were auction items donated by businesses and individuals. It was like nothing I had ever imagined. I knew my friends had gone to so much trouble and effort to put this event together. It was amazing. I had never pictured myself in a position where people would have to raise money for me, but if I had to be in that position, I couldn't imagine being around anyone other than the people in that room.

There was a lot of emotion that night. I am really sure it was love that kept me going and love that wore me out. It's a powerful, emotional experience to be in a room of people who care, who are giving of themselves for you and are cheering you on. My daughter was overcome with emotion that night, and I know it was because she could feel it too. The funds raised that night supported me while I was still trying to get my disability pay. It still hadn't been approved, and although it would eventually work out, the money my community raised ended up being necessary for me to continue treatments while being denied insurance. I don't think the people in that room had any idea about the timing and importance of that fundraiser. I don't think I even realized it myself. I feel like I must have been living in a haze, because looking back, we realized we were likely months or weeks from either selling our home or giving up my treatments altogether at that time. If you live in the Lyme world, you know that happens daily. Many lose their homes, many can't afford their apartments and move in with family, and others are simply homeless.

This hit me once, and I wondered how many people living on the street were struggling with Lyme. It was a place you could end up when misdiagnosed for years or decades like thousands are. You don't have energy to support yourself, and the pain and misery could force you to find ways to numb the struggle. There is absolutely nothing to say that I would not have ended up there had it not been for the people around me. I know the average person will think I am being dramatic, but I know that not one Lyme patient will think I am. It's a quite real possibility. When doctors won't help you, and family easily think you are just lazy or not motivated, and all of them start to think you are a hypochondriac whining about all these small illnesses that are impossible to prove, you might turn to drugs or alcohol because existing as you are is impossible. I wouldn't blame one person for taking that route in that situation. I would actually suggest they had found the best possible survival mechanism in the situation they were in. The majority of people with Lyme who are not believed by their loved ones are treated as if they have psychiatric issues. How many stories have we heard of such people ending up on the street or committing suicide? The rates of suicide are high in Lyme. It's not an overreaction. I can tell you that even with all the support in the world, there are periods of time when suicide seems like a real option. It was only the support that surrounded me that pulled me through.

I was actually lucky in a few very unique ways. I was hyperactive as a child. You could maybe even say I was hyperactive as an adult too. I did a lot, including a lot of crazy things. I was always active, overdoing it, and trying something new. I loved being social, being part of a new event, or starting something new. I believe this fact saved me and proved to the people I love that I was really struggling—because although my decline seemed gradual to me, in many others' eyes I had changed in a very short time. I became quiet and less involved, I dropped out of things and stopped doing my fitness programs, and then I stopped exercising altogether. I became overridden with anxiety and avoided many of the things I would normally do. To everyone around me, I was changing rapidly, and there seemed to be no explanation. But they also knew I wasn't faking it. I didn't want to be this way. I wanted to do all those things so badly that I kept trying, and it kept getting worse. The people who knew me the best knew something major had to be happening to take me away from all I loved.

That is not the case for every Lyme patient. If you are someone who is more intellectual or less physically active then the symptoms may not be as obvious as early on. I don't know how you could convince someone else it was affecting you, if you weren't challenging yourself daily and seeing the subtleties that illness shows for awhile. If you'd had it for decades and it just didn't hit you as hard and as fast as it did me, then how could you prove it? Some people may be born with it. There are professionals who say that is not possible, but science has been showing this possibility for decades. I know people who are eventually going to win this battle to prove it true. What about those infected children who don't have parents who know to fight? It may seem like the children were just born that way—lazy, crazy, or lost. My heart breaks for anyone who is struggling with Lyme while the professionals around them are not picking up on it. It happens every day. I pray for the day when it all comes to light and the medical profession is no longer fooled by the people who made this mess in the first place. It will happen, and the truth will come out, but not in time to save thousands, maybe millions, who have suffered over the years, needlessly. I think of those people every day. I often feel guilty for being blessed with a diagnosis, money for treatment, and loved ones all around me. But I can't focus on the guilt. I must focus on the change, or the guilt will be all-consuming. Why should I find a solution and not someone else? Everyone deserves proper care, treatment, and love. No one is beneath that basic right.

Lori Dennis is author of the book *Lyme Madness*, and she perfectly describes why we are all in this insane situation. I am so grateful to her for the time, effort, and pain she went through to put that book together after her eyes were opened during the process of trying to help her adult son. Without her book, I believe many families would not understand that Lyme is a crime and that people are neglected and mistreated daily. I never would have believed something like this was possible. In an interview by Cindy Kennedy, Lori Dennis was asked "what ticks her off," to which she perfectly replied:

> What ticks me off? I'll tell you what ticks me off. Medical ego. It lights a fire under me like nothing lights a fire under me. So what I mean by that is doctors—and there are just too many of them—who are blind to this, who don't listen, who don't respect their patients, who listen to the propaganda that's been fed to them, who don't open their minds and their hearts to what's in front of them and therefore turn their backs on people who are really sick ... And even worse, telling them that it's all in their head. Really ticks me off because it's a sick, shaming thing to do. It's not helpful. And it's blaming the victim. (Dennis 2018)

She is so right. I truly believe everyone deserves kindness, and the way medical professionals treat people who present Lyme symptoms, suggest they might have Lyme, or even treat themselves after a diagnosis of Lyme is appalling. Lyme patients are treated like shit by the very professionals who are paid to be somewhat compassionate, to try everything in their power to help people, and to yes, maybe sometimes consider that they don't know everything or that there is more to learn. But only a select few doctors in the Lyme world, a very select few, do these things as they should. It's not okay. It has to stop. And I believe there are some very powerful people out there who are getting closer to making it stop for all time.

It is hard in this game to try to help yourself but not be overcome with guilt for those who can't. I believe that is what drives many Lyme advocates I have come to know. You are shocked that such inhumanity can exist in Canada. But when you dig deeper, you realize that big money won over some vile people, and they are okay watching thousands suffer. I believe kindness always wins in the end. I don't know how or when it will happen. It seems the Lyme wars have been going on for decades, and people have been fighting for the truth to be revealed for decades, but it hasn't happened yet. I can't stop believing in kindness winning in the end. I have to believe the truth will prevail, or all I have believed in my whole life is wrong. I know it's not wrong. I know the truth will come out. Sometimes I think the truth is closer than we know. We just have to keep believing.

I have also decided that with that belief, I must continue to believe in gratitude. I believe gratitude to be one of the most powerful and healing emotions you can have. I also believe that sometimes with Lyme it can be one of the hardest emotions to experience. How can you be grateful when in a short amount of time, it is possible to lose health, wealth, family, and friends, all while being ridiculed by the professionals who are supposed to help you? Gratitude is not the first emotion that comes to mind. But I also believe that may be some of the purpose in all of this. If you can find true gratitude in all that is wrong with this disease and the treatment that surrounds it, you can find gratitude under any circumstances. It's not an easy thing to do. It may be easier for me than some because I had a community of support that I truly believe was beyond anything I ever imagined possible. But Lyme patients themselves are a great community of support. They have all been through similar experiences of loss, mistreatment, and suffering. So they know how to treat others who suffer like them, with true kindness. So for them I was also grateful.

I will continue to strive to see only what I am grateful for in my life and to be grateful that it comes so easy. I am truly lucky for everything in my life. I am lucky I finally found good doctors. I am lucky for financial support all around me. I am more than blessed by amazing people in my life. And I am forever grateful for a truly compassionate husband and amazing children who made treatment as tolerable as it can be and for a dog who suffered alongside me. I was truly equipped as best as anyone could be to take on this fight. So I must also find a way to help those who may not be as well equipped. It has to stop, and when it does, I promise to be eternally grateful for the truth.

# CHAPTER 19

# Conclusion

As I write this, I have been living the longest healthy streak of my recovery, which is so promising, but I am also starting to experience what I know is a setback. I can't do what I have been doing. I am sick more and tire easily again. I am trying to remain calm as I see it coming. It's a helpless feeling because I have learned there is not much I can do but ride it out. The last setback lasted over two months, but afterward, I experienced the best two months I have known in years. So as it is starting to rain, I know there will be sun again.

Is this as good as I'm going to get? It's possible. But I believe there to be more healing. Am I responsible for this setback? It's possible. It's so hard to know when or why it happens, and maybe I *was* doing too much and caused it to happen. Or maybe it would have happened anyway, as the doctors suggest. It is part of healing, which means I am still healing. I also know that I need to recover from this my way, and sometimes, it just feels so good to do a bit of what I used to do, to show signs of who I used to be, to feel like me, that I just want to feel that forever. It's not the smartest way to recover, but it feels right for me. This time, I am going to do things my way.

People aren't always going to agree with me. People aren't always going to believe me. But that will no longer influence how I treat myself. My goal will forever be to help others find that part of themselves too, the part where they are no longer dependent on things outside of themselves to know who and how they are. We deserve so much more from ourselves.

I want women especially to learn to treat themselves with the same care, dignity, and respect as they so often treat others. I believe it to be the only way to find peace in your life. I believe we all deserve that.

As Ellen DeGeneres once said about coming out and going through the toughest part of her life, "it was so important for me to lose everything, because I found what the most important thing is—to be true to yourself."

I believe I will always be healing, not just from Lyme but from all that life hands us. I think we are all healing from something. I decided I was okay with that. Maybe it was a good way to look at myself. Maybe I would spend my whole life trying to get "there." And I eventually became okay with that too. Because as I learn, I believe I can help others do the same. And as much as some of the lessons seem unbearable at the time, they always seem worth it when I make it to the other side. There is nothing better to help you through than knowing there are people there to support you, knowing you are never alone, especially when you have yourself backing you.

We all need to feel safe in knowing that when things are not okay, we can tell someone who will listen—knowing that professionals will take us seriously, and friends and family will trust us even if the pain or problem is not obvious. I wonder what would happen to our mental health crisis if everyone knew there was somewhere safe to go, someone safe to go to, if they could not say that things were okay: a place without judgment, maybe even without solutions, just a gentle place to go when you ask yourself the question, "Am I okay?" and you can't answer yes. I believe we owe it to ourselves to ask that question every day and to know that the answer may not always be yes but that this happens to everyone. We don't need to answer yes every day—that's normal—but when there are more days when the answer is no and the frequency starts to increase, we need to feel safe to tell someone. No one should suffer alone.

We all have periods when we need to reach out for help. That is not a sign of weakness; it is a sign of being human. No one feels they are okay every day, and no one should feel there is something wrong with them if they don't. But when the no days outweigh the yes days, we need to know that the strong thing to do is ask for help. And if the person we ask doesn't believe us or won't listen, we need to keep searching until we find someone who will. The most powerful thing we can do for ourselves is admit when we are not handling things. Not only will this get us the help that we deserve; it also will make it okay for the next person to do the same. I am not sure when it became normal to hide our low times and fight to make it look like we are managing when we are not. It didn't get me anywhere but worse off than I would have been.

I have to think the world would be a better place to live if we could just be there for people when they aren't okay and help them find a way to honestly say, "I'm okay." We all have differing abilities, but if we all use what comes naturally to us to help others, then we all may get through this a lot easier. There is always the other side of any problem, but sometimes we just need some help getting there, some support to remind us there is another side, and sometimes someone just being there as we muddle through can make all the difference in the world. And if your profession is to help or provide support in some way, you must ask yourself what you can do to help that person be okay. Maybe you don't have all the answers, maybe your expertise is not what the person needs, or maybe you don't believe in the person's problem, but you must not make a bad situation worse. Dismissing them, treating them like they are making the problem up, or patronizing them is not the way. They just may be right; they may be telling the truth and may be truly struggling. Please, do whatever is in your power to help them be okay; that's all I ask.

If we can all travel through these storms together, knowing there is another side and knowing we are not alone, we can start to find the things that serve us, heal us, and feed us. We can't all have the answers all of the time, but we can be open-minded and consider possibilities, and even if we don't understand, we always have the ability to help in some way. Then we not only would be okay but even could start to thrive in our own lives. Life is not just about living; I believe it's about thriving. And I believe when we thrive, we help others thrive too. It's never going to be a straightforward battle, but what could be better than knowing that you have the ability to help others when you are thriving and that you deserve their hand when you are not?

As I learned to look forward with peace, there was one little element of my journey that still haunted me, and I wanted to let it go. I repeatedly relived those two weeks following my bite. I relived each step and the misinformation about removal, infection, testing, and treatment. I pictured myself standing at that mirror in that campground years ago, looking at those bugs, and wondered about how it all could have been different. Maybe I would not have lost my passions, my abilities, my health, and most of all, my energy. But at some point I had to stop looking back and reliving those moments, those steps, those weeks.

I asked myself what I would like to see when I relived that memory in the mirror and the two weeks that followed. I decided I wanted to remember how strong I was to keep trying to survive when everything was going wrong, how determined I must have been to eventually get help for myself, and how much endurance I must have had to last through a horrible recovery. I decided I wanted to remember how I had learned to thrive in life.

I decided the best way to make sure those were my memories whenever I looked back was to literally tattoo over the spot where the ticks had attached, including specifically where the last tick had attached and infected me. The art covers the part of my back that I have viewed in that mirror so many times, but now I see there a bright, beautiful, vibrant tree of life—because that is what I have been given after all this struggle. It represents the logo for my fitness business, which I longed to get back to; it is a symbol of all the parks I managed and hiked over the decades; and it is a strong, powerful example of longevity, just as my life is becoming. This tattoo is the best way I can erase the memory of those ticks on my back. They are gone now, and I imagine the Lyme, Babesia, and Bartonella gone from my body too. I am becoming strong, powerful, and full of life. My life is coming back.

There is only one way to look now, and it is forward—with faith. This process, this disease, this challenge has given me the gift of seeing life more clearly than I had ever been able to see it before. It's like I've thrown out the rearview mirror for the bright, clean, clear front windshield, and there is so much life in that view. Maybe the key is to always live as though I am in that two-week window. From this point on, I am always checking with myself for my truth and gathering information from the experts, but always deciding for myself what feels right for me. What if every day in that two-week window, I consider what serves my highest good and what actions provide the most good to me and others? What if I live in that two-week window as though I need guidance from God to keep me on the right path, knowing He guides me when I have no idea which way to go? Maybe that two-week window passed once for me, but this time the opportunity will not be lost. I will live as though I have the opportunity again and again.

My window is much bigger and brighter now. I have the vision of my father traveling down the road in his fifth-wheel truck with the largest, clearest windshield there could be. He was always so adamant about keeping it clean, and now I am too. A lot of self-care can help make sure that you can see the way and that the path is clear. No wonder he always took the time. It feels like he's been with me all along, helping me see the way. I once felt like he had abandoned me when I needed him the most. Now I feel like he was right along for the ride, helping me see but letting me figure it out for myself. That is how the greatest teachers in life do it, isn't it? I guess that's how God does it too.

Because of all of that, I am now full of hope, promise, and the knowledge that I am blessed beyond belief. I now have freedom in knowing who I was and who I want to be and in knowing that I will let no one sacrifice me for their own ignorance ever again. I also have faith that the truth about this illness will come to light and many will be saved from my demise. It won't happen overnight—I have learned that. But it will happen, and I won't stop speaking the truth until it does. I know of amazing Lyme advocates working on the same goal, and it is going to happen because of them. I know their passion and drive, because without the truth we cannot stop, or too many more will be affected. So I will continue, just as they do, to fix a wrong that has had too many years to develop. I have been blessed by amazing support, and because of that I have been able to weather this storm that many have not. So for them, I can't stop until the truth is out. I won't stop until doctors, educators, and other medical professionals all see chronic Lyme for exactly what it is and provide the best care possible to those suffering and those who may suffer.

The same personality, motivation, determination, and so on that probably played a role in getting me into this situation are also the same characteristics that I believe carried me through, and I see similar characteristics in many Lyme warriors I meet. I know that from the outside someone with Lyme may look weak or whiny or overreactive to small issues. But I can promise you, from the inside they are the toughest, most resilient, determined, and motivated people you will ever meet. The challenges inside are mountainous, the issues are numerous, and the roadblocks are endless, but their mindset and desire to fight are often more resilient. It's the only reason they go on. They are warriors in every sense of the word. Never let what appears to be going on outside fool you.

I have support all around me: my friends, my family, my husband, and God. Nothing is stronger than that. I became powerful and strong not from working out, but from having confidence that I could handle whatever life tried to throw at me. It tried so hard to cripple me, break me down, and wear me out. Sometimes I was sure it would get the best of me, but more times I and others believed it wouldn't, so it didn't. There is so much peace in knowing yourself, trusting yourself, and eventually loving yourself. Anything else just muddles the view.

It makes you realize that those bumpy paths, the hard-fought challenges, and the seemingly never-ending battles in life have a purpose. I realized before all of this that I was struggling with purpose. I wanted to be able to help others in ways that I could never seem to manage. I guess the saying is true: "be careful what you wish for; you just might get it." I certainly don't think I was asking for this, but maybe in a roundabout way, I was. If that's the case, there is only one thing to do, and that is to use the experience—to find a way to do better, give more, and be of service with what I have learned. It is the only way to make it all mean something.

There will be many times when life knocks you down, but it can also build you up: higher, better, and stronger than you could ever imagine being. It can truly teach you how to thrive. Sometimes it's hard to remember or even imagine that that is what life's battles are meant to do. Sometimes they feel like nothing more than a cruel punishment. But when they do come—and they do for everyone—if you just keep believing, asking for help, living in gratitude, and knowing there is purpose in all of this, you eventually see what you are meant to see. And when you do, it will almost feel like the pain, fear, sadness, and frustration were all worth it—almost.

Maya Angelou said, "My mission in life is not merely to survive, but to thrive; and to do so with some passion, some compassion, some humor, and some style." I hope you thrive!

# REFERENCES

ABC News, 2017. "CDC Advises You May Need Multiple Lyme Disease Tests After a Tick Bite" http://abcnews.go.com/GMA/video/cdc-advises-multiple-lyme-disease-tests-tick-bite-48364357).

Appel, M. J., S. Allan, R. H. Jacobson, T. L. Lauderdale, Y. F. Chang, S. J. Shin, J. W. Thomford, R. J. Todhunter, and B. A. Summers. 1993. "Experimental Lyme Disease in Dogs Produces Arthritis and Persistent Infection." *Journal of Infectious Diseases.* 167, no. 3: 651–64.

Balmori, A. 2014. "Electrosmog and Species Conservation." *Science of the Total Environment* 496: 314–16.

Baranchuk, Adrian. 2017a. "Electrocardiographic Presentation of Acute Lyme Disease." *American Journal of Emergency Medicine* 35, no. 7: 1040.e5–1040.e6.

Baranchuk, Adrian. 2017b. Presentation: Lyme Carditis and Management of High Degree AV Block. Lyme Disease Association, Inc. Conference.

Bell, S. J., and B. Sears. 2003. "Low-glycemic-load diets: impact on obesity and chronic disease." *Critical Reviews in Food Science & Nutrition,* 43(4), pages 357-77.

Burgess EC, Amundson TE, Davis JP, et al. 1986. "Experimental inoculation of Peromyscus spp. with Borrelia burgdorferi: evidence of contact transmission." *American Journal of Tropical Medicine and Hygiene.* 1986; 35(2): 355–9.

Burgess EC, Patrican LA. 1987. "Oral infection of Peromyscus maniculatus with Borrelia burgdorferi and subsequent transmission by Ixodes dammini." *American Journal of Tropical Medicine and Hygiene.* 36(2): 402–7.

Burgess EC. 1989. "Experimental inoculation of mallard ducks (Anas platyrhynchos platyrhynchos) with Borrelia burgdorferi." *Journal of Wildlife Diseases.* 25(1): 99–102.

Burgess EC. 1992. "Experimentally induced infection of cats with Borrelia burgdorferi." *American Journal of Veterinary Research.* 53(9): 1507–11.

Burgess EC. 1986. "Experimental inoculation of dogs with Borrelia burgdorferii." *Zentralbl Bakteriol Mikrobiol und Hygiene A.* 263(1-2):49-54.

Burgess EC. 1988. "Borrelia burgdorferi infection in Wisconsin horses and cows." *Annals of the New York Academy Sciences.* 539:235-43.

Burrascano, J. 2008. *Advanced Topics in Lyme Disease, Diagnostic Hints and treatment Guidelines for Lyme and Other Tick Borne Illnesses,*16th edition, October, 2008 http://www.lymenet.org/BurrGuide200810.pdf.

Canadian Lyme Science Alliance. 2017. "Lyme in the Media: Fact Checking AMMI President Dr. Caroline Quach." Facebook, March 13, 2017. https://www.facebook.com/notes/canadian-lyme-science-alliance/lyme-in-the-media-fact-checking-ammi-president-dr-caroline-quach/1502680299762884/.

Cerri D, Farina R, Andreani E, Nuvoloni R, Pedrini A, Cardini G. 1994. "Experimental infection of dogs with Borrelia burgdorferi." *Research in Veterinary Science.* 57(2):256-8.

Cameron DJ et al. 2014. "Evidence Assessments and guideline recommendations in Lyme disease: the clinical management of known tick bites, erythema migrans rashes and persistent disease." *Expert Review of Anti-infective Therapy.* 12(9):1103-35.

Clarke, H. 2006 "Cleanses and Cleanups." Last modified 2006. https://www.drclarkinfocenter.com

Connor, D.M. 2017. "Lyme Disease Patients File Federal Antitrust Suit Against Infectious Disease Specialists & Health Insurers." *Huffington Post*. November 15, 2017. https://www.huffingtonpost.com/entry/lyme-disease-patients-file-federal-antitrust-suit-against_us_5a0c1905e4b060fb7e59d4db

Cook MJ. 2015. "Lyme borreliosis: a review of data on transmission time after tick attachment." *International Journal of General Medicine*. 8:1-8.

Davidson, J. 2017. "Don't Feed the Parasite: Best Natural Cleanse Solutions." Accessed March 12, 2018. http://drjaydavidson.com/dont-feed-parasites/.

Dennis, Lori. 2017. *Lyme Madness: Rescuing My Son Down the Rabbit Hole of Chronic Lyme Disease*. Ontario, Soulwork Publishing.

Dennis, L. 2018. "A Mother's Journey – Rescuing a Son from Lyme Disease." Interview by Kennedy, Cindy. *Living with Lyme*, January 24, 2018. http://livingwithlyme.us/2018/01/episode-17-mothers-journey-rescuing-son-lyme-disease.

Faber, Sue. Dec. 2017. "LymeHope Presents: Pregnancy & Gestational Lyme Disease." Youtube, May 31, 2018. https://www.youtube.com/watch?v=SLFRYVcGeR4&feature=youtu.be

Embers ME, Barthold SW, Borda JT, Bowers L, Doyle L, Hodzic E, Jacobs MB, Hasenkampf NR, Martin DS, Narasimhan S, Phillippi-Falkenstein KM, Purcell JE, Ratterree MS, Philipp MT. 2012. "Persistence of Borrelia burgdorferi in Rhesus Macaques following Antibiotic Treatment of Disseminated Infection." *Public Library of Science ONE* 7:e29914. https://doi.org/10.1371/journal.pone.0029914.

Embers ME, Hasenkampf NR, Jacobs MB, Tardo AC, Doyle-Meyers LA, Philipp MT, et al. 2017. "Variable manifestations, diverse seroreactivity and post-treatment persistence." Public Library of Science ONE 12(12): e0189071. https://doi.org/10.1371/journal.pone.0189071.

Government of Canada. 2018. "Surveillance of Lyme disease." Accessed May 31, 2018. https://www.canada.ca/en/public-health/services/diseases/lyme-disease/surveillance-lyme-disease.html.

Greene RT1, Levine JF, Breitschwerdt EB, Walker RL, Berkhoff HA, Cullen J, 21Nicholson WL. 1988. "Clinical and serologic evaluations of induced Borrelia burgdorferi infection in dogs." *American Journal of Veterinary Research*. 49(6):752-7.

Grauer GF, Burgess EC, Cooley AJ, Hagee JH. 1988. "Renal lesions associated with Borrelia burgdorferi infection in a dog." *Journal of American Veterinary Medical Association*. Jul 15;193(2):237-9.

Hawkins, R. 2017. Testimony, HESA Federal Standing Committee on Health 42nd Parliament, 1st Session, Meeting No. 60, June 8, 2017, Audio, http://parlvu.parl.gc.ca/XRender/en/PowerBrowser/PowerBrowserV2/20170608/-1/27612?Language=English&Stream=Video&useragent=Mozilla/5.0%20(Macintosh;%20Intel%20Mac%20OS%20X%2010_13_6)%20AppleWebKit/605.1.15%20(KHTML,%20like%20Gecko)%20Version/11.1.2%20Safari/605.1.15\.

Hoskins, Eric Ontario Ministry of Health and Long Term Care. 2016. "Minister's Letter to Doctors - Ontario College of Family Physicians", Accessed June 10, 2017. https://ocfp.on.ca/docs/default-source/default-document-library/minister-letter-to-docs-re-lyme-2016-07-29_english.pdf?sfvrsn=582df889_0.

Hodzic E, Imai D, Feng S, Barthold SW. 2014. *"Resurgence of Persisting Non- Cultivable Borrelia burgdorferi following Antibiotic Treatment in Mice."* Public Library of Science ONE 9:e86907–12.

Horowitz, Richard. 2017. *How Do I Get Better? An Action Plan for Treating Resistant Lyme & Chronic Disease.* New York: St. Martin's Griffin.

Horowitz, R, "Meeting Two of the Tick-Borne Disease Working Group." Facebook, December 13, 2017. https://www.facebook.com/ drrichardhorowitz/posts/meeting-two-of-the-tick/1569992886422837/

Hunfeld KP, Ružić-Sabljić E, Norris DE, Kraiczy P, Strle F. 2005. "In Vitro Susceptibility Testing of Borrelia burgdorferi Sensu Lato Isolates Cultured from Patients with Erythema Migrans before and after Antimicrobial Chemotherapy." Antimicrobial Agents and Chemotherapy 49:1294–1301.

Hynote ED, Mervine PC, Stricker RB. 2012. "Clinical evidence for rapid transmission of Lyme disease following a tickbite." *Diagnostic Microbiology and Infectious Disease* 72:188–192. doi: 10.1016/j.diag microbio.2011.10.003.

Institute of Medicine (US) Panel on Micronutrients. 2001. *Dietary Reference Intakes for vitamin A, vitamin K, arsenic, boron, chromium, copper, iodine, iron, manganese, molybdenum, nickel, silicon, vanadium, and zinc. Institute of Medicine*, D.C., National Academies Press.

International Lyme and Associated Diseases Society. 2018. "Peer-Reviewed Evidence of Persistence of Lyme Disease Spirochete Borrelia burgdorferi and Tick-Borne Diseases." Accessed March 12, 2018. http://www.ilads. org/ilads_news/wp-content/uploads/2017/02/CLDList-ILADS.pdf.

Kaiser R. 2000. "False negative serology in patients with neuroborreliosis and the value of employing of different borrelial strains in serological assays." *Journal of Medical Microbiology* 49(10): 911-915.

Kosik-Bogacka DI, Kuźna-Grygiel W, Jaborowska M. 2007. "Ticks and mosquitoes as vectors of Borrelia burgdorferi s. l. in the forested areas of Szczecin." *Folia Biolica* (Krakow). 55(3-4):143-6.

Krause Pj, Feder HM, Jr. 1994. "Lyme disease and babesiosis." *Advances in Pediatric Infectious Disease*, 9, 183-209.

Lam, Michael. 2017. "Chronic Lyme disease Symptoms and Adrenal Fatigue." Accessed March 12, 2018.

Liegner, K. 2017. "Interview with Kenneth Liegner." Accessed May 1, 2018. http://lyme-basics.com/2017/08/12/interview-kenneth-liegner/

Luché-Thayer, Jenna et. al. 2017. *Updating ICD11 Borreliosis Diagnostic Codes:* Edition One ISBN-10: 1978091796 ISBN-13: 978-1978091795 CreateSpace Independent Publishing Platform October 7, 2017.

Luche-Thayer, J. 2017. "Addressing Systemic Obstacles in the Borelliosis Pandemic." 18th Annual ILADS Scientific Conference, Boston, MA, Presentation.

MacLeod, I. 2017. "Lyme's a Human Torture Chamber" LinkedIn, June 25, 2017 https://www.linkedin.com/pulse/lymes-human-torture-chamber-isabella-macleod/.

Melaun C, Zotzmann S, Santaella VG, Werblow A, Zumkowski-Xylander H, Kraiczy P, Klimpel S. 2015. "Occurrence of Borrelia burgdorferi s.l. in different genera of mosquitoes (Culicidae) in Central Europe." *Ticks and Tick-Borne Diseases.* 2016 Mar;7(2):256-63. doi: 10.1016/j.ttbdis.2015.10.018. Epub.

Mercola J. 2018. "Basic Steps to Your Emotional Freedom." Accessed March 12, 2018 https://eft.mercola.com.

Middelveen MJ, Burke J, Sapi E et al. 2014. "Culture and identification of Borrelia spirochetes in human vaginal and seminal secretions." *F1000Research,* 3:309. doi: 10.12688/f1000research.5778.1.

Moody KD, Barthold SW. 1991. "Relative infectivity of Borrelia burgdorferi in Lewis rats by various routes of inoculation." *American Journal of Tropical Medicine and Hygiene.* 1991; 44(2): 135–9.

Neustadt, J., & Pieczenik, S.R. 2008. "Medication-induced mitochondrial damage and disease." *Molecular Nutrition and Food Research*, 52, 780-788.

Nicholas A. Crossland, Xavier Alvarez, Monica E. Embers. 2017. "Late Disseminated Lyme Disease: Associated Pathology and Spirochete Persistence Post-Treatment in Rhesus Macaques." The American Journal of Pathology. **2017**; doi: 10.1016/j.ajpath.2017.11.005.

Outbreak New Today. 2016. "Lyme Discovery: Borrelia Bacteria Hides Inside Parasitic Worms, causing Chronic Brain Diseases." Released may 23, 2016http://outbreaknewstoday.com/lyme-discovery-borrelia-bacteria-hides-inside-parasitic-worms-causing-chronic-brain-diseases-13216/.

Patient Centered Care Advocacy Group. 2016. "Lyme Bacteria Hides Inside Parastitic Worms, causing Chronic Brain Disease" Released May 19, 2016 https://www.prnewswire.com/news-releases/lyme-bacteria-hides-inside-parasitic-worms-causing-chronic-brain-diseases-300270742.html.

Pieczenik, S.R., & Neustadt, J. 2007. "Mitochondrial dysfunction and molecular pathways of disease." *Experimental and Molecular Pathology*, 83, 84-92.

Rudenko N et al. 2015. *"Isolation of live Borrelia burgdorferi sensu lato spirochaetes from patients with undefined disorders and symptoms not typical for Lyme borreliosis."* Clinical Microbiology and Infection. pii: S1198-743 14)

Rudenko N, Golovchenko M, Vancova M, Clark K, Grubhoffer L, Oliver JH Jr. 2016. "Isolation of live Borrelia burgdorferi sensu lato spirochaetes from patients with undefined disorders and symptoms not typical for Lyme borreliosis." *Clinical Microbiology and Infection* 22:267.e9–267.e15.

Segerstrom, Suzanne C, Miller, Gregory E. 2004. "Psychological Stress and the Human Immune System: A Meta-Analytic Study of 30 Years of Inquiry." *Psychological Bulletin,* Jul; 130(4): 601–630.

Sensi, M., Pricci, F., Andreani, D., et al. 1991. "Advanced Nonenzymatic Glycation Endproducts AGE): Their Relevance to Aging and the Pathogenesis of Late Diabetic Complications, Diabetes Research." 16(1), 1991, pages 1-9. human primates exposed to Borrellia burgdorferi by tick feeding. *Public Library of Science ONE* 12(12): e0189071. https://doi.org/10.1371/journal.pone.0189071.

Stone, Judy. 2015. "Lyme Deaths From Heart Inflammation Likely Worse Than We Though." *Forbes,* September 4, 2015. https://www.forbes.com

Stricker, RB & Fesler, MC. 2017. "Chronic Lyme Disease: A Working Case Definition." *Chronic Diseases - International,* 4(1), 1025. http://www.prweb.com/releases/2017/05/prweb14305710.htm

Thomas RJ, Dumler JS, Carlyon JA. 2009. "Current management of human granulocytic anaplasmosis, human monocytic ehrlichiosis and Ehrlichia ewingii ehrlichiosis." *Expert Review of Anti-infective Therapy.* Aug;7(6):709-22. doi: 10.1586/eri.09.44.

Woodrum JE, Oliver JH Jr. 1999. "Investigation of venereal, transplacental, and contact transmission of the Lyme disease spirochete, Borrelia burgdorferi, in Syrian hamsters." *Journal of Parasitology.* 1999; 85(3): 426–30.

Wright SD, Nielsen SW. 1990. *"Experimental infection of the white-footed mouse with Borrelia burgdoreri." American Journal of Veterinary Research.* 1990; 51(12): 1980–7.

Zhang, Y. 2017. Interview - Ying Zhang, John Hopkins University, Accessed August 23, 17. http://lyme-basics.com/2017/08/07/interview-ying-zhang/.

# RECOMMENDED READING

Axe, Josh. 2016. *Eat Dirt: Why Leaky Gut May Be the Root Cause of Your Health Problem and 5 Surprising Steps to Cure It.* Harper Collins.

Buhner, Stephen. 2015. *Healing Lyme: Natural Healing of Lyme Borreliosis and the Coinfections Chlamydia and Spotted Fever Rickettsiosis.* 2nd ed. Raven Press.

Davidson, Jay. 2015. *5 Steps to Restoring Health Protocol: Helping Those Who Haven't Been Helped with Lyme Disease, Thyroid Problems, Adrenal Fatigue, Heavy Metal Toxicity, Digestive Issues, and More!* Milwaukee: Jay Davidson Publishing.

Dennis, Lori. 2017. *Lyme Madness: Rescuing My Son Down the Rabbit Hole of Chronic Lyme Disease.* Soulwork Publishing.

Ferrie, Heike. 2010. *Ending Denial: The Lyme Epidemic, A Canadian Public Health Disaster.* Caledon: KOS.

Horowitz, Richard. 2017. *How Do I Get Better? An Action Plan for Treating Resistant Lyme & Chronic Disease.* New York: St. Martin's Griffin.

Lam, Michael. 2015. *Adrenal Fatigue Syndrome: Reclaim Your Energy and Vitality with Clinically Proven Natural Programs.* Adrenal Institute.

Liegner, K. B. 2015. *In the Crucible of Chronic Lyme Disease: Collected Writings and Associated Materials.* Retrieved from http://books.google.com.

Ortner, Nick. 2018. *The Tapping Solution for Manifesting Your Greatest Self: 21 Days to Releasing Self-Doubt, Cultivating Inner Peace, and Creating a Life You Love*. Hay House.

Ober, C., S. Sinatra, and M. Zucker. 2014. *Earthing: The Most Important Health Discovery Ever?* Columbus: Basic Health.

Rawls, William. 2017. *Unlocking Lyme: Myths, Truths, and Practical Solutions for Chronic Lyme Disease*. Vital Plan.

Spector, Neil. 2015. *Gone in a Heartbeat: A Physician's Search for True Healing*. Triton Press.

Strasheim, Connie. 2017. *New Paradigms in Lyme Disease Treatment: 10 Top Doctors Reveal Healing Strategies That Work*. South Lake Tahoe: BioMed Publishing Group.

Wahls, Terry. 2014. *The Wahls' Protocol: A Radical New Way to Treat All Chronic Autoimmune Conditions Using Paleo Principles*. New York: Penguin.

## Website Links

http://www.lymehope.ca

http://lymeontario.com

https://canlyme.com

http://www.ilads.org

http://www.klinghardtacademy.com

# Recommended Documentary

Under Our Skin (June 19, 2009)

Director: Andy Abrahams Wilson

Film series: Under Our Skin Documentary Series

Producer: Andy Abrahams Wilson

Cast: Mandy Hughes, Dana Walsh, Willy Burgdorfer

Open Eye Pictures, Inc, USA

CPSIA information can be obtained
at www.ICGtesting.com
Printed in the USA
LVHW092304300419
616203LV00001B/7/P

9 781982 211325